The politics of frustration

Harry Midgley
and the failure of Labour
in Northern Ireland

To my parents

Graham S. Walker

The politics of frustration

Harry Midgley
and the failure of Labour
in Northern Ireland

Manchester University Press

Published by Manchester University Press
Oxford Road, Manchester M13 9PL, UK
and 51 Washington Street, Dover,
New Hampshire 03820, USA

British Library cataloguing in publication data
Walker, Graham S.
  The politics of frustration: Harry Midgley
  and the failure of Labour in Northern Ireland.
  1. Midgley, Harry   2. Politicians – Northern
  Ireland – Biography
  I. Title
  941.6082′092′4   DA965.M/

Library of Congress cataloging in publication data
Walker, Graham S.
  The politics of frustration
  Bibliography: p. 224.
  Includes index.
  1. Midgley, Harry, d. 1957. 2. Trade-unions –
Northern Ireland – Officials and employees – Biography.
3. Trade-unions – Northern Ireland – Political activity –
History. 4. Commonwealth Labour Party (Northern
Ireland) – History. 5. Northern Ireland – Politics and
government. I. Title.
HD6665.M53W35   1985   331.88′092′4 [B]   85–10684

ISBN 0–7190–1821–8   *cased*

Photoset in Linotron Ehrhardt by
Northern Phototypesetting Co., Bolton
Printed in Great Britain
by the Alden Press, Oxford

Contents

	Acknowledgements	*page* vi
1	Belfast beginnings and thoughts from Flanders (1892–1919)	1
2	Trying times (1919–1923)	14
3	Labour's Standard-bearer (1923–1925)	28
4	'The Workers' Champion' (1925–1932)	41
5	Street riots and a passage to Stormont (1932–1936)	58
6	Spain: The press, the pulpit and defeat (1936–1938)	85
7	NILP showdown (1938–1942)	114
8	Cabinet and Commonwealth (1942–1947)	147
9	Unionist evangelist (1947–1950)	181
10	Minister of Education (1950–1957)	198
11	Conclusion: Success or failure?	216
	Appendix	222
	Primary sources	224
	Secondary sources	226
	Interviews	230
	Index	231

Acknowledgements

My greatest academic debt is to Alex Robertson who supervised the thesis out of which this book evolved. He offered many helpful suggestions, tendered sound advice, and, most importantly, made sure it got written. I am also grateful to Dr. A. T. Q. Stewart and Dr Tom Gallagher for their comments and suggestions on improving the book. I of course bear sole responsibility for the shortcomings which remain.

The Institute of Irish Studies, Queen's University of Belfast, kindly gave me a grant to help with typing costs, and I benefited greatly from my period there as a research fellow. I am very grateful to Miss Sandra Maxwell for typing the manuscript so speedily.

The book could not have been written without the help and co-operation of Mrs. Elizabeth Ireland and Mr John Midgley, both of whom kindly gave me access to private material, and offered encouragement throughout. I also thank all the people listed at the end of the book who took the trouble to see me and answer my questions.

My greatest overall debt is to my parents who have given me unfailing encouragement and support. The book is dedicated to them both as a small token of my gratitude.

Chapter One

Belfast beginnings and thoughts from Flanders (1892–1919)

I

Henry Cassidy Midgley was born at 59 Seaview Street in North Belfast on 8 September 1892. He was the third child of Elizabeth Cassidy and Alexander Midgley, both born and raised in Lurgan, County Armagh. Sometime in the 1830s Harry (as he came to be known) Midgley's great-grandfather, John Midgley, came to the North of Ireland from his native Yorkshire.[1] He came to instal and to operate flax-spinning machinery and by at least 1846 he had established his own steel reed manufacturing business in Belfast.[2] By 1852 his son James had set up a similar concern in Lurgan.[3]

Alexander Midgley, born in 1860, does not seem to have become involved in the linen business. Around 1880 he and Elizabeth travelled to Australia where their first two children (Minnie and Elizabeth) were born. In 1890 they returned to Ulster, this time to settle in Belfast where Alexander secured employment as a labourer in the city's other major industry of the time: shipbuilding.[4] The giant of the shipbuilding industry was the firm of Harland and Wolff which increased its labour force fivefold between 1870 and 1910.[5] A smaller firm, Workman and Clark, went into business in 1879, making Belfast one of the world's premier shipbuilding centres.

By the second half of the nineteenth century two distinct economies were beginning to crystallise in Ireland: an industrially-orientated economy in the North centring on the staple industries of shipbuilding, heavy engineering and linen; and a rural agrarian economy in the rest of the country. This can be qualified by acknowledging that the only part of the North – and Ireland – to become fully industrialised was Belfast and its environs, the area generally known as the Lagan Valley. Belfast's growth as a city during this period was truly astonishing: from a population of some 87,000 in mid-century, it boasted over 350,000 at the turn of the century.[6]

By the time of Harry's birth, the Midgley family was established in the archetypal Victorian working class housing conditions of Belfast. Seaview Street was one of many rows of small four-roomed back-to-back houses in an area which, like many others in Belfast at this time, suffered acutely from over-crowding, disease, high infant mortality, and bad sanitation. This was one of the most densely populated parts of Belfast with its proximity to mills and warehouses and to the docks and shipyards.[7] It became known, in electoral terms, as the Dock Ward, and the name of Harry Midgley was to become inseparably identified with it.

Accompanying Belfast's rapid industrial expansion was the problem of sectarian conflict between Protestants and Catholics in competition for work. From the early Victorian years large numbers of Catholics had flocked to the city and had begun to form what might be described as a 'lumpen proletariat'. They formed a disproportionate part of the unskilled and semi-skilled work-force, and their availability as cheap labour enabled employers in many cases to lower wage rates. Sectarian tensions were omnipresent and occasionally yielded to fierce communal rioting especially between the Protestant Sandy Row and Catholic Pound areas.[8] In the Dock area the sizeable Catholic community lived just north of the city centre on either side of York Street amidst a cluster of factories and warehouses. Seaview Street was further north in the Protestant area commonly known as 'Tiger's Bay'.

In August 1899 Alexander Midgley died at the age of 39 after years of ill-health. In conditions of severe privation it was left to his widow Elizabeth to raise five children (two boys – Eddie and Alex – being the last addition to the family) with an income largely derived from her own skills in stitching handkerchiefs.[9] The young Harry was profoundly affected as he watched his mother battle against the odds. In later years he was often to remark that he was receptive at an early age to those calling for the alleviation of poverty because of what he saw his mother go through.[10]

Her influence on his early life was unmatched by anyone else. She instilled in him a love of learning, encouraged him to read widely, and, in spite of the family's relative poverty, insisted that he stay on full-time at Duncairn Gardens National School until he had turned 12 years of age. Midgley was thus spared the status of 'half-timer' which so many children of his generation in industrial cities such as Belfast had to assume. This meant that they attended school for half a day and worked the other half in a mill or a factory or elsewhere.

After leaving school Midgley's first employment was as a helper in a grocery store. He later claimed that he was paid four shillings a week for a working week of never less than 60, and frequently up to 80, hours.[11] This was at a time when twelve to fifteen shillings a week was an average wage for labourers.

By the time, at the age of 14, he entered Workman and Clark to begin his apprenticeship as a joiner, Midgley had become even more aware of the inequality and injustice which surrounded him and had become more interested in politics. He had met Keir Hardie some time earlier and it was the kind of genuine, burning desire on the part of Hardie, and those in the Labour movement in Belfast, to end poverty and social injustice, which so impressed and inspired this precocious young radical.[12] Midgley was thus attracted to the Independent Labour Party (ILP), the campaigning vanguard of Belfast Labour politics.

II

The emergence of a significant Labour movement in Belfast in the Edwardian era[13] owed much to the foundations laid by the trade union movement in the city, especially during the period 1880 to 1900.[14] These two decades saw a signal growth in trade union organisation epitomised by the Belfast Trades Council, established in 1881, and the focus of industrial and, to a lesser extent, political activity during these years. In the 1880s Belfast tasted the flavour of British evangelical socialism by way of the message brought by Henry George and the Fabians. In 1893 a branch of the ILP was set up in the city, largely at the promptings of the British TUC. The ILP attracted those progressive leading figures in the trade union movement of whom William Walker, later to become the most important Labour personality in the North of Ireland, was one. The ILP held propaganda meetings and swam resolutely against Belfast's treacherous sectarian currents in its bid to foster a sense of class consciousness among workers.

It was at the Custom House Steps, Belfast's equivalent of Hyde Park Corner, that Midgley made his debut as a public speaker at the age of 14, at meetings held by the ILP.[15] The ILP mushroomed during the period 1905 to 1907 when, at the climax of the dockers' strike in the latter year, it consisted of five branches. The most notable of these was probably that of North Belfast – William Walker's branch – where Midgley and several other Labour activists who would later rise to prominence, cut their political teeth.

Midgley was thus brought into close contact with Walker[16] of whom he wrote later: 'He was a man of inspiring personality, a magnificent orator, a veritable giant among men'.[17] It was through the efforts of men like Walker that a Labour tradition was built up in Belfast and inherited by such as Midgley. This tradition was forged in a climate of sectarianism and it could not avoid confronting, and to some extent reproducing, the conflicting ideological strands spawned by Nationalism and Unionism. Walker's form of socialism, concentrating as it did on municipal affairs and identifying closely with the general outlook of British Labour, was shaped largely by his own opposition to Irish Home Rule, and, it can be argued, by the strength of his own identification with the Protestant community in the North. Walker certainly shared the general view within this community that a Home Rule parliament in Ireland would come strongly under the influence of the Roman Catholic church.[18] His conception of progress was synonymous with the continuation of the Union and he stood for the integration of the Irish Labour movement into that of the rest of the United Kingdom, a stance which was to prove politically untenable in the light of British Labour's sympathy for a Home Rule settlement.

Walker fought unsuccessfully three times, in 1905, 1906 and 1907, for the Westminster seat of North Belfast, and on the third occasion Midgley assisted his campaign.[19] Taken together these contests constitute a milestone in the history of Belfast Labour. Walker had stormed a hitherto impregnable Unionist citadel and had almost captured it, especially in 1906 when he came within 291 votes of doing so. Walker's performances proved that Labour had become a meaningful force in politics, but with their overtones of sectarianism the contests also indicated how formidable an obstacle the Home Rule issue was proving to be for an alternative political force which attempted to concentrate totally on social and economic issues.[20]

During the period of Walker's pre-eminence as Belfast Labour's most renowned advocate, Irish nationalist sentiment was present only to a very limited extent in the Northern Labour movement. Labour in the South, however, came increasingly to assume the character of 'radical nationalism', a process set in train by James Connolly and his Irish Socialist Republican Party during the period 1896 to 1903. Connolly departed for America in 1903 and did not return to Ireland until 1910 when – by now a convinced syndicalist[21] – he took up a post in Belfast for the Irish Transport and General Workers' Union (ITGWU).

Connolly returned to Ireland convinced that Labour must unite on an all-Ireland basis and prepare to stage an effective challenge in the new Ireland after Home Rule, an eventuality he considered inevitable. The years 1910 to 1912 were thus to witness a confrontation between 'traditionalist' (British) Labour thinking in Belfast personified by Walker, and those led by Connolly who held a united Irish perspective. The ramifications of this conflict for Belfast Labour were to be felt in the decades after the eventual partition of Ireland in 1921.

The question of Home Rule had been the subject of over two decades of controversy and agitation. The Irish nationalist movement continually voiced the demand for self-government and held the image of a united, indivisible Irish nation as 'the political article of faith'.[22] Nationalist ideology insisted that an Irish nation had once existed and was destined to exist again, freed from the fetters of an alien (British) administration to recover a distinct Gaelic cultural identity which had been eroded but was by no means extinct.

The nationalist outlook, with its insistence on the 'divine destiny' of a self-governing Ireland, found it difficult to confront the vexatious question of the Protestant population largely concentrated in the north-east of the island. This group's position was never considered in terms other than of the Irish nation. Its stubborn resistance to inclusion in this nation was seen as an aberration, a travesty of the true nature of Protestant Ulster. For Irish nationalists the latter was embodied by those Ulster Protestants who had participated in the 'United Irishmen' rebellion of 1798.

To the Protestants of the North, and most of those in the South, Ireland's prosperity was viewed as bound to that of Britain, and their article of faith was the Union. Unionism, as it came to be known, developed as a movement out of the first Home Rule crisis of 1885–6. At first there was no question of its 'Irish' identity; Unionists considered themselves true Irishmen in fighting to save their country from what they saw as the disaster of Home Rule. In the early phase of anti-Home-Rule agitation Southern Unionists played a prominent role.[23] Not surprisingly, given the concentrated density of the Protestant population in the North, the movement became steadily more identified with the Province of Ulster. The economic disparities between this area and the rest of Ireland served to give the Unionists a persuasive rationale to their case.

Related to Unionism was the phenomenon of Orangeism, a movement based organisationally on the Orange Order. Ideologically Orangeism stressed the principles of the Reformation and identified Protestantism with material progress, civil liberty and spiritual purity. Perhaps more importantly, the negative side to the ideological coin conveyed a strident anti-Catholicism in which Catholicism was synonymous with backwardness, superstition and spiritual enslavement. In social terms the Order thus came to insist upon Protestant vigilance with all the implications of this in the workplace and in domestic life.

III

By 1910 Labour in Belfast was in difficulty. Walker's election campaigns had consumed much of its finance, and as the controversy over the third Home Rule Bill intensified it found itself on the defensive, attempting to stress social issues to audiences fired with sectarian passion. In addition, British Labour's increasingly pronounced Home Rule stance proved irritating to such as Walker who continued to press for stronger links between the Irish and British Labour movements. In September 1909 Connolly, writing from America, astringently criticised Northern Labour's attitude as 'destructive to the hopes of a real revolutionary labour movement in Ireland', and derided its 'intellectual bias' towards 'the Fabian opportunism of England'.[24]

In 1911 both Connolly and Walker put their respective cases with regard to the question of an all-Ireland labour movement or integration with British Labour. In this controversy,[25] neither man distinguished himself, both resorting to personal abuse, and there are grounds for suspecting that Walker bore a grudge against Connolly on account of the latter's scathing criticisms of Northern Labour alluded to above. In addition, it might be argued that Walker's defensive retort to Connolly's opening broadside regarding the parts played by Protestants in Ireland's radical past suggests that he resented Connolly's apparent attempt to portray radicalism as monopolised in Ireland by Catholics. Walker and other Protestant Labour activists were not prepared to have their identity or their own tradition of social agitation subsumed into a nationalist-inspired radicalism which reflected distinct cultural traditions. Connolly, for his part, failed to see why Labour in Ulster should be inclined towards Unionism at all and had little respect for the degree to which it was firmly rooted in the British Labour tradition.[26]

However, by the time the controversy exploded on to the pages of *Forward*, the Glasgow ILP paper, Walker's defensiveness on this question gave the appearance of being a 'head in the sand' attitude given the apparent imminence of Home Rule. The Labour ranks were divided into those who stood by Walker and those who were either firmly against him or felt that, despite their ambivalence towards nationalism, a time of choice had come and that Home Rule would soon be a reality with which they would have to live. Walker took pains to distance himself from the Tory outlook of the Unionist leaders of Ulster's resistance to Home Rule, Sir Edward Carson and Sir James Craig. In practice, however, Walker's socialist ethos stood in danger of being overwhelmed by the profoundly Orangeist and anti-Catholic nature of the Unionist rhetoric which rose to a virulent pitch during the Home Rule crisis years of 1910 to 1914. Many Belfast socialists balked at the prospect of appearing to be in alliance, however uneasily, with such a force and feared for their movement in the event of Carson and the massive support he claimed in the Protestant community taking up arms in defiance of Home Rule. Even before Connolly arrived in Belfast in 1911, the initiative in the city's labour politics had passed to a group who favoured his approach. The major figures in this group were Thomas Johnson, later to become the leader of the Irish Labour Party after partition, David Campbell and William McMullen.

Meanwhile Walker's position became increasingly isolated. By 1910 he was, in fact, only supported by a band of admirers in the Belfast ILP.[27] However, this did not prevent him from waging a vigorous fight against attempts to build an all-Ireland Labour party. At the Irish Trades Union Congress in 1910 and in 1911 he won the day on this issue. In 1912, however, Congress gave its blessing to a new party set up by Connolly, the Independent Labour Party of Ireland (ILP(I)). In the same year Walker took his leave from politics, accepting a government post in Belfast administering the new National Insurance scheme. His supporters formed a dejected rump caught in a limbo between the rest of the Labour movement which had opted to accept Home Rule and the majority of Protestant workers who were preparing to defy it.

IV

Midgley, like the majority of those in the Belfast Labour movement, saw in Connolly's strategy the best hope for socialism in Ireland after Home Rule. By this time Midgley was engrossed in politics – committed to socialism and attracted by the glamour of public speaking at which he excelled.[28] He had a combative style which, when combined with his somewhat impetuous tendencies, occasionally led him to launch personal attacks which were not always forgiven. His opposition to Walker in this period seems to have taken such a personal form.[29]

Midgley's pro-Connolly attitude of this period is attested to, if obliquely, by letters written by one of his friends in the ILP, George Irwin. Irwin was a stalwart of the early Labour movement in the North and a strong Home Ruler and his friendship with Midgley was to endure after he had settled in New York after the First World War. Irwin's letters to Midgley were written in 1936–7 but, as well as observing political events of that time, he frequently reminisced about the past. In one letter he wrote: 'No matter how much we are opposed to war, there come times when we must fight. Connolly in the GPO and the Spanish Government are examples of this.'[30] The significance of the obviously laudatory reference to Connolly is the way in which Midgley's endorsement of Irwin's viewpoint is implicitly assumed.[31]

Midgley may have joined Connolly's ILP(I) in 1912, but there is no surviving evidence to say for certain. Walker's supporters were by now all concentrated in the North Branch of the ILP which held aloof from the new party. The ILP in Belfast thus split – the other branch being pro-Connolly.[32] The years 1912 to 1914 saw the cause of Labour in Belfast, of whatever hue, totally overtaken by the national question. Labour's weakness was painfully exposed in July 1912 when sectarian rancour climaxed in the explusion of Catholic workers from the shipyards. The Labour movement was utterly ill-equipped to show any meaningful resistence to rampant sectarian forces.

Such turmoil in Belfast may have been among the reasons which led Midgley, in the winter of 1912–13, to emigrate to America. His work in the shipyard did not enthral him and he had few qualms about leaving before his apprenticeship had been fully served. Midgley went to America with George Irwin who later recalled in his letters the initial hardships they had faced. Work was hard to come by and the less than welcoming attitude of some American socialists proved deeply disillusioning.[33] Eventually both men found labouring jobs and joined the American Federation of Labor (AFL), striking up friendships with labour activists who were in later years to visit Belfast to deliver lectures to the ILP.

Midgley may thus have joined the AFL more out of personal than political considerations. None the less it fits uneasily in relation to the influence exerted on him by Connolly. The AFL was bitterly opposed to syndicalism, espoused in America at this time by the Industrial Workers of the World (IWW) for whom Connolly had been an organiser before 1910.[34] It can only be concluded that while Connolly clearly made an impression on Midgley during these years, it seems that at no time could Midgley be viewed as a total convert to the full-blooded doctrinal approach typified by Connolly whether in his anti-imperialist and revolutionary nationalist, or in his syndicalist, outlook.

V

In the summer of 1914 Midgley returned home to Belfast on holiday. He found the situation if anything more charged with tension than when he left. An all-party conference at Buckingham Palace on 21 July had failed to produce agreement between Unionists and Nationalists, and matters seemed set to slide into the furnace of civil war. The Ulster Volunteer Force (UVF) stood at the ready to seize the Province and to declare a provisional government in defiance of Home Rule. The mood of the Nationalists, meanwhile, had grown more implacable and embittered on account of British troops opening fire and killing three people amidst disturbances in Bachelor's Walk in Dublin.

With numbing suddenness, however, came the outbreak of war with Germany and the consequent suspension of wranglings over Home Rule. Both Carson on behalf of the Ulster Volunteers, and John Redmond for the Nationalists, pledged the services of their men to the British army. At last, on 18 September, the Irish issue was put to one side when the Home Rule Bill became law with an accompanying bill suspending its operation until the end of the war and allowing for an Amending Bill to be introduced to alter it in respect of Ulster.

The 36th (Ulster) Division was organised soon after this. Along with his brothers, Eddie and Alex, Midgley joined up, choosing to enlist in the Royal Inniskilling Fusiliers. This is further evidence that Midgley was not a Connolly acolyte in the sense that contemporaries like William McMullen were. The act of enlisting cannot, whatever the circumstances and the personal reasons he may have had, be construed as anything but an indication that Midgley did not accept Connolly's view of the war as simply a product of conflicting imperialist designs in which the workers of the countries involved were to be used as exploitable cannon fodder. Serving with the Ulster Division, Midgley fought alongside many members of the UVF and in predominantly Protestant company. A deep attachment to the community in which he was reared, and whose ties he could not, or would not, loosen or break, seems to have been behind his behaviour.

The initial illusions that the war would be a brief one and that action would be somehow glamorous were very abruptly shattered in the mud of France. If Midgley had not been quite so naive as this at the outset, what transpired none the less stunned him to the quick. No-one who went to fight in the war could have had any conception of the unprecedented carnage which was to ensue. In addition to the deaths of friends known from Belfast, and of friends made in service, Midgley suffered the loss of his brother Alex who died of wounds on 6 July 1917.[35]

Midgley was wounded and gassed at some point during the war,[36] possibly on the Somme. He was also transferred from the Royal Inniskilling Fusiliers to the 150th Field Company of the Royal Engineers, another section of the Ulster Division.[37] In the later stages of the war he saw action in Flanders, at Ypres, at the Battle of Messines in June 1917, and at Kemmel Hill in Belgium. Official records of Midgley's war service do not survive. It is doubtful if he got beyond the rank of lance-corporal, and the medals he emerged with were for general service.[38]

Midgley recorded his feelings and impressions during the war by writing poetry. Eventually, in 1924, the poems were published in Belfast under the title *Thoughts from Flanders*. The style of the verses owed much to Kipling and it is clear that 'the soldier's poet' was a literary companion of Midgley's.

The poems indicate that Midgley's idealism emerged defiantly fortified from the war despite its tribulations. He seemed to consider the 'utopian socialist' ideal of a brotherhood of man and international peace more easily attainable in the wake of the cataclysm of the war than before. It is as if he considered the suffering to be a horrendous prelude to the world at last coming to its senses. In 'Joy Cometh with the Morn' he writes: 'Yet from the grief which has come to your hearts this day/Ye mighty mothers of earth/Shall emerge love's triumphant eternal ray/ The morn of the glad new birth'.

Midgley possessed a reinforced and intensified sense of mission after the war. He was determined that his comrades should not have fallen in vain. Equally, he believed in man's essential goodness and in his capacity to bring about a better world. Midgley seemed to hold a firm belief in God and, perhaps more importantly, in a kind of 'divine will' which was manifest in the 'wondrous plan' of nature which so entranced him. There is no hint of agnosticism or inner doubt anywhere in his poetry.

As well as thus articulating Midgley's basically Christian beliefs and values, the poems were often written in biblical language and with a plainly religious tone. Some were redolent of popular hymns and psalms which, significantly, Midgley often quoted in his political addresses. One of his favourite verses, employed in the perorations of many speeches during his political career, could have fitted very congenially into *Thoughts from Flanders*:

These things shall be: a loftier race,
Than e'er the world has known, shall rise;
With flame of freedom in their souls,
And light of knowledge in their eyes.
New arts shall bloom of loftier mould,
And mightier music thrill the skies,
And every life shall be a song
When all the earth is paradise.

Some of the poems expressed less idyllic and grandiloquent sentiments. The war may not have diluted Midgley's idealism but it certainly fired him, on several occasions, with righteous indignation. The activities of those who profited materially by the war, when set against the appalling loss of life, constituted an abomination about which Midgley railed publicly for a long time after the end of the war. During the war he was critical of those in government and bitter with regard to perceived incompetence on the part of those in office and in positions of military command. In an election campaign in West Belfast in 1923, Midgley, standing in the Labour interest, was accused by a supporter of his Unionist opponent of 'writing and trying to get letters sent through to Belfast' in wartime which were 'full of sedition'. His accuser further stated that the letters had been stopped by a censor and that someone in Belfast had been contacted in order to tell Midgley to stop sending such material.[39]

If the war brought suffering, it also made Midgley more appreciative of all he had left behind, particularly his sweetheart, Eleanor Adgey, and Ireland, the two 'fancies' of one of his poems. Eleanor was born in 1895 and grew up in the same area of Belfast as Midgley. They married on 22 August 1918 when he was home on leave and lived at first, on his return from the war, with the Adgey family in Hillman Street.

Midgley was not demobilised until around May of 1919. He returned to his work as a shipyard joiner, this time with Harland and Wolff,[40] but he clearly had no intention of staying there long. A firm foothold in the world of Labour, politically and industrially, was his immediate goal, and by the end of the year he had achieved part of it by becoming organising secretary of the Irish Linenlappers and Warehouse Workers' Union.

Notes

1 The Midgley name originated from the Midgley township of Halifax in the West Riding of Yorkshire.
2 *Henderson's Belfast Directory 1846–47*, Belfast, 1846.
3 *Belfast and Province of Ulster Directory 1852*, Belfast, 1852.
4 This, and subsequent information on Midgley's parents, is derived from the document entitled 'The strength of faith', an account written by Midgley himself in his later years about his early life. The document is contained in the collection of Midgley's personal papers, hereafter referred to as *Midgley Papers*.
5 See J. M. Goldstrom, 'The industrialisation of the north east' in L. M. Cullen, *The Formation of the Irish Economy*, Cork, 1968.
6 See E. Jones, 'Late victorian Belfast' in J. C. Beckett and R. E. Glasscock, *Belfast: The Growth of a City*, Belfast, 1967.
7 E. Jones, *A Social Geography of Belfast*, Oxford, 1960, pp. 133 ff.
8 See P. Gibbon, *The Origins of Ulster Unionism*, Manchester, 1975, chapter 4.
9 Document entitled 'Biographical comments re Harry Midgley', *Midgley Papers*.
10 A good example of this is Midgley's speech on widows' pensions in the Northern Ireland parliament 20 March 1934. N.I. House of Commons Debates XVI, 635–6.
11 Notes on 'Portrait gallery' BBC Radio programme 1956, *Midgley Papers*.
12 See Midgley's speech 6 March 1934. N.I. House of Commons Debates XVI, 436.
13 'The Labour movement' in Belfast at this time comprised the ILP, the Trades Council and Trades Union movement, the Labour Representation Committee (founded 1903), and two small groups of activists, the Belfast Labour Party and the Belfast Socialist Society.
14 See D. W. Bleakley, 'Trade union beginnings in Belfast and district', MA thesis, Queen's University Belfast, 1955, Introduction.
15 See pen picture of Midgley written by Bob McLung in *The Labour Opposition in Northern Ireland* September 1925.
16 For a brief outline of Walker's career see J. W. Boyle, 'William Walker' in J. W. Boyle, *Leaders and Workers*, Cork, 1967. For a considered appraisal of Walker's politics see A. Morgan, 'Politics, the Labour movement and the working class in Belfast 1905–1923', Ph.D. thesis, Queen's University Belfast, 1978, chapter 7.
17 *Belfast Telegraph* 26 March 1941.
18 See, for example, an article by Walker in the Belfast Trades Council newspaper, *The Belfast Labour Chronicle* January 1905. Walker expressed his views regularly in this paper which took an anti-Home Rule position.
19 *Labour Opposition in Northern Ireland* September 1925.
20 For a full account of the 1905–7 contests see Morgan op.cit. chapter 7.
21 See B. Ransom, *Connolly's marxism*, London, 1980, chapter 2.
22 Morgan op.cit. p. 5.
23 P. Buckland, *Irish Unionism* I, Dublin, 1972 *passim*.
24 'Learning their lesson', in O. D. Edwards and B. Ransom (eds), *James Connolly: Selected Political Writings*, London, 1973.

25 *The Connolly–Walker Controversy*, Cork, n.d. See Morgan op. cit. chapters 7, 8; Ransom op. cit. pp. 30–35; and H. Patterson, *Class Conflict and Sectarianism*, Belfast, 1981, pp. 79–80.

26 The strong links were evident through such phenomena as the visits paid by leading British Labour figures to Belfast, the emergence of branches of the Fabian Society, and the development of such a uniquely British socialist institution as the Socialist Sunday School. As a boy Midgley attended the Socialist Sunday School in Belfast run by the ILP.

27 Morgan, op. cit., p. 288.

28 Midgley spent long hours perfecting his speaking techniques, paying attention to his manner of delivery and gestures. In relation to his vocabulary he would pore endlessly over a dictionary of synonyms to find suitably stirring words and phrases. Information from Murtagh Morgan at a meeting of the West Belfast Historical Society 12 June 1981.

29 Interview with William Walker Logan 16 June 1981. Logan's father was a friend and supporter of Walker (hence his son's middle name) and recalled to his son that Walker had been hurt by Midgley's attacks and that Midgley had written to apologise.

30 Letter dated 20 July 1937, *Midgley Papers*. 'Connolly in the GPO' refers to the Easter Rising of 1916 which Connolly led in the cause of an Irish Republic. He was executed for his part in the rebellion. The reference to the Spanish government concerns the Spanish civil war which was then raging.

31 At the time Midgley was engaged in a propaganda struggle in Belfast on behalf of the Spanish government's cause. It is unlikely that Irwin would have coupled this cause with Connolly's in 1916 had he not had reason to believe, from the past, that Midgley admired Connolly's course of action.

32 Morgan op. cit. pp. 335–6. The other branch was Central Belfast.

33 Letter from Irwin to Midgley 27 February 1935, *Midgley Papers*.

34 Ransom, op. cit., p. 2.

35 *Soldiers Died in the Great War 1914–19* Part 4, Corps of Royal Engineers, HMSO, 1921.

36 London *Evening Standard* 22 October 1944.

37 'Biographical notes re Harry Midgley', *Midgley Papers*.

38 Information from W. J. Midgley.

39 *Irish News* 4 December 1923. See chapter 3.

40 *Labour Opposition in Northern Ireland* September 1925.

Chapter Two

Trying Times (1919–1923)

I

Midgley commenced his duties as a trade union organiser on 1 January 1920. He was the Linenlappers' first full-time permanent official.[1] He was to revel in the experiences of negotiations with individual employers and, on occasion, employers' associations and such institutions as the Chamber of Commerce. In his first year as an official he concluded a successful wage agreement which resulted in the basic wage of male workers in the trade being raised from 55s. to 76s. 6d. per week.[2] This triumph ensured his re-endorsement after his first three years of service. He was re-elected by 289 votes to seven at the Union's annual general meeting, and a resolution of warm appreciation of his efforts was carried unanimously.[3]

Midgley had no illusions with regard to the magnitude of Labour's task in overcoming the political obstacles of Belfast, or about the effort and strength of character and mind which would be required of him personally if he was to play a leading part in this endeavour. In the Northern Ireland House of Commons in 1942 he revealingly, if rather gratuitously, described the purposefulness of his behaviour on his return from the war: 'I had to train myself and discipline my mind. I spent night after night, year after year, without efficient intellectual control trying to drill my mind and train my mentality, and I have achieved just what I have achieved simply by determination to do it.'[4] To his natural energy and drive, therefore, Midgley grafted, by his self-application, a capacity to absorb and digest facts and figures and relevant information, and to construct and argue persuasively a logical case. He possessed an alert and enquiring mind, and if he cannot be termed an intellectual, he was certainly more than capable of deep thought and of original and stimulating analyses of some of the day's greatest political issues.

It could never be said that Midgley shirked work or responsibilities. He realised that there are few, if any, short cuts to prominence, and that to take on a heavy burden and work determinedly through it was the only sure way of making an impression. Hence, on his return from the war, he started to work on behalf of those ex-servicemen who did not get their jobs back after the war ended. In addition to this he took a leading role in the activities of the Belfast Labour Party and the North Branch of the ILP which he represented at the ILP conference in Glasgow in April 1920. He seems also to have involved himself straight away in the affairs of the Belfast Co-operative Society, and he was on the Committee of Management by 1923.[5]

II

As noted earlier, the Labour movement in Belfast suffered from the crisis surrounding the national question before the war. During the war there was little activity in terms of propaganda, but trade union membership grew substantially.[6] In 1917 a conference of trade unions and ILP representatives was held in Belfast and out of it emerged the reconstituted Belfast Labour party.[7] This latter party put forward four candidates at the 'coupon' election in 1918, one of whom was Sam Kyle, a prominent member of the North ILP branch. All four were defeated but none were humiliated.[8] The Belfast Labour party had also to compete, in two cases, against the Ulster Unionist Labour Association (UULA). This organisation had grown out of the dissatisfaction of many Protestant trade unionists over the Belfast Trades Council's attempts, in 1914, to represent the Home Rule cause as supported by a majority of the working class in the North.[9]

The problems which had bedevilled the Belfast Labour movement before the war had not disappeared and were about to once more expose Labour's weaknesses. Related to the conflicting ideologies of Unionism and Nationalism and to the sectarianism they spawned, were structural impediments to the development of a Labour movement along lines based on class identification. The most important was the character of the labour market in which Protestants maintained a stranglehold on many crafts and skilled occupations which in effect became their preserves. Catholics were often rigorously excluded from these occupational sectors and were correspondingly over-represented in proportion to their overall numbers in the semi- and unskilled manual sectors. This Protestant domination of the skilled sector entailed an ambiguous mixture of sectarianism, a limited sense of class consciousness, and a pronounced sense of craft consciousness. The trade union movement in

Belfast was forced from the outset to compromise with the reality of this situation and indeed could be said to have unintentionally strengthened the sectarian division by its application of craft and occupational controls.

Another obstacle to working class unity was the religiously segregated residential pattern which obtained in Belfast, the most salient feature of which was the existence of a Catholic ghetto community largely concentrated in the Falls Road area of West Belfast. This community had developed from the early Victorian years when large numbers of Catholics flocked into the city to find work. The Catholics formed a tightly knit, often embattled, grouping in which the Church's influence was all-pervading and most notable in the spheres of education and politics.[10] In this milieu the Nationalists established their political machine and produced the consummate 'ghetto boss' in Joseph Devlin.[11] Devlin played the role of 'broker' in the community, dispensing patronage on behalf of his party and receiving the solid support of the Catholic people in return. His populism united the mass of the labouring poor and the small Catholic bourgeoisie, and he was careful to identify the Nationalist cause with urgently-needed social and economic improvements. Trade union organisation, moreover, was conspicuous by its relative absence in Catholic areas, a fact which greatly facilitated Devlin's operations.

At the end of the war the prospects of Northern Labour making significant progress seemed fair. The national question was still in the balance with constitutional wranglings about to begin anew, this time with the spectre of Sinn Fein,[12] triumphant in the 1918 election, hovering threateningly in the background. The Nationalist Party had been devastated in the election, their only notable success being that of Devlin in shrugging off Eamon de Valera's challenge on his home ground of West Belfast. The Unionists won twenty-six seats, all but three of which were in the six north-eastern counties of Armagh, Antrim, Down, Derry, Fermanagh and Tyrone. While Sinn Fein's victories in the South resulted in increased tension there, the North, as far as the national question was concerned, remained for the moment relatively peaceful.

In the realm of industrial and economic struggle, however, it was aroused as never before. It became clear very quickly that there would be no sudden post-war social transformation. Wartime changes in the shipbuilding and engineering industries had bred some resentment: dilution had taken place and skilled jobs had been taken in some cases by unskilled and semi-skilled Catholic workers, some of whom came from the South. Pay differentials had narrowed between skilled and unskilled,[13] and in general the sense of 'caste' felt by Protestant shipyard workers had been undermined. In January 1919 they expressed their frustrations by striking in demand of a forty-four hour working week. The working week at this time was fifty-four hours.

The 44 Hour Engineering Strike practically paralysed Belfast.[14] New peaks of Belfast working class militancy were scaled, and, related to a background of developments in Soviet Russia and the impending war in the South of Ireland, this level of agitation seemed to bode ill for the Unionist establishment. The strike, however, should not be viewed in this context. It was an important demonstration of the Protestant workers' ability to take forceful independent action when they perceived their material welfare to be in some jeopardy. It was not an attempt to uproot the established order or in any way a hint that they had modified their stance on the national question. The strike committee was adamant that their action be conducted responsibly, and the committee included two Unionist representatives, William Grant and Robert Weir, both of whom participated in the name of the UULA.

The strike ended unsuccessfully on 14 February after lasting three weeks. The episode, however, was arguably indicative of the existence of an undercurrent of social discontent which other concurrent happenings seem to suggest was fairly widespread in Britain in the immediate post-war period. The soldiers' strikes and demonstrations against delays in demobilisation, for example, greatly alarmed the establishment. It was up to the Labour movement to channel these feelings to its own advantage. The omens seemed good when, in May 1919, Belfast witnessed the largest May Day rally seen in the city.

Gradually ex-servicemen returned to find themselves unemployed and unrewarded for their sacrifices. They came to constitute a large disaffected group seemingly receptive, at first, to the Labour message. On 1 December 1919 Midgley spoke on behalf of these ex-servicemen as part of a deputation from the Textile Trades Federation to the Belfast Corporation. The deputation stressed the worsening unemployment situation in the city and demanded that the corporation put into operation an Act of Parliament which would enable it to feed hungry children. Midgley himself referred to the wages paid in the linen trade which he described as 'a disgrace to civilisation'.[15]

In January 1920 the Belfast Labour Party won ten seats out of sixty at the municipal elections. It had put forward twenty-two candidates. The

contests were the first and last council elections to be conducted on the
system of Proportional Representation, a fact which had a lot to do with
Labour's success.[16] Most of the seats were won in Protestant areas with
the Labour Party again careful to avoid the national question and to
concentrate on economic issues.

Another well-attended May Day parade was held in Belfast in 1920.
Midgley spoke in favour of a resolution congratulating the German and
Russian workers in their recent struggles, excoriating profiteering,
protesting against the 'unfair treatment' of ex-servicemen and proposed
rent increases, and urging a range of social measures including municipalisation by the Belfast Corporation of coal, milk and bread.[17] By this
time Lloyd George, the British Prime Minister, had introduced the
Government of Ireland Act which proposed two separate parliaments in
Ireland: one in Dublin with jurisdiction over twenty-six counties; the
other in Belfast with authority over the six north-eastern counties. The
Act was ignored in the South where Sinn Fein had set up a provisional
parliament, the Dáil Éireann, while Ulster Unionists granted it grudg-
ing acceptance: they had never asked for a parliament of their own,
simply continued integration with Britain. The Belfast Labour
movement was about to be once more sucked into the cauldron of
controversy surrounding the issue. At the same May Day meeting, S. C.
Porter, who had been a Labour candidate in the 1918 election,
denounced the proposals as an attempt to fragment Irish Labour by 'a
small clique of Orange capitalists'.[18]

In general those in the Labour movement were aghast at the prospect
of partition. They took their cue from Connolly's denunciation of the
idea in 1914 as a recipe for two capitalist, reactionary states.[19] A Home
Rule settlement with the maintenance of close ties with the rest of the
United Kingdom had been desired by the majority, including Midgley.
Sam Kyle, by no means an ardent nationalist, wrote bitterly eight years
later of the 'dismembering' of the country.[20] Belfast Labour, however,
did not make its position officially plain in regard to partition, preferring
to voice general support for the policies of the British Labour party
including Home Rule for Ireland.

Midway through 1920 baleful effects of the Southern war between
the Irish Republican Army (IRA)[21] and the British Army began to
manifest themselves in the North. The IRA extended its operations
North for the first time since the outbreak of hostilities and Northern
Catholics became objects once more of grave suspicion. The common
belief among Protestants was that the IRA was operating a well

organised cell in Belfast from which base it would launch a concerted attack on Ulster. Gradually, the wrath of the unemployed ex-servicemen turned on those Catholic workers who, as they saw it, had taken their jobs. The ex-servicemen's organisation soon assumed a militantly Loyalist character, working closely with the British Empire Union.

By the summer of 1920 the economic boom was well and truly a spent force with reduced production in the linen, shipbuilding and engineering industries resulting in increased unemployment. The mood in Belfast was tense on 12 July when Sir Edward Carson chose to deliver a stinging attack on Labour as the ally of Sinn Fein in seeking to bring about 'disunity amongst our own people'.[22] On 20 July the first Catholic workers were ejected by angry Loyalists from the shipyards, soon to be followed by Protestants with known Labour sympathies. This wave of expulsions, in intensity and numbers, far exceeded those of July 1912.[23] It was to be the prelude to over two years of murderous sectarian strife in Belfast.

In the course of this reign of terror, the Labour movement was routed. The North Belfast ILP hall in Langley Street, which Midgley helped to build in 1910, was burned to the ground by a Loyalist mob in the rioting which followed the shipyards expulsions. Leadership of the Protestant working class in the industrial realm passed from trade unionists with a Labourist outlook to hard-line Loyalists. Propaganda meetings were forced to cease, and Protestant Labour men, including Midgley, were targets of abuse in their own community.[24]

On 28 July 1920 an Expelled Workers Relief Committee was set up, and, perhaps inevitably given that Catholics formed a majority of those expelled, it was organised in Catholic areas and mainly by Catholics. Two exceptions, however, were James Baird and John Hanna, two Protestant trade unionists who had also been hounded from their jobs. Both men, especially Baird, whipped up sympathy for the plight of Expelled Workers by means of representations to the British Labour Party and the British TUC. The latter body subsequently attempted, without success, to have the workers reinstated. In August 1920 Baird was among those who urged a blockade of Belfast to cut off essential imports of steel, coal and other industrial raw materials. Baird was soon in league with Sinn Fein who had called for an economic boycott in the South of all Belfast goods. This boycott began late in 1920 and continued into 1922. It failed in its objective to have the expelled workers reinstated, and also in its attempt to expose partition as damaging to

Ulster. Recent work, however, shows that the boycott did hurt Belfast's trade: 5 million pounds' worth was lost in 1921.[25]

How deeply Midgley was involved with Baird and Hanna at this time is difficult now to tell. He is not on record as having supported the Southern economic boycott or as having helped to canvass in Britain with a view to cutting off supplies of steel and coal, although he was accused of the latter activity by his opponent in an election campaign in 1923.[26] His involvement in the Expelled Workers Committee seems probable,[27] but it may only have been of a marginal nature. This is suggested by recent work in the Belfast Labour movement which states that Baird and Hanna were the particular targets of Loyalist abuse.[28] That Midgley shared the same general political outlook as the other two, however, was clearly illustrated by events surrounding the first elections for the new Northern Ireland parliament in May 1921.

III

The Belfast Labour Party decided not to contest the election. It had been much reduced in strength by the defections of those who, in Sam Kyle's words, 'could not stand up to the perpetual strain'.[29] In Belfast, however, four Independent candidates stood in the Labour interest: the Rev. J. Bruce Wallace in North Belfast; Baird in the South; Hanna in the West; and Midgley himself in the East division. Their decision to stand in a climate of such virulent hostility was an act as personally brave in each case as it was politically futile.

Significantly, Midgley fought his campaign in conjunction with Baird and Hanna. They placed advertisements in the newspapers signed by all three. On 16 May the *Irish News* carried the following: 'We stand for an unpartitioned Ireland based on the goodwill of all who love their native land – north to south and east to west.' And on 21 May, again in the *Irish News:* 'We are completely against partition. It is an unworkable stupidity, as the inner circle of political wire-pullers well know, but it is considered sufficiently good to fight an election on.'

Midgley, therefore, had come out explicitly against partition. This did not mean, however, that he (or Baird and Hanna) wanted too many Protestant voters to know: the above adverts appeared only in the *Irish News*, the traditional morning newspaper of the Catholic community in Belfast. In the Unionist *Northern Whig* and *Belfast News-Letter* the trio inserted the somewhat more anodyne and less controversial message:

'Civil and Religious Liberty! In Belfast. Vote for Baird, Midgley and Hanna.'[30]

They need not have bothered to be so circumspect. If Midgley's stance on the national question was not common knowledge, that of Baird and Hanna certainly was. On the evening of 17 May the three candidates attempted to hold a large meeting in the Ulster Hall, an ambitious venture for Labour in Belfast even in the most peaceful of times. Before they could mount the platform the hall had been stormed by Loyalists indignant that what they regarded as something of a Protestant temple was about to be 'desecrated' by 'Sinn Feiners'. Having been informed that they would only be allowed to speak provided they made no 'disloyal utterances', the three men decided to abandon the meeting.[31] Instead, a meeting was held by the gatecrashers during which a telegram from Sir James Craig was read out congratulating them on their action. The Loyalist workers had contacted Craig earlier to tell him that they had captured the Ulster Hall from the 'Bolsheviks'. The chair at the Loyalist meeting was taken by a Mr R. Tregenna who claimed to have seen the three Labour men in the City Hall the previous Friday, 'smiling and sneering with their Nationalist and Sinn Fein friends'. Baird in particular was vilified at the meeting.[32] Ironically, as far as Midgley was concerned, the Loyalist demonstration had been organised by the Ulster Ex-servicemen's Association. This organisation had broken away, late in 1919, from the main ex-servicemen's organisation, 'The Comrades of the Great War'.[33] The day after their abortive rally the three candidates decided reluctantly to cancel all other planned meetings 'owing to official hooliganism'.[34]

Votes were cast amidst much intimidation and violence. Personation, a traditional feature of Irish elections, was predictably rife. The Unionists raised the temperature to fever pitch with their appeal to the voters to save the Protestant way of life and leave no doubt as to where Ulster stood. The Nationalists, for their part, beat the opposite drum: 'We are Irish first, Irish last and Irish all the time', exclaimed Devlin.[35]

All the Labour candidates were crushed and lost their deposits. Midgley received 645 first preference votes and came bottom of the poll.[36] Baird fared little better in South Belfast with 875, while Hanna obtained a derisory 367 in the West. In North Belfast the Rev. Wallace received 926 first preferences, and his campaign was notably trouble-free. Wallace had deliberately distanced himself from the other three and on the issue of the constitution he made it clear that he believed Ulster Protestants should not be forced under an all-Ireland parliament

against their wishes.[37] A Labour candidate, Alex Adams, stood in
County Down, but he too lost his deposit, obtaining 1,188 first preference votes. The Unionists got the decisive majority they required
winning forty seats out of fifty-two. The Nationalists and Sinn Fein won
six seats each, neither group having the intention of taking their places in
the new parliament. Midgley, Baird and Hanna had also promised not to
take their seats if elected.[38]

In the aftermath of the election an obviously disgusted Midgley
complained bitterly of 'the way in which defenders of civil and religious
liberty had conducted themselves', and defiantly pledged to 'carry on
the fight until democracy was cured of the blindness which afflicted it at
present'. Finally, with scant regard now for tactical discretion, he stated
that: 'they of the Labour movement did not believe that the partition of
the working classes of Ireland would ever solve the problems of the
country, and for that reason they were going to work for that unity which
would bring about political and economic emancipation'.[39]

There can thus be little doubt that Midgley meant what he said about
partition. If he had wanted to try and avoid the national question and
concentrate on social and economic issues, he, like Wallace, could have
run an individual campaign. By campaigning with Baird and Hanna he
gave the appearance of support for such actions as the attempt to have
British Labour organise a blockade of Belfast. When Midgley split with
the Northern Ireland Labour Party in 1942, some ex-colleagues, Jack
Beattie in particular, took the chance to embarrass him by recalling
Midgley's advocacy of a 'Socialist Republic' for Ireland during this early
stage in his career.[40] In 1923 and 1924 Midgley addressed meetings
demanding the release of Republican prisoners interned by the
Northern Unionist government.[41] It has even been said that Midgley
frequently delivered speeches, at this time, from platforms bedecked in
Irish tricolours.[42]

All this cannot be ignored but, arguably, it is still wrong to try to
categorise Midgley as an Irish Republican in this period. His ultimate
ideal may have been an Irish Socialist Republic but too much in his
background and too many of his other political activities suggest that in
practice Midgley was clearly not a rigid Republican. There was his war
service and the deep sense of comradeship which he took out of it and
which undoubtedly motivated him to work on behalf of ex-servicemen
who were predominantly Protestant and fervently in favour of the
British connection. There was his involvement in the affairs of the
Belfast Co-operative Society, a Unionist-dominated body in which

Midgley never seems to have felt uncomfortable. There was his trade union job in which most of his members were Protestants and Unionists. And there was also his immersion, from boyhood, in a British Labourist tradition he at no time wished to distance himself from. The complexities and apparent contradictions in Midgley's politics mirrored the state of the Labour movement in Belfast which comprised a range of differing, and conflicting, tendencies.

IV

The circumstances in which the Northern Ireland state came into being established a sectarian political mould which determined Labour's minor status as a political force. Labour's equivocation on the national question ensured that it would pay only a peripheral role in the state's politics as long as the issue overrode all others. Labour's dilemma was a very real one and it would be simplistic and deceptive to argue that it brought its problems upon itself by not making its position clear. For the facts were that there was no unity within the movement on the constitutional question, and there were strong objections, based on the need to try and unite Protestant and Catholic workers, to be made against declaring in either a Nationalist or a Unionist direction.

It should also be remembered that the whole constitutional future of Ireland – both North and South – was riddled with uncertainty in the trouble-torn years of 1920–3. A Boundary Commission was appointed to redefine the hastily drawn border of 1920, and it was generally expected to make substantial adjustments in accordance with the wishes of the local populations. Many observers felt that in the wake of a redefined border, the Northern state would prove to be unviable as a political unit. The whole future of the South – 'The Irish Free State' as it had now become – as a political entity appeared similarly insecure. Continual friction there exploded into a brutal civil war in June 1922 between those who were prepared to accept the Anglo-Irish Treaty concluded in December 1921, and those Republicans for whom a 26-county state with limited sovereignty did not begin to meet their aspirations. This civil war ended in defeat for the Republicans in the spring of 1923.

Belfast Labour was effectively disowned at the moment of partition by both the British and Southern Irish Labour movements. The former had long wanted to be rid of Irish problems and for the most part displayed a woeful inability – or unwillingness – to come to terms with the intricate realities of the matter. Life was made much easier by identifying all of Ireland's ills in the Tory persona of Carson.[43] For its part, Labour in the South displayed a similar tendency to favour facile analyses of what should have occasioned serious debate. Typical examples of this abound in the Southern Labour newspapers of the time. In the *Watchword and Voice of Labour*, a paper edited by an old associate of Connolly's, Cathal O'Shannon, the Protestant workers were constantly being pilloried as 'gullible' and 'deluded' while at the same time being assured of their Southern comrades' faith in their eventual conversion to Connollyite socialism.[44]

It might also be argued, however, that Belfast Labour learnt little from its pre-World War I experience. In 1920–2 it again chose not to address itself to realities. Its spokesmen predictably fulminated about Craig and Carson and the innumerable acts of Tory iniquity; they also subscribed – in a barely modified form – to the prevailing theory in the Southern Labour movement that the bosses were manipulating gullible Protestant workers to malevolent ends. The pogroms of 1920–2 were, in Sam Kyle's opinion, deliberately 'engineered' after the shock waves of the 1919 Strike had shattered Unionist complacency.[45] This narrow perspective on what was a wide and complex issue may have allowed Labour to adopt a righteous posture while sectarian strife erupted all around, but it supplied them with no clear way forward when the time came to emerge into the reality of the new Northern Ireland State.

The Protestant skilled workers had reasserted themselves in 1920 and their domination of the crafts remained unimpaired after the sectarian troubles petered out in 1922. In fact, polarisation in all aspects of life became even more rigid. Many Catholics and some Protestants had been forced out of their homes to take refuge in 'safe' ghetto areas, thereby strengthening the existing segregated residential pattern. The Roman Catholic church's insistence on separate schooling found an echo in fundamentalist Protestant attitudes. Catholics in the new state found themselves accorded second-class citizenship, and completed the vicious circle themselves by disclaiming all allegience to the State. The Nationalist Party maintained a policy of complete abstention from the Northern Ireland parliament until 1925, and attended only irregularly thereafter. Protestants, for their part, felt that their way of life had only been preserved by their willingness to shed blood. Eternal vigilance had to remain the order of the day, given the unrepentantly Nationalist minority in their midst.

The Labour movement had only to consider the case of the large numbers of unskilled and semi-skilled Protestant workers to realise that Orange ideology was not monopolised by the skilled, and supposedly privileged, workers. It had only to take the Unionism of the Protestant working class seriously to realise that it was not synonymous with craven loyalty to the bosses. It had only to examine the strength of the respective community folk cultures to appreciate how deeply the sectarian roots were sunk and how impeccably-reasoned exposés of sectarian ideologies would not of themselves be enough to break their cultural grip on the mass of the people.

No searching examination was conducted by Labour into the acute problems it faced; neither was there any fruitful debate about how best to cultivate support in such a divided society. Instead, future endeavours came to be increasingly governed by the principle of political expediency.

Notes

1 Union file (A22), 'Memorandum re Mr. H. Midgley', USDAW Records, Manchester. Linenlappers folded linen after it had passed through the various stages of manufacture.
2 *Belfast Telegraph* 26 March 1941.
3 Undated newspaper cutting in *Midgley Papers*. The meeting probably took place late in 1922.
4 N.I. House of Commons Debates XXV, 2806–7.
5 Harry Midgley's Election Address, West Belfast 6 December 1923, *Midgley Papers*.
6 See S. Kyle, 'Labour in the north of Ireland', *The Irishman* 31 March 1928.
7 J. Harbinson, 'A history of the Northern Ireland Labour Party', M.Sc. thesis, Queen's University Belfast, 1966, p. 36.
8 Morgan, op. cit. pp. 375–80.
9 For information on the emergence of the UULA see 'Particulars of my life', autobiographical details written by Joseph Cunningham, Protestant trade unionist and member of the Northern Ireland senate from 1921. PRONI D1288.
   For a detailed account of the history of the UULA and its significance in relation to the Unionist movement see Morgan op. cit. chapter 13. The UULA's importance lies in the way it was integrated by Carson into the Unionist Party in 1918 in an attempt to preserve pan-class Unionist unity.
10 See S. Baker, 'Orange and green', in H. J. Dyos and M. Wolff, *The Victorian City*, London, 1973.
11 See Morgan op. cit. chapter 10 for an analysis of Devlin's political role within the Catholic community.
12 Sinn Fein, 'Ourselves Alone', was a revolutionary political force which desired the establishment of an Irish republic, completely separated from Britain.

13 See Patterson op. cit. p. 95.
14 This strike is admirably chronicled and analysed by both Patterson op. cit. chapter 5, and Morgan op. cit. chapter 5.
15 *Belfast News-Letter* 2 December 1919.
16 See A. Wilson, *P.R. Urban Elections in Ulster, 1920*, London, 1972, and C. O'Leary and I. Budge, *Belfast: Approach to Crisis*, London, 1973 pp. 136–40.
17 *Northern Whig* 3 May 1920.
18 Quoted in A. Clifford, 'Labour politics in Northern Ireland' Part 3, *The Irish Communist* No. 162 June 1979.
19 See, for example, 'The exclusion of Ulster' in *Ireland Upon the Dissecting Table*, Cork, n.d.
20 Kyle op. cit.
21 The military wing of Sinn Fein.
22 See M. Farrell, *Northern Ireland: The Orange State*, London, 1976 pp. 27–8.
23 For detailed accounts of the expulsions see Patterson op. cit. chapter 6, and Morgan op. cit. chapter 6.
24 See Midgley's speech, N.I. House of Commons Debates XVII, 139.
25 See D. S. Johnson, 'The Belfast boycott 1920–22', in J. M. Goldstrom and L. A. Clarkson (eds), *Irish Population, Economy and Society*, Oxford, 1982.
26 *Northern Whig* 27 November 1923.
27 During the 1938 Northern Ireland election campaign, Midgley claimed to have been one of the Expelled Workers' delegation which went to Britain to raise money for those workers who had been thrown out of their jobs. See chapter 6.
28 Morgan op. cit. p. 397.
29 Kyle op. cit.
30 *Belfast News-Letter* and *Northern Whig* 18 May 1921.
31 *Irish News* 18 May 1921.
32 *Northern Whig* 18 May 1921.
33 Morgan op. cit. p. 218.
34 *Irish News* 19 May 1921.
35 Ibid. 23 May 1921.
36 For a full breakdown of the results see S. Elliott, *Northern Ireland Parliamentary Election Results 1921–1972*, Chichester, 1973.
37 See A. Clifford op. cit.
38 *The Voice of Labour* 19 November 1921. This was a Southern Labour newspaper edited by Cathal O'Shannon.
39 *Northern Whig* 27 May 1921.
40 See, for example, Beattie's speech at Stormont 11 May 1943, N.I. House of Commons Debates XXVI, 478–9: 'That was the time [i.e. the early 1920s] he [Midgley] was going up and down from Dundalk to Dublin and West Belfast with your humble friend and when I was afraid to sit on the platform with him because of the outrageous speeches he was making about the Tories of the North.'
41 The first time Tommy Watters, a prominent member of the Communist Party of Ireland in the 1930s, heard Midgley speak was at a release meeting for the Republican prisoner Frank Thornbray. Interview with Tommy Watters 11 July 1980. See also next chapter.

42 Interview with J. P. Kyle 25 March 1981.
43 See F. D. Schneider, 'British Labour and Ireland 1918–1921: the retreat to houndsditch', *Review of Politics* 40, 1978, pp. 368–91.
44 See, for example, *Watchword and Voice of Labour* 20 November 1920.
45 Kyle op. cit.

Chapter Three

Labour's Standard-bearer (1923–1925)

I

With Midgley as secretary, the Belfast Labour Party slowly began to recover from the demoralising effects of the inter-communal violence of 1920–2. There was no attempt to contest any seats at the 1922 General Election, but by January 1923 the climate had sufficiently cooled to allow participation in the municipal contests. Only two Labour candidates were elected, however, a loss of nine seats in all on the 1920 performance.

In the spring of 1923, the Belfast Labour Party decided to make a start in building up its organisation at grassroots level. It met to draw up a constitution for divisional parties, the object being to enrol individual members as well as affiliated societies. By the end of the year there were two divisional parties: East and West Belfast.[1] This was in addition to, and separate from, the existing ILP organisation in the city which comprised two branches: North and Central.[2]

Two happenings near the end of 1923 gave the Labour movement a renewed sense of vigour and self-confidence. On 12 October, Belfast's pre-war practice of playing host to speakers from the British Labour movement was resumed with a successful meeting in the Ulster Hall addressed by Col. J. C. Wedgewood MP. The meeting was well attended and passed off peacefully. Wedgewood delivered an inspiring address and reflected the drive and the optimism of the British Labour Party, poised as it then was to issue a powerful and, in the event, partly successful electoral challenge. Writing a few months after the meeting, Midgley claimed that Wedgewood had 'helped very materially to create a more healthy atmosphere in Belfast'.[3] At the same meeting Midgley himself had drawn loud applause by declaring: 'I notice the orthodox politicians in Northern Ireland are at present preparing their new bogey for the next election – that is the Border Question ... I tell you, both from the international point of view, and also from the point of view of the love that ought to dwell in our hearts, there is no border on God's earth worth losing one's life over.'[4]

The second event which boosted Labour's fortunes had Midgley as its focal point: the decision to contest the seat of West Belfast at the General Election of 6 December 1923 with Midgley as the party candidate. This decision was not taken lightly. The weight of opinion in the party at the time of its annual meeting had been against contesting elecuons and in favour of strengthening organisation and increasing propaganda activities until such times as the omens seemed fair for the party to fight. The legacy of the recent troubles evidently rested heavily on many in the party who, understandably, did not wish to risk another humiliation along the lines of 1921 before the party had even begun to build up its resources.

Midgley was among those who considered the party's policy of keeping a low profile to be self-defeating. It could not be in Labour's interest to leave the political field to the Unionists and Nationalists, both of whom, in the absence of a third force, would certainly be better able to tighten their grip on their respective communities by virtue of their appeal to respective national loyalties and sectarian traditions. It was vital to show that Labour would not be deterred by violence and intimidation and that it meant to carve a non-sectarian position for itself on the political spectrum in the material interest of the working class. As Midgley wrote in March 1924: '. . . it became increasingly evident that some attempt would have to be made to gauge the state of the public mind by challenging the powers that be in an electoral contest.'[5]

II

The constituency of West Belfast had been redefined in 1921. The old Falls Ward which had been controlled by Joe Devlin was merged into a larger division which included the strongly Protestant areas of the Shankill Road and Sandy Row. The Nationalists viewed this with good reason as a cynical piece of gerrymandering on the part of the Unionists with the intention of depriving them of representation at Westminster. They chose, as a protest, to boycott the 1922 election, and in 1923 they again declined to participate. Midgley, therefore, was left as the sole challenger to the Unionist incumbent, Sir Robert Lynn.[6]

The election campaign was memorable. Midgley worked hard to win the votes of both Protestant and Catholic areas of the division. In his election address Midgley waxed boldly eloquent: 'As a Labour candidate I challenge the whole conception of economic relationships underlying our present economic system', going on to claim that the Labour Party alone had a 'positive remedy' for unemployment. He urged national work schemes with adequate provision made for those who could not be employed. Turning to the war debt, he declared himself in favour of a Graduated War Debt Redemption Levy, better known as the Capital Levy, on all individual fortunes in excess of five thousand pounds, the revenue from this to be devoted solely to the reduction of the debt. The war still prayed on Midgley's mind and, perhaps with Protestant voters also in mind, he emphasised his own service and the sacrifices of those who gave their lives. With regard to social issues, Midgley adumbrated the expected demands, among them a National Minimum Wage, an eight-hour day, and widows' pensions.[7] In fact, Midgley's programme repeated practically word for word large parts of the British Labour Party's election manifesto.[8] He obviously had the intention, if elected, to work closely with the Labour Party at Westminster.

Not surprisingly Lynn and his supporters attempted once again to equate Labour with Sinn Fein in the eyes of Protestant voters. This was only one 'scare' tactic, however: the 'red menace' of bolshevism was also played up for all it was worth. The *Northern Whig*, for example, carried a notice: 'The Socialist Party is the close ally of the blood-stained Soviet tyranny in Russia, the only atheistic Government in the world.'[9] Lynn himself told a meeting that socialism and bolshevism were one and the same and produced nothing except 'long hair and long speeches'.[10] Lynn communicated his confidence through the pages of the *Northern Whig*. Perhaps convinced of the certainty of Catholic abstentions, the latter newspaper assured its readers that the result was 'a foregone conclusion'.[11] Lynn also accused Midgley of being party to the attempts made in 1920 to deprive Belfast of necessary raw materials.[12] Some of Lynn's supporters went further and severely stretched the credibility of his campaign by peddling what they knew to be outright falsehoods. Thompson Donald, who had known Midgley personally in the shipyards, claimed at a Lynn meeting that Midgley had received a convent school education! He further declared, significantly, that he would rather Joe Devlin was returned for West Belfast than Midgley.[13] Herbert Dixon, a Unionist MP, saw much in common between Midgley and de Valera: 'both are rank, rotten republicans', he declared with an alliterative flourish.[14]

Such desperate tactics betrayed the Unionists' anxiety. Thompson

Donald was astounded to find himself being heckled in of all places, the Shankill Road: 'What's gone wrong with the Shankill?', he despairingly asked the crowd, a large portion of which obviously favoured Midgley.[15] Lynn himself had to cope with interjections at some of his meetings; in the middle of one attack on 'Red Flaggers', he was reminded that Midgley was 'a good trade unionist'.[16] The *Northern Whig* had to admit that Midgley's meetings in Protestant areas were, for the most part, 'enthusiastic and well-attended',[17] and consequently redoubled its efforts to make the 'Sinn Feiner' charge stick:

The electors of West Belfast and particularly those who reside in the Sandy Row and Shankill Road districts, will be interested to learn that Mr Midgley's canvassers visiting the Falls area of the West state that their candidate not only favours an Irish Republic but the establishment of Republics generally. Those who suffered at the hands of the Sinn Fein gunmen will also read with interest that the same canvassers state that the release of the Falls Road gunmen now in prison is one of the planks of their platform.[18]

Midgley's campaign was, in fact, a masterly exercise in appearing as all things to all men. He attempted as much as he could to concentrate on social and economic issues but soon proved that he was ready to deal with the more emotive issues surrounding the national question. On the Shankill Road Midgley was asked the inevitable question about where he stood with regard to the border, a question he parried as follows: 'I agree with Sir James Craig when he says that the Boundary question should be settled without the loss of a single life on either side.'[19] 'Where's your flag?', he was then asked. 'Flying over the grave of my brother on the Western Front', he replied. 'Are you in favour of the old flag [the Union Jack]?', someone else enquired. 'I am out to uphold all the good that old flag stands for by creating better conditions', answered Midgley adroitly, going on to say that he was a member of the Agnes Street Presbyterian Church and a good Protestant.[20] As the uproar continued a voice asked why he didn't have a band with him to which Midgley gave the defiant reply: 'I could have had bands, but the bandsmen were afraid to come in case they would lose engagements on the 12th of July.' Challenged to name the bands, Midgley cited the Colonel Bernard Flute Band, a claim which elicited a denial from this band's secretary the following day. Midgley was eventually drowned out by the strains of 'Derry's Walls', and took himself off to the Falls Road where it was claimed by the *Northern Whig* the next day that he had been joined by a Hibernian band which accompanied him round the area.[21]

In the Catholic Falls Midgley gave his audience there what they wanted to hear. Asked whether, if elected, he would vote against money being sent from England to continue the internment of prisoners, Midgley replied: 'I am not in favour of men being interned in any part of the world, whether it is in Sandy Row, Larne, Wexford or Cork. If there is a charge let it be put against them. I stand for freedom for Protestant and Catholic alike.' Without saying so in as many words, Midgley's rhetoric conveyed the clear impression that he shared the national aspirations of his Falls audience: '[they all should work] to make North, South, East and West brothers and sisters regardless of the creed they belonged to.'[22] The Falls of course was also fertile territory for scathing attacks on the Unionists, and Midgley's ferocious rhetoric in this regard contrasted notably with his more respectful references to Unionist leaders such as Craig in Protestant areas.

The skill with which Midgley played off one sectarian force against the other was reflected in the final vote. Midgley amassed an impressive 22,255, losing narrowly to Lynn by just 2,720 votes. The number who polled was 47,230 out of a register of 67,162, and it seems that at least half of those who did not vote were Catholics. The *Irish News* estimated that there were around 12,000 Catholic abstentions,[23] and lamented the fact that no organised effort was made by any Nationalist organisation to get people to the polls to vote for Midgley.[24] It is impossible to deduce with any degree of precision the religious mix of Midgley's total vote, but given that there were around 23,000 Catholic voters in the ward,[25] and assuming that the Catholics who did vote voted virtually '*en masse*' for Midgley, it would appear to be a fair estimate that Midgley's total comprised some 12,000 Catholic votes, and some 10,000 Protestant votes. The *Northern Whig*, somewhat chastened by Midgley's performance, admitted that he had won considerable Protestant working class support. It referred disparagingly to, 'that element of Labour which, refusing to follow the lead of their legitimate advisers, preferred to support the scarlet banner of the English Socialist party, as represented in this instance by Mr. Harry Midgley'.[26] Personation was again widespread, with both sides condemning the other for practising it. Midgley was predictably delighted with his showing and described the vote he received as 'stupendous'.[27]

Midgley's candidature in West Belfast has been seen as an opportunist attempt to exploit the 'ready protest vote of the Catholic community'.[28] Opportunist it certainly was, but arguably in the best sense of that word. Midgley took the chance to give both Protestant and Catholic workers an alternative to Tory Unionism, an alternative denied them in the previous election. In so doing he enhanced significantly the political standing of the Belfast Labour movement. He took on the sectarian forces which were inevitably directed at him, and emerged with a personal triumph having won votes in roughly equal numbers from Protestants and Catholics. Midgley's vote indicated that a substantial portion of the working class was responsive to the politics of Labour and not in thrall to the respective ideologies of Nationalism and Unionism. Coming so soon after the troubles of 1920–2, Midgley's achievements in these respects were quite remarkable. His belief that Labour had to contest elections and carry on the fight for class politics in the full glare of the public eye, seemed to have been vindicated. For Midgley the cause of Labour should not – and did not – have to wait.

It should be remembered, however, that Midgley's impressive performance was partly the result of his skill in being able to pander, to some degree, to the prejudices of Protestant and Catholic voters. He did it superbly and, to his credit, always sought to convince his audience, whoever they were, that declarations of national loyalty would not, at the end of the day, alter their economic circumstances. On this occasion his social message probably struck the right note, but even so he still lost, and, crucially for Labour, it was plain that reliance on an appeal to people's social and economic needs would not be enough against the deeper stirrings evoked by the border question. Some of those who voted for Midgley this time would revert to old loyalties another day, depending on circumstances and personal foibles. Midgley's showing was encouraging for Labour but it was none the less clear that its room for manoeuvre was still acutely restricted by the parameters of the national question.

The West Belfast result further stimulated Labour's process of reorganisation. Midgley at this time seems to have been the most dynamic figure in the movement although Sam Kyle, Jack Beattie and William McMullen were probably all as well known to the public. In October of 1923, a report on Belfast Labour's progress appeared in *Forward*, the Glasgow ILP paper, and the correspondent singled out Midgley for special praise: 'The Secretary [of the party] is Comrade Harry Midgley. If ever there was a man for the job young Midgley is that man. Of a most winning and likeable nature, a man to evoke friends and hold them, a dynamo of energy, a love for his work and the cause, that man is Midgley.'[29]

In January 1924, following the local elections at which Labour made two gains, Midgley announced that a conference was to be held at which the Belfast Labour Party would become the Labour Party (Northern Ireland) with its own constitution.[30] This conference was duly held on 8 March and was attended by over forty delegates representing the country districts and the party locally, and also by representatives of the Shipbuilding and Engineering Federation. The question of a full constitution was left to a future conference, but the party, in renaming itself, pledged to extend its operations as far as possible throughout the six counties. Kyle was elected president for the coming year, Robert Dornan vice-president, and Midgley secretary.[31]

In effect Labour in the North had decided to face the reality of partition and had begun to make a serious attempt to gain political power in the new parliament. It made no firm commitment on the national question, however, refusing to make any explicit declaration of loyalty to the new state or any intimation of desire to see a united Ireland brought about. The new party was independent of both the British and Irish Labour parties, although it clearly modelled its aims and its approach on the former, and had an indirect link with the latter by virtue of a number of trade unions and other organisations being affiliated to the ITUC of which the Irish Labour Party was a part.[32] However, most of the trade unions affiliated to the new party were British-based unions.

III

In October 1924 there was another general election and Midgley was chosen again to represent Labour, this time under the auspices of the Northern Ireland Labour Party (NILP),[33] in West Belfast. Lynn of course was defending the seat, and this time there was a third candidate: Patrick Nash, an internee in Larne, who was put forward by Sinn Fein. The Nationalists again abstained. Sam Kyle withdrew his candidature from North Belfast and all Labour efforts were directed at securing victory for Midgley. The election took place in the long shadow cast by the Boundary Commission whose recommendations regarding the border were expected to be made soon after. Even before the election the Unionists had begun to foster resolve among the Protestants to yield 'Not an Inch' and to hang on to the territory which they then had control of. 'The Border bogey' had come back to haunt Labour well and truly.

Midgley found this out to his cost early on in his campaign. He tried to hold a meeting in Sandy Row but it was broken up by an angry mob and he was forced to beat the first of several retreats to the sanctuary of the Catholic Falls.[34] Later he tried his luck in the Shankill Road and had his brake rushed. Missiles were thrown and Midgley's election agent, Jack Beattie, sustained an ugly head wound.[35] The treatment meted out to Midgley got so bad that even the *Northern Whig* was forced to adopt a censorious tone to the mobs,[36] while simultaneously fuelling the fires with its vilification of Midgley as a 'Sinn Feiner' and a 'Bolshevik'. It appeared that the result in 1923 had been too close for comfort for the Unionists, and this time there were to be no punches pulled in respect of propaganda and campaign work. Intimidating tactics, if not encouraged, were at least winked at. Passions were deliberately inflamed over the question of the border, and no less a figure than Carson entered the fray to proclaim that the election was Ulster's 'most crucial hour' during which 'any wavering, dissension, or division will be construed as a victory for Sinn Fein'.[37] The *Northern Whig* was not averse to distorting the truth in its desperation to see Lynn elected. It published an advertisement which stated: 'The Boundary Commission has been appointed by the Socialist Government. Vote against Socialism!'[38] Lynn made much of Midgley's appearance at a meeting in May 1924 in support of Republican internees, and said that Midgley had written to Ramsay MacDonald asking him to influence the Northern Ireland government on this issue.[39] Midgley did not deny this. Less malevolently, the Unionists made some capital out of Mary MacSwiney's[40] campaign on behalf of Nash. The *Northern Whig* published a rhyme entitled 'Midgley's Appeal to Mary MacSwiney': 'I'm sitting on the stile, Mary / I should be on your side / But I want to gull the Orangemen / And so I try to hide / the Green Flag underneath the Red / Till polling day goes by / the Red is on my lips Mary / But the green flag's in my eye.'[41]

After the Shankill Road incident, Midgley seems to have riveted his attention to the Catholic areas of the ward in a bid to stave off defections to Nash and if possible to lure out those Catholic voters who had abstained in 1923. Certainly he made a positive effort to pose as the Catholic voters' champion. Speaking in the Falls, he said: 'I desire with all my heart and soul, no matter what the result of this election may be, to lay my tribute at the shrine of comradeship, love and respect that the people of a different religious persuasion in West Belfast have meted out to me since I came into the constituency.' 'You are worthy of it all', came the reply from a voice in the crowd.[42] Midgley once again spoke out against internment: '[the Internees] had been put on the *Argenta*, and later in the Larne workhouse, on trumped-up charges, but really on account of their religion.'[43]

Midgley, with the full backing of the *Irish News* which had always opposed Sinn Fein in favour of the constitutionalist nationalists, could do little wrong in Catholic eyes. He was even cheered on the Falls when he told his audience that a republic for Ireland would not mean freedom for Ireland.[44] He was of course trying to discredit Sinn Fein and, significantly, he had little difficulty in winning the crowd to his viewpoint. In Devlin's traditional stronghold, Sinn Fein republicanism had not made its electoral mark and the vast majority followed the middle-of-the-road nationalist line of the *Irish News*.

Midgley was once again fighting on the programme of the British Labour Party and he stoutly defended the Labour government's record since they had taken office in January 1924.[45] This was made easier by comparing it to the record of the Unionist government under Craig. Midgley also reiterated the cruder nationalist theories regarding the Unionist Party and the Protestant workers: 'I know, and you know, that the periodic outbursts of insane bigotry and intolerance in Belfast were instigated by the Ulster Tory Party so that the people of all creeds and classes would be kept at each other's throats.'[46] However much truth there was in this, Midgley had demonstrated, by saying it, that, for the moment at least, he had given up on the Protestant workers and had condemned them as dupes of the Unionist Party.

He may have been forgiven for doing that in the light of his reception in the Shankill Road, but there is evidence that he still enjoyed considerable Protestant support. The *Irish News* columnist 'Slemish' claimed to have received a letter from an Orangeman in which the writer complained about the declaration of the District Master of his Orange Lodge that Orangemen who helped Midgley should be expelled from the Order. The correspondent wrote that he and other Orangemen had as much right to support Midgley as the District Master had to support Lynn, and that they were going to continue to support Midgley in spite of the threats.[47] Midgley also had three Protestant socialist clergymen speak for him: the Rev. Edgar J. Fripp, the Rev. J. Bruce Wallace, and the Rev. A. L. Agnew.[48]

The result was declared on 30 October and was as follows: Lynn 28,435, Midgley 21,122, and Nash 2,688. The total vote was 52,410 out of an electorate of 66,010. Again personation had been rife, and this time it seems to have been more prominent on the Unionist side. Intimidation had also been in evidence, and Midgley's agents had had to leave the polling booths in Sandy Row.[49] Midgley had lost some ground among the Protestant voters and any gains made among Catholics were probably offset by the republican vote for Nash. The *Irish*

News estimated Catholic abstentions to be 'many thousands'[50] but there were probably fewer than in 1923. Midgley's performance was more than creditable. He had again scored something of a personal triumph and proved his ability to win substantial support in both communities. Given the curtailment of his campaign in Protestant areas early on, it is probably surprising that he obtained as many Protestant votes as he obviously did. This was proof again that the Unionists could not afford to be complacent, and that their so-called manipulative tactics had failed completely in a great many cases.

Midgley was undaunted by the setback. After the election, in a rare moment of humility, he averred: 'Time is on our side, and whether Harry Midgley is the candidate in the future it does not really matter, for the Labour cause is greater than Harry Midgley.'[51] Labour's cause had received another boost, albeit a less spectacular one than in 1923. It was also painfully evident, however, that sectarian battle cries had prevailed again and that as the temperature of the controversy surrounding the national question rose, Labour's hopes of cutting a significant swathe in the political landscape fell in accordance.

At the end of November, Midgley vented his suppressed anger concerning the circumstances of the election in the pages of *Forward*: 'Seldom has an election atmosphere been so charged with putridity, slander, spite, violence and denial of the right of free speech as that created in Belfast on this occasion.' He further complained that the Unionists 'proceeded to point out to the Tory working classes of Belfast that we were in league with the Catholic Church', and stressed Labour's urgent need for money to build up an 'electoral machine' for the future.[52] No electoral machine of Labour's, however, no matter how efficient, could win over a majority of 'the Tory working classes' while the party continued to equivocate on the constitutional issue. And, as Labour would find out, there were few electoral machines as efficient as Joe Devlin's in the Catholic community.

Labour's equivocation on the national question was, after 1924, largely theoretical. In practice it accepted the reality of the new state which, despite continuing uncertainty over the Boundary Commission, had survived and was going to be viable, in some form, after all. Labour in Northern Ireland recognised the importance of checking the Unionist domination in every possible way. It urged that Northern Ireland enjoy parity with the rest of the United Kingdom in the realm of social services.[53] Midgley's conscious adoption of the British Labour programme in his election contests and his part in shaping the new party constitution along the same lines as that of the British Labour Party,[54] suggest that he believed that politics in Northern Ireland had to be fought on a British basis.

Midgley's approach, however, begged a political framework in which Northern Ireland could participate on equal terms with the rest of the United Kingdom, with the people able to vote for the parties that were likely to govern them from Westminster. It was from Westminster that the social reforms demanded by the Labour Party in Northern Ireland would emanate, and in this respect the party found its appeal to be blunted. For it was not the policy of the Unionist government to deviate from the rest of Britain in the realm of social legislation; the government's guiding principle quickly became that of 'step by step', a policy which was generally followed.[55] One of the most important effects of this was to weaken the provincial basis for the development of class politics. In such circumstances politics in Northern Ireland focused on the question of the Constitution while social and economic issues were decided at Westminster. Devolved government was thus of itself an advantage to the Unionists.

IV

In January 1925 Midgley finally won an election: he defeated the Unionist, Thomas English, for the Belfast Council seat of Dock by 2,676 votes to 2,637. Midgley had of course been brought up in the Dock area and knew it inside out. There was a sizeable Catholic vote and it is likely that Midgley secured it virtually intact, in addition to the minority of Protestant votes he was able to pluck from English to give him his paper-thin victory.

During his campaign, Midgley put the case for 'Labour's municipal charter': the extension of municipalisation in the city to cover such as coal and the supply of milk. The Unionist press viewed such aims as the thin end of the wedge, and joined with the *Irish News* in denouncing socialism. This combined opposition of Unionists and Nationalists against Labour was to be a common feature of municipal elections. In the traditionally Nationalist wards of Smithfield and Falls the Labour candidates complained of the sectarianism of their Nationalist opponents.[56] Sam Kyle claimed that the Unionists had urged electors in these divisions to vote Nationalist and had quoted with approval the Pope's directive to his flock to fight the dangers of socialism and communism.[57] The *Northern Whig* suddenly forgot the menace of Rome in its fear of the 'Red Peril': 'All the great leaders of Christian thought, whether they be Roman Catholics or Protestants, have warned their followers of the blighting influence of socialism.'[58]

While the press thus declaimed, Midgley extended his sphere of influence and took another important step in his political career. It was to be the beginning of a long and eventful political association with the Dock ward of the city.

Notes

1 *The Labour Party (Northern Ireland) Annual Report 1923–24.*
2 The North branch was much the stronger and contributed more financially to party funds. See Morgan op. cit. p. 369.
3 *The Labour Party (Northern Ireland) Annual Report 1923–24.*
4 *Irish News* 13 October 1923.
5 *The Labour Party (Northern Ireland) Annual Report 1923–24.*
6 Lynn was at this time editor of the Belfast morning newspaper, the *Northern Whig.*
7 Harry Midgley's election address West Belfast 6 December 1923. Included in the papers of Mr Sam Napier.
8 See R. Miliband, *Parliamentary Socialism*, London, 1961 pp. 98–9.
9 *Northern Whig* 28 November 1923.
10 Ibid. 1 December 1923.
11 Ibid. 27 November 1923.
12 Ibid. 29 November 1923.
13 *Belfast News-Letter* 28 November 1923.
14 *Northern Whig* 4 December 1923.
15 *Belfast News-Letter* 30 November 1923.
16 *Northern Whig* 1 December 1923.
17 Ibid. 27 November 1923.
18 Ibid. 1 December 1923.
19 Ibid. 5 December 1923.
20 *Irish News* 5 December 1923.
21 *Northern Whig* 5 December 1923.
22 *Irish News* 28 November 1923.
23 Ibid. 8 December 1923.
24 Ibid. 7 December 1923.
25 *Northern Whig* 7 December 1923.
26 Ibid.
27 Ibid. 8 December 1923.
28 Morgan op. cit. p. 720.
29 *Forward* 13 October 1923.
30 *Northern Whig* 11 January 1914.
31 *The Labour Party (N.I.) Annual Report 1923–24.* The party's new constitution did not become operative until 1 February 1926.
32 The Irish Labour Party paid the Northern Party a subsidy during the 1920s.
33 The name Northern Ireland Labour Party (NILP) seems to have been

adopted from around the end of the 1920s. For the purposes of convenience
it will be used here throughout.

34 *Northern Whig* 13 October 1924.
35 *Irish News* 16 October 1924.
36 *Northern Whig* 17 October 1924.
37 Ibid. 24 October 1924.
38 Ibid. 25 October 1924.
39 Ibid. 28 October 1924.
40 Daughter of Terence MacSwiney, the Mayor of Cork, who died on hunger
    strike in 1920.
41 *Northern Whig* 25 October 1924.
42 *Irish News* 15 October 1924.
43 *Northern Whig* 15 October 1924.
44 *Irish News* 29 October 1924.
45 Harry Midgley's election address West Belfast 29 October 1924. *Midgley
    Papers*.
46 *Irish News* 29 October 1924.
47 Ibid. 25 October 1924.
48 Ibid. 28 October 1924. The Rev. Agnew – a Unitarian minister – was well
    known at this time for his strong Labour congregation at his church in York
    Street. Midgley himself attended services at the church.
49 *Irish News* 30 October 1924.
50 Ibid.
51 Ibid. 31 October 1924.
52 *Forward* 29 November 1924.
53 See A. Clifford, 'Labour politics in Northern Ireland Part 5', The *Irish
    Communist* No. 165, September 1975.
54 See 'Notes re the Labour movement in Northern Ireland', *Midgley Papers*.
55 There were significant discrepancies between Northern Ireland and the rest
    of the UK in certain social respects. Relief rates paid to the poor, for
    example, were lower in Belfast than any other British city. See chapter 6.
56 *Northern Whig* 13 January 1925.
57 *Forward* 31 January 1925.
58 *Northern Whig* 13 January 1925.

Chapter Four

'The Workers' Champion' (1925–1932)

I

Midgley attached great importance to his election to the City Council. He looked upon it as a stepping stone to a parliamentary career,[1] while believing that local government could do much to benefit the community. He took his seat with a double purpose: to press for urgently needed social reforms, and to enhance his own position both within the Labour movement and in the public eye.

Midgley well understood the informal nature of Belfast politics and it suited him perfectly. He was an affable and outgoing personality who made friends easily and who was quick to try to help others. He knew that to build up a strong base of personal support he could use his position of influence to do favours for people. His seat on the council and his position on the board of management of the Co-operative Society he used to good effect to widen his circle of contacts. The Belfast political scene – and indeed that of Northern Ireland as a whole[2] – was small enough to ensure that politics would be conducted in a personal style, a state of affairs which conferred advantages on an individual like Midgley whose strength of character enabled him to make a powerful impact.

As a councillor Midgley concentrated much of his energy on educational questions and commenced the battle he was to wage for several years on the issues of free school books and the provision of meals for necessitous children.[3] This was an area in which Ulster lagged behind the rest of the United Kingdom. Midgley fought Labour's cause on a whole range of other issues too: wage increases, resistance to cuts in corporation employees' wages, rent reductions, housing schemes, the rate of Outdoor Relief paid by the Poor Law Guardians, and the establishment of a municipal bank for Belfast. As a representative of Dock Ward, Midgley had much to complain about: this ward had more one-roomed houses than any other in the city, and many of these houses accommodated upwards of six persons.[4]

In Northern Ireland as a whole unemployment was steadily rising: in 1925 it stood at 23.9 per cent, over twice the United Kingdom rate.[5] Rates of Poor Law Relief were much lower than in the rest of the UK and relief was only granted in cases of the most extreme hardship.[6] By 1925 a severe economic depression had set in, especially in the textile industry.[7] The shipbuilding industry too had begun to contract, a process which was to lead to a reduction in the number of employees from the 1924 figure of 20,000 to 2,000 in 1933.[8]

By the end of his first three-year term in the council, Midgley had made his mark. He had been instrumental in securing additional money to provide free school books and meals for more poor children than before; he had secured workmen's fares on the trams until 8.30 a.m., instead of 8 a.m.; and he had secured cheaper tram fares for all children.[9] Determined to make life difficult for the business and commercial interests which ran the city, he had involved himself in controversy,[10] and had assiduously cultivated the role of 'the Workers' Champion', his slogan in 1928 when he stood for re-election.

II

It is much more difficult to assess the impact made by Midgley on the Northern Ireland Labour Party (NILP) during the late 1920s. He certainly appears to have adopted a lower profile in comparison with the period 1920–5, and he did not hold office in the party from 1925 until 1932. He claimed that his main objective when elected to the council was to become immersed in municipal politics and to use this experience for future benefit as a parliamentary representative, a goal he never seems to have doubted he would attain. He sought to prove his abilities as Labour's leader in the council and to become recognised as Labour's most renowned advocate in the city.

There are, however, grounds for suspecting that, his relatively low profile notwithstanding, Midgley was jockeying for position within the party during this period and seizing every opportunity to improve his chances of challenging effectively for the leadership. Although he bore him no personal grudge, it seems that Sam Kyle, leader of the Parliamentary Labour Party after the 1925 election,[11] was the man whom Midgley perceived as the main obstacle in his path to the top.

Born in 1884, Kyle was still very much in his prime and he could boast of over twenty years of uninterrupted service to the Labour movement in Belfast. He was a much-respected and popular figure both within and outside the Labour movement. Kyle was an able man and a staunch socialist. He believed just as strongly in parliamentary democracy and attempted while in parliament to mould a responsible image for the Labour Party, a mirror image, in fact, of the British Labour Party led by Ramsay MacDonald. Kyle was a moderate man in temperament and in outlook, and believed that the pejorative notions held by many people in Northern Ireland about Labour could only be dissolved if the party, as in Britain, proved itself 'fit to govern'. As will be shown, Midgley's views in this respect did not differ significantly from Kyle's. He simply desired that Harry Midgley, and not Sam Kyle, should lead this responsible and mature political party.

On 5 May 1926, in response to the General Strike in Britain, Kyle made an emollient speech in the Northern Ireland parliament expressing the hope that the situation in Ulster would stay normal.[12] At a Labour meeting on Sunday 9 May, Kyle reiterated his appeal for calm, and urged workers not to deviate from 'constitutional methods'. Following Kyle, Midgley contrived a stark contrast in tone. Using all his rhetorical flair, he urged support for the miners and went on to say that soldiers who took up guns against strikers were 'dogs and damned low despicable dogs'. He added: 'If they were men, a more manly and Christian thing to do would be to turn the guns on those who gave the orders.'[13]

This militant posturing on Midgley's part would probably have been motivated to some extent by a genuine feeling of solidarity with the strikers in general and the miners in particular.[14] In addition Midgley may not, like Kyle, have regarded with dismay the prospect of the strike spreading to Northern Ireland. In the circumstances, however, it is possible to interpret this episode in terms of Midgley attempting to undermine Kyle's leadership credentials. Midgley could afford to say reckless things; he was not in parliament and held no office in the party. He was free to use his oratorical prowess to stir things up and to advance himself as the kind of man who would provide inspiring and uncompromising leadership. His outburst can be seen as an attempt to draw support from those elements in the party who were far from happy with its moderate leadership.

In June 1928 the British Labour movement was thrown into a storm of controversy by the publication of the Cook–Maxton manifesto.[15] The miners' leader, A. J. Cook, and the chairman of the ILP, James Maxton, produced the manifesto largely in response to the Mond–Turner discussions in the wake of the General Strike and the consequent anti-Labour legislation. These discussions between an employer (Mond) and a trade unionist (Turner) were denounced as collaborationist, and Cook and Maxton decided to initiate a campaign which they hoped would result in Labour serving a renewed – and rigidly socialist – challenge to the status quo. Their manifesto, however, was widely interpreted as either an attempt to wrench the Labour Party from its reformist road, or the first step to the establishment of a new party.[16] The ILP was divided with several of its leading figures reacting unfavourably to the manifesto which they saw as unrealistic and fanciful.

On 7 July *Forward* published a resolution passed by the North Belfast ILP branch of which Kyle was secretary. The resolution called on Maxton to be more 'explicit' regarding the charges he was making against the leaders of the Labour Party. Following this, *Forward* published a letter from Kyle two weeks later in which he invoked Cook's speech at the 1927 TUC in which the miners' leader had dismissed the idea of Europe as one economic entity as 'unpracticable idealism', and unmistakeably indicated that he (Kyle) viewed the Cook–Maxton manifesto in the same terms.[17]

One week later *Forward* published a notice submitted by the Dock Ward Labour Party in which it was stated that a resolution had been passed approving of the action of Maxton and Cook.[18] Midgley, of course, was in the Dock Ward party and was also a regular contributor to *Forward*. Nothing concerning the Dock Ward party specifically had appeared in the paper before, and there are, therefore, some grounds for suspecting that Midgley was largely responsible for publicising the Dock Branch's resolution in order to be seen to be out of step with the views expressed by Kyle and the North Belfast ILP in the previous weeks. At the very least it can be said that Midgley did nothing to dissociate himself from his branch's resolution which exposed a clear fissure in the ranks of Labour in Northern Ireland.

Again it may have been the case that Midgley sincerely believed in the manifesto as a progressive development for the Labour movement, and certainly his support for it would have been consistent with his militant outbursts during the General Strike. It was, however, consistent with very little else he seemed to hold with at the time, and tends to fit awkwardly with his earlier defence of the British Parliamentary Labour Party – much reviled by Maxton – and his later repudiation of the ILP decision to disaffiliate from the Labour Party in 1932.[19]

During the late 1920s Midgley contributed frequently (book reviews, political reports, poems, and biographical sketches of Belfast trade unionists) to his trade union journal. These contributions offer insights into his political thinking during this period. In the course, for example, of a three-part review of the works of Anatole France, Midgley drew upon the French novelist to affirm his belief in the eventual triumph of a socialist order, but also to reveal that he was under no illusions about how quickly or easily this would be brought about. From *The Gods are Athirst*, Midgley divined the moral that, 'No man should preach the doctrine of armed revolution unless he understands, and accepts, all the implications of his own philosophy'.[20] He went on to recommend the book to those who wished to see into the mind of an individual gripped by 'revolutionary fervour', and who, like himself, 'know nothing of the workings of the mind dominated by an idea to the exclusion of all finer sentiments, such as family ties, blood relationship, and bonds of comradely affection'. Midgley much admired Anatole France's 'sublime touch' in 'recognising and reconciling the inevitabilities of life, laughing at the idiosyncracies of men, and shattering their superstitions with a withering but graceful scorn'.[21] For Midgley, to read France's works was to be inspired with magnaminity towards all men. He summarised the inspiration he derived from France as follows: 'To strive to know all helps one to forgive much, and to be at least charitable to almost all human failings.'[22]

From this it might be said that Midgley had come to hold a less simplistic outlook on life than many in the Labour movement who tended to see matters in a black–white perspective with little or nothing in between. These quotations suggest that by this time Midgley had come to recognise that the complexities of human nature could not be overridden or wished away to accommodate the requirements of any set of political doctrines and dogmas. He seemed to believe that the triumph of socialism would be a long and difficult process in which the importance of a humane, tolerant and open-minded disposition on the part of those engaged in trying to bring it to fruition, was paramount. In a review of Upton Sinclair's *Oil*, Midgley referred regretfully to the American Labour movement as 'still more concerned with doctrinaire divisions than with a unity for a common purpose'.[23] Midgley thus appears to have had little time for factionalism, or for doctrinal arguments about what constituted 'pure' and 'true' socialism. According to these writings, he abhorred anything which threatened the unity of the Labour movement, and, equally, he seemed to take a jaundiced view of those whose idealism precluded a realistic and effective approach to the problems of the day.

The reflective and more private side of Midgley comes across in these articles which contain much common sense and sound reasoning. Such qualities were sometimes lacking in public when he unleashed a tide of flowery or vituperative rhetoric. In this kind of situation Midgley exercised the romantic in him and conveyed a sense of dynamism, fighting-spirit, and evangelism which was probably unmatched by anybody else in Northern Ireland politics. Patrick Shea, in his autobiography, has recalled that, as a young man in Belfast in the late 20s and early 30s, Midgley impressed him as: 'the vociferous radical, the most compelling and uncompromising home-grown advocate of socialism; a small black-haired, swarthy man, a restless, impatient man whose days and nights were spent preaching and reading and arguing, disputing actions of employers or decisions of the Ministry of Labour. To me, in those early days, he was the one Socialist in our community who could be said to have fire in his belly.'[24]

Aside from his fiery speeches, it could not be said that Midgley displayed the characteristics of an extreme socialist. He, along with Kyle and others, had accepted with some alacrity the chance to get involved in the workings of the Northern Ireland State,[25] and he had never disguised his admiration for the progress made by the British Labour Party. His ambitions were to attain a parliamentary seat, and to lead the Northern Ireland Labour Party, ambitions he knew he could not harmonise with a consistently militant stance. In this light, therefore, it is difficult not to conclude that any support he may have expressed for the Cook–Maxton manifesto contained, like his General Strike speech, an element of opportunism. Midgley's outlook was in essence that of Kyle: a belief in progressive changes effected by a reformist Labour Party leading ultimately to the creation of a socialist society. In this period, however, it suited Midgley to appear occasionally as more radical than Kyle in order to boost his own credibility as a potential leader. It has, moreover, been said that Midgley, despite his preoccupation with municipal politics, looked with some envy on the Labour men in the Northern Ireland parliament from 1925 to 1929, namely Kyle, William McMullen[26] and Jack Beattie.[27]

III

Labour had taken heart at the 1925 election result. Beattie topped the poll in East Belfast, Kyle was elected on the second count in North Belfast, and McMullen on the fourth count in West Belfast. Both

Beattie and Kyle had obviously won substantial Protestant support although they would also have received a large share of the Catholic vote concentrated in the Short Strand and Oldpark areas respectively. Labour had only put forward these three men who, in the absence of the Nationalists, became the official opposition in the new parliament, Sam Kyle assuming the role of leader. The election saw the Unionists lose eight seats, something of a setback given that a resounding victory had been eagerly sought to impress the Boundary Commission.[28] However, it made no difference for, in November of 1925, the Commission concluded its deliberations by recommending that the border be left virtually unaltered.

By the time of the 1925 election, Labour had clearly stated its intention to supply a non-sectarian opposition to the Unionists in parliament. In March 1925, a month before the election, there appeared the first issue of the newspaper *The Labour Opposition in Northern Ireland*, published by the North Belfast ILP and edited by Hugh Gemmell.[29] This issue set out Labour's election programme, the first item being 'to provide an opposition in the Northern Parliament'. The other items concerned social issues such as old-age pensions, widows' pensions, the establishment of a Ministry of Health, and the nationalisation of the railways.[30] The party's equivocal attitude to the border was reflected in Sam Kyle's election address in the following issue in which he declared that the only boundary which concerned him was that between the rich and the poor. He did add, however, in a sentence which perhaps summed up the pragmatic strain of thought within the party: 'Until the Free State [the Irish Free State] is prepared to give the same conditions to teachers, OAPs and Unemployment Insurance as we have in Northern Ireland we in the North should not permit any worsening of our position.'[31]

It is not easy to draw definite conclusions about the nature of the NILP during the 1920s. The party was a rather hybrid organisation, deriving inspiration from the two conflicting traditions personified by Connolly on the one hand, and Walker on the other. The national question continued to pose serious problems for the party both from the outside and from within. The way in which the party coped with these difficulties perhaps signified the triumph of a 'third tradition' which had been forged out of the turmoil in the movement precipitated by the pre-war Home Rule crisis. This tradition, if such it can be called, was a pragmatic response to what was perceived to be the inevitable establishment of a Home Rule parliament in Ireland. As was noted in chapter

1, a majority of those in the Northern Labour movement favoured a
Home Rule settlement as the most democratic way of settling the
question in Ireland while preserving close ties with Britain. This outlook
was not prompted by strong Nationalist sympathies; most of Labour's
activists in the North were Protestants and had been steeped in the
British Labourist/ILP tradition which in turn had spawned its Northern
Ireland variation epitomised by William Walker.

After the war this line of thinking was reflected in the anti-partitionist
stance of most people in the Labour movement, but, significantly, this
anti-partitionism gradually became a nominally, rather than a fervently,
held view. The Northern state, after the first year or two of its existence,
was looked upon as a reality which Labour could ignore only at the cost
of total political impotence. A new pragmatism emerged, perhaps best
embodied in the steady persona of Kyle, but shared as much by the
stormy petrels of the movement such as Hugh Gemmell and Midgley
himself. This school of thought seemed to attempt to unite the party by
venerating simultaneously the respective legends of Connolly and
Walker in terms of both men's dedication to the cause of Labour.

Thus Walker could take place of honour as the first in *Labour
Opposition*'s pen portrait series, 'Labour Men of the North'.[32] In the
case of Connolly, Hugh Gemmell objected to 'the tawdry tinsel of
"only" Nationalism with which some people have surrounded Connolly', and insisted on his being viewed as 'Ireland's first socialist
martyr'.[33] Walker's rejection of any kind of Home Rule settlement, and
Connolly's tendency towards mystical nationalism after 1914, were
carefully overlooked. Connolly commemoration meetings and Walker
commemoration meetings were held at different times during the
1920s.[34]

Austen Morgan has argued that Walker's legacy was manifest in the
NILP of the 1920s while Connolly's was by and large absent.[35] This
view should be qualified. In practice the Walkerite emphasis on identifying closely with the British Labour movement was very much adhered
to, but once Labour had decided to involve itself in the political life of
Northern Ireland, this was surely not surprising. The party had to
address itself to the political issues of the state in which it found itself
and was obliged to adopt the British Labour programme in its attempt to
prevent the Unionists from governing in a narrow, parochial and self-
interested fashion. To a large extent Walker was celebrated as a Belfast
man and as someone who, until 1912, and given his all in building up the
Belfast Labour movement in conditions of the utmost difficulty and, at

times, danger. Nobody – at least in written form in the Labour press of the time – was prepared to praise Walker's Unionist stand. Connolly's influence, ideologically, was far greater than that of Walker, and there was no shortage of Labour activists in the 1920s who identified themselves as 'Connollyite Socialists' or 'Republican Socialists', and who held a passionate belief in a united Irish republic. Such men included William McMullen, Murtagh Morgan, James Grimley and Tommy Geehan.[36] Men such as Midgley and Gemmell were also influenced in their thinking by Connolly but they regarded him in a more detached way. They paid tribute to his ideals while proceeding to deal with the questions of the day for which Connolly's corpus of writings supplied no ready answers.

Midgley's state of mind on Connolly and the national question at this time is difficult to define. According to Patrick Shea, Midgley's speeches of this period indicated that 'his political thinking was pretty near James Connolly's concept of an Irish Workers' Republic'.[37] In June 1927 Midgley spoke in Dundalk in support of the Irish Labour candidates for the constituency of Louth in the Free State election of that month. He was reported as saying:

When the people of Ireland were fighting for Home Rule on constitutional lines, he was proud at that time to have taken his stand with his friends in the North as a Home Ruler, and he would fight again in similar circumstances for the right of the Irish people to manage their own affairs.[38]

In 1929 Midgley wrote to *Forward* to complain about the tactics employed by Nationalist politicians against William McMullen in the West Belfast contest of that year's election. He said:

As a young man he [McMullen] received a large amount of inspiration from the late James Conolly [sic], and as a consequence he holds very advanced views on the question of Irish Nationality. In the Parliament of Northern Ireland he held aloft, time and again, the ideal of a United Irish race, even at times when it was both difficult and dangerous to do so . . . This was the man against whom Joseph Devlin and the Nationalist Party flung themselves with savage fury.[39]

The latter statement is sufficiently ambiguous to be open to opposing interpretations, but the lyrical style in which McMullen's 'advanced views' are referred to tends to suggest, to put it no stronger, that Midgley at this time still sympathised with Connollyite ideals.

Against this has to be acknowledged another example of the more reflective Midgley: a short story written for his trade union journal in 1928 entitled, 'The Carnalea Republic'.[40] This piece was a clever allegory the moral of which Midgley underlined at the end as follows:

The members of the Carnalea Brotherhood are beginning to realise that there is no fundamental difference between their Republic and the old system of monarchy. Under each taxes must be paid, and ground rent forthcoming. The change of flag doesn't change the system, for the fault lies not with the flag but with the system of ownership under the flag.

Midgley had also said, in a previous article, that 'Nationalism is not enough',[41] and with this, and his 'Carnalea Republic' moral, Connolly would not of course have found fault. By such writing, however, it could be argued that Midgley was revealing a certain scepticism with regard to a Workers' Republic actually coming about, and an impatience with those, like Connolly in the end, whose nationalism tended to obscure their socialism. Moreover, praise for McMullen's 'advanced views on Irish Nationality' was by no means incompatible with the view that to be identified totally, like McMullen, with such ideals, was to be too politically restricted in the context of Northern Ireland.

This 'third tradition', therefore, seemed to steer a course between the Connollyite and Walkerite strains within the party. It did so in a way which suggests that the former tended to pull more ideological, if far less practical, weight. Connolly's socialist ideal of an Irish Workers' Republic was held aloft, the militaristic nationalism of his later years buried. Walker's contribution to the history of the Belfast Labour movement was often praised, and his policy of close identification with the British Labour movement was carried out in accordance with circumstantial demands. Walker's unionist Labour ideals, however, could only have been espoused by a small group. The party was, in general, anti-partitionist, but the adoption of the British Labour approach to politics, and the more pronounced estrangement between North and South after 1921, gradually reduced the strength of the anti-partitionist feeling in the party during this decade.

The party in effect walked a political tightrope between Unionism and Nationalism, but its image was such that the Unionists had no difficulty in convincing Protestant voters that it was no friend of the British link, while the Nationalists, for their part, were able to criticise it quite legitimately for not coming out unequivocally against partition. The ideological splits within the party cannot be summed up in terms of a revolutionary nationalist/reformist unionist division. The lines of identification regarding these splits were often blurred: there were nationalist-minded members of the party who adopted a revolutionary approach[42] and nationalist-minded members who repudiated such a perspective; there were those who admired the British Labour reformist tradition but who would have disavowed the label 'unionist'.

The NILP remained very much a Belfast-centred party throughout the 1920s. Despite the declared intention of extending operations the length and breadth of the six counties, the only other notable centre of activity was in Londonderry, Nothern Ireland's other city. Here the local party had a measure of local government success despite similar hostility – of both the Unionist and Nationalist kind – to that in Belfast.[43] The Derry party was probably more clearly anti-partitionist in outlook than its Belfast counterpart. There were also Labour organisations in North Antrim and in Newry by 1930, but neither was very strong.[44] As the 1920s wore on more branches were organised in Belfast, namely Shankill, Clifton, Court, Smithfield, Pottinger and Dock. The strength and level of activity of these branches varied enormously,[45] the most active, in terms of propaganda and social activity, being Dock. Dock also gloried in the name of 'Red Ward', so conferred because of the number of municipal election successes achieved there by Labour.[46] Two of the branch's hardest workers were Annie Loftus and John Campbell, both of whom were to be great helpers and supporters of Midgley inside the party during the years to come.

IV

In May 1929 Lord Craigavon (James Craig) called an election, the first to be fought under the system of a majority vote in single-member constituencies. Earlier in the year Craigavon and the Unionists had abolished Proportional Representation in an attempt to draw the parliamentary lines clearly between Unionists and Nationalists, most of the latter having by now taken their seats. Craigavon considered the Labour and Independent Unionist members something of a nuisance, and it was their elimination – or at least their reduction in numbers – which was the purpose of the measure.

It had the desired effect as far as Labour was concerned. Only Beattie was returned, this time for the constituency of Pottinger, one of the four East Belfast wards. Kyle was beaten by 189 votes in Oldpark by the Unionists, while McMullen lost in Falls Ward to the Nationalist Richard Byrne after a vehemently sectarian contest. Labour also suffered defeat in Dock where Dawson Gordon lost to the Unionist, and in Ards where Alex Adams finished a poor second, again to the Unionist.

The four Labour candidates in Belfast polled 20,516 votes,[47] a total which, translated into PR terms, would have probably implied success. The Unionists won thirty-seven seats, the Nationalists eleven, and Independent Unionists three.

Midgley had wanted to fight a seat at the election but had not been able to obtain the official backing, and financial aid, of his trade union, the National Union of Distributive and Allied Workers (NUDAW).[48] In protest at the Union Executive's decision not to adopt Midgley as a candidate, the President of Belfast Number Five branch of NUDAW wrote to the Industrial General Secretary. In the letter he said that the branch members 'deeply regret[ted]' the decision which, he added, had come as a surprise since it had been assumed for four years that Midgley would have stood as a candidate.[49] The letter paid dividends. Midgley was adopted officially in August 1930 as a Northern Ireland parliamentary candidate for the next election.

In January 1928 Midgley was re-elected as Councillor for Dock, defeating the Unionist, William Douglas, by 500 votes. One year later he secured the aldermanship for the same ward, beating another Unionist, Samuel Gray, by a similar margin.[50] These and other local election campaigns of the time were notable for the kind of anti-socialist propaganda and unscrupulous tactics employed by both Unionists and Nationalists.

During the 1928 elections the *Irish News* blasted away any trace of sympathy it may previously have possessed for Labour in a barrage of scaremongering outbursts. According to the editorial of 9 January, Socialism and 'extreme' Protestantism were 'inseparable' and a 'conspiracy against their [Catholic] religion'. Of the Falls and Smithfield wards which Labour candidates proposed to contest, the *Irish News* stated: '. . . they never returned any member who was not an avowed and professed Catholic, standing as a Catholic and returned because of [sic] his fidelity to Catholic principles was unquestioned by any side.'[51]

The Unionists were not slow to take note of this decided hostility to Labour, and to make use of it for their own ends. In Dock there was no Nationalist candidate; simply a straight fight between Midgley and the Unionist. In an effort to dissuade some Catholics from voting for Midgley, the Unionists had a handbill circulated which reiterated many of the *Irish News*'s points about Socialism and Catholicism. It ended as follows: 'Remember what Bolshevism and Socialism have done against the Catholic Church in Mexico, China, Russia and France. Don't support Socialism at any cost. Don't vote for Midgley.'[52]

Midgley triumphed over such tactics but other candidates were not so fortunate. Murtagh Morgan, a Catholic, was defeated by a Nationalist in Smithfield after a campaign in which his opponent's canvassers had assigned to him an Orange Lodge number with which to impress the almost exclusively Catholic electorate.[53] Press reports of the elections also reveal how large a part the Ancient Order of Hibernians was playing on behalf of Nationalist candidates at this time.[54] Indeed the AOH had always formed the backbone of Joe Devlin's political machine.

Midgley's victory in 1929 followed a relatively clean fight during which he put the emphasis on education. After vowing to fight for free school books for all children, he revealed his dream 'of an educational system under which the broad highway of educational opportunity would be opened up to all the workers, and, beginning at the elementary school, they would march progressively to the secondary school, and then to the university'.[55]

The Nationalists' election behaviour confirmed Midgley in what had become a reproachful attitude towards them. He had been unimpressed by the political outlook held by most of the Nationalist councillors, the majority of whom were small businessmen. In an article in *Forward* he wrote that 'there is but a step, if indeed as much as a step' between them and the Unionist councillors.[56] Midgley claimed that it was the Labour group which was the real oppressed minority in the city, pointing out that not one Labour representative had been selected to serve as Chairman or Vice-Chairman on a single council committee.[57] In January 1930 his relations with the Nationalists deteriorated further. The Labour group decided to put Midgley forward for the office of Lord Mayor, but in the event he got only the votes of the Labour councillors. The Nationalists either voted against him or abstained, and seemed happier to see a Unionist, Sir William Coates, assume the honour.[58]

The new decade brought only grim economic hardship for Northern Ireland. The unemployment total rose until, by 1931, it stood at almost a quarter of the insured population.[59] Midgley continued, in the City Council, to fight for measures to alleviate the lot of those on Poor Relief, and he helped prevent, in 1931, the planned round of wage cuts of corporation employees. He also continued to wage his personal battle for free school books, offering, in January 1931, to resign and fight his seat on the Corporation on this issue.[60]

The NILP limped into the 1930s, its morale low after the 1929 election. It gave the appearance of drifting along, rather than stridently proclaiming its message, and it seemed to lack the inspiring kind of leadership which Midgley believed he could supply. Consequently, in 1931, after years of being an ordinary party member, he challenged for the Chairmanship of the party along with Bob Getgood, Gemmell and Kyle.[61] Gemmell was elected at the annual conference but it was clear that Midgley would not be kept in the wings much longer. He had led the Labour group in the Council with some tenacity and much publicity;[62] he had built for himself a personal reputation which by the 1930s made him look veritable leader 'material'.[63] His personal support within the party was now strong, as were his connections with all parts of the Labour movement including the trade unions and the Co-operative Society. In addition he was now the official candidate of his trade union for a parliamentary seat.

V

By the 1930s Midgley was settled with his wife and four children (two sons and two daughters) in Duncairn Gardens, again not far from where he was born and raised. Midgley was a proud father and sought to pass on his own learning to his children. He encouraged them to read widely and to learn musical instruments. Midgley himself was passionately fond of classical music and listened with rapture to Grand Opera.[64] Despite pressures of political work he continued to devour novels, especially those by writers with a socialist outlook like Upton Sinclair, and he continued to pen his own verse for publication in his trade union journal. On the sporting front he took a close interest in his boyhood football team Linfield.

It should also be noted that Midgley did not keep in the best of health. *Labour Opposition* in November 1925 reported that 'Comrade Harry Midgley is again ill', and throughout his career Midgley's exertions periodically took their toll. He was a man who could never involve himself half-heartedly in anything; as a result he often found himself overworked and exhausted. It was, however, a price he paid with little compunction.

Notes

1 See N.I. House of Commons Debates XXVI, 1947.
2 See P. Buckland, *The Factory of Grievances*, Dublin, 1979 pp. 17–18, 32–5.
3 See, for example, Minutes of Belfast City Council, Education Committee 27 February 1925 and 6 March 1925. In January 1929 Midgley attempted to

get the council to increase the estimates in respect of free school books from
£1,750 per year to £20,000 to ensure that all children attending elementary
schools would be so provided. He was defeated and lost out again on the
issue in September 1929. See minutes of monthly meetings of Belfast City
Council 1 January 1929 and 2 September 1929.

4 *Forward* 28 August 1926.
5 Ibid. 28 May 1927.
6 See next chapter.
7 By 1930 there were 20,000 unemployed linen workers in Belfast. See Budge
   and O'Leary op. cit. pp. 144–5.
8 Budge and O'Leary pp. 144–5.
9 Harry Midgley Election Address 16 January 1928, *Midgley Papers*.
10 He was outspoken, for example, on matters involving corruption. In 1925 an
   inquiry disclosed that corruption and maladministration had taken place in
   relation to house-building schemes. Midgley alleged that the whole affair
   was then 'whitewashed'. See *Forward* 24 February 1928.
11 See below pp. 70–1.
12 *Irish News* 6 May 1926.
13 Quoted in M. Milotte 'Ireland and the Great Strike', *Irish Times* 10 May
   1976. Only in the first couple of days did the strike spread to Northern
   Ireland and even then it was confined to the docks.
14 Midgley wrote a poem entitled 'The Cry of the Miners' for his trade union
   journal *New Dawn* 26 June 1926.
15 See R. E. Dowse, *Left in the Centre*, London, 1966 pp. 141–6.
16 Ibid. pp. 141–2.
17 *Forward* 21 July 1928.
18 Ibid. 28 July 1928.
19 See *Forward* 30 July 1932.
20 *New Dawn* 20 August 1927.
21 Ibid.
22 Ibid. 23 July 1927.
23 Ibid. 14 April 1928.
24 P. Shea, *Voices and the Sound of Drums*, Belfast, 1981 p. 162. Shea worked in
   the NI Civil Service and eventually became only the second Roman Catholic
   to reach the rank of Permanent Secretary.
25 Midgley and Kyle gave evidence before a Government Committee of
   Inquiry in October 1921 regarding the workings of the Trade Boards. In
   1922–3 Midgley served as a member of the Departmental Committee on the
   Cost of Living, and on the Rents Restriction Committee.
26 McMullen was born in 1892 in the same area of Belfast as Midgley; he was a
   Protestant and worked in the Harland and Wolff shipyard. He worked
   closely with Connolly in Belfast in 1911–13, and became organiser of the
   Irish Transport and General Workers' Union in the city. He moved to
   Dublin in 1932 and became President of the ITGWU. He died in 1982.
27 Beattie was born in 1886. He was a Protestant and worked in the shipyard as
   a riveter. He was an early member of the ILP in Belfast. Became Northern
   organiser of the Irish National Teachers' Organisation from 1934. He died
   in 1960.

28 The Unionists lost four seats to Independent Unionists and one to the Unbought Tenants' Association, as well as three to Labour. See S. Elliott op. cit.

29 Gemmell came to Belfast during World War I from Scotland to avoid being conscripted. His parents came from Conlig, Co. Down. He was a leading member of the North ILP and the West Belfast Labour Party during the 1920s. He wrote for several Labour newspapers under the pen name 'Hotspur'.

30 *Labour Opposition in NI* March 1925.

31 Ibid. April 1925.

32 Ibid. March 1925.

33 *The Irishman* 19 May 1928.

34 A large Walker meeting was held on 29 November 1923 at which Midgley paid tribute to Walker's 'glorious work'. See *Irish News* 30 November 1923. For details of Connolly meetings see, for example, *The Irishman* 19 May 1925, and *Labour Opposition* June 1926. Dock Ward party held a Connolly Memorial Meeting on 12 May 1926.

35 Morgan op. cit. pp. 365–9.

36 Geehan was a Catholic textile worker and secretary of the Court Ward party. In 1927 he became associated with the Workers' Party of Ireland (WPI), a Communist Dublin-based group led by Connolly's son, Roddy. In 1929 he left the NILP and started to campaign against its 'reformist' approach.

37 Shea op. cit. p. 164.

38 *Belfast Telegraph* 6 June 1927.

39 *Forward* 8 June 1929.

40 *New Dawn* 18 August 1928.

41 Ibid. 9 June 1928.

42 Such as Tommy Geehan and his followers who agitated against those who were effectively in control of the party. See the revolutionary–reformist debate between Geehan(?) and Gemmell in *Labour Opposition* February and March 1926.

43 Sixteen Labour councillors were returned in 1926. See 'The Labour movement in Derry', *The Irishman* 12 May 1928.

44 *The Irishman* 27 September 1930.

45 Ibid.

46 Between 1925 and 1930 Midgley, Kyle, Dawson Gordon, Margaret McCoubrey and Sam Hazlett were all elected.

47 Farrell op. cit. p. 115.

48 In February 1926 the Linenlappers' Union was absorbed into NUDAW, a move in which Midgley played an instrumental role. See Industrial General Secretary's Report (1926) 21 February 1926 No. 57, USDAW Records, Manchester.

49 Industrial General Secretary's Report (1929) 7 May 1929 No. 150, USDAW Records, Manchester.

50 The results were: *1928* – Midgley 3,080; Douglas 2,580.
                              1929 – Midgley 2,781; Gray 2,273.

51 *Irish News* 9 January 1928.

52 Ibid. 13 January 1928.

53 *The Irishman* 25 January 1930.
54 See, for example, *Irish News* 8 January 1929.
55 Ibid. 11 January 1929.
56 *Forward* 24 February 1928.
57 Ibid.
58 Minutes of Belfast City Council, Meeting of Council in Committee, 20 January 1930.
59 Budge and O'Leary op. cit. p. 145.
60 *Belfast News-Letter* 3 January 1931.
61 He was nominated for the Chair by the Belfast Trades Council. See Belfast Trades Council minutes 5 march 1931. PRONI MIC. 193.
62 See *Belfast News-Letter* 3 March 1931 and 2 April 1931 re voluble exchanges involving Midgley at City Council meetings.
63 Midgley of course had his skills as a speaker to draw on in order to cut a leadership figure. In *Forward* 31 May 1930 a Midgley speech was described thus: 'Brilliant oratory; caustic biting wit; an unassailable armoury of facts, figures and illustrations; and a stirring appeal that Midgley alone can muster.'
64 *New Dawn* 10 July 1926.

Chapter Five

Street riots and a passage to Stormont
(1932–1936)

I

The international economic crisis which set in after 1929 affected Northern Ireland severely. As in the UK as a whole, this was particularly so during the years 1931 to 1933. Essentially an exporting country, Northern Ireland suffered a steep decline in these years as the value of her exports fell to approximately £20 million below the average figure for the 1920s. The staple industries of shipbuilding, engineering and linen were hit hardest: in 1932 only two vessels were launched from the Belfast shipyards with a tonnage of 5,749. This contrasted starkly with the figure of twenty-nine vessels in 1930 with a tonnage of 168,068. The value of the output in both the linen and engineering industries also slumped, if less dramatically.[1] The depressing corollary to all this was the unemployment rate: the official figures were 28.1% in 1931; 27.2% in 1932; and 26.7% in 1933,[2] but these figures do not include the many thousands out of work who were not registered as such. It has been estimated that the jobless total in Northern Ireland in 1932 was 100,000.[3]

The British Labour government, under the premiership of Ramsay MacDonald, responded to the financial crisis by proposing a programme of cuts, including a 10 per cent reduction in unemployment benefit.[4] This proposal split the Labour Cabinet and MacDonald consequently resigned. To the consternation of the movement, however, he then agreed to stay on as Prime Minister of a National Coalition government with the Conservatives and Liberals. The programme of cuts was duly introduced after the National government won a landslide election victory in October 1931.

MacDonald's action was regarded by those in the Labour movement as the 'Great Betrayal'. In Belfast, Midgley joined in the chorus of denunciation. In his opinion the movement would in the long term be better for having cast out 'the scoffers, the doubters and those who never really believed in socialism'. 'Capitalism', he added, 'cannot much longer be patched up. The future is ours.'[5]

There was another group of people in Northern Ireland who shared Midgley's view that the demise of capitalism was imminent. They were Communists and they opposed the NILP as vehemently as they opposed the Unionist government. The hostility was mutual with leading figures in the NILP such as Gemmell very prone to anti-Communist speeches and writings. In response to the growing social and economic crisis, the Communists, going under the name of the Revolutionary Workers' Groups (RWGs), concentrated their energies and their small numbers in Belfast. Their leaders included Tommy Geehan, Tommy Watters, Loftus Johnston, and Jimmy Kater, the latter two being Belfast Protestant shipyard workers.[6] The RWGs sought to capitalise on working class anger over unemployment, cuts in unemployment benefit, and the hardships of the Poor Law system. They were active from the summer of 1931 in Belfast, holding meetings in both Protestant and Catholic working class areas. Their aim was to inspire a strong revolutionary working class movement across sectarian lines which would have no use for the reformism and constitutionalism of the NILP.

The NILP, in conjunction with the trade union movement and the Belfast Trades Council, waged its own campaign of protest over the crisis and its effects on working people. Their spokesmen, of whom Midgley was one of the most renowned, took care to stress that they adhered strictly to peaceful, constitutional methods. In so doing they hoped to distinguish themselves clearly from the small Communist group. At a meeting organised by the trade union movement in September 1931, Midgley said: 'We believe in fighting at the ballot box and not using physical force', while Bob Dorman urged his listeners to 'put our case in a peaceful and constitutional manner'.[7]

At the NILP conference in March 1932, Midgley was elected chairman of the party, a victory probably due to his obtaining the block votes of the larger trade unions such as the Amalgamated Engineering Union. He was now in a strong position to steer the party in the direction he wanted to go. This position was strengthened still further with the departure later in the year of Sam Kyle and William McMullen to take up trade union posts in the South. Kyle and McMullen, along with Midgley, were the most able men in the party at this time. Conference proceedings seemed to reflect Midgley's outlook very closely. John Campbell, re-elected as secretary, rejected a call for a General Strike against the Means Test: 'The people had their remedy and that was the ballot box. A one day strike would be of no avail; let the working people get down to brass tacks and realise their strength.'[8] For the first time the British Labour Party was officially represented at the conference, G. R. Shepherd, the party's National Agent, being the fraternal delegate. Shepherd expressed the hope that contacts between the two parties would be strengthened in the future.[9]

For Midgley and most of the NILP, the fortunes of the British Labour movement were of the utmost importance in relation to Northern Ireland. The relationship between the two parties was a subject which would receive, under Midgley's guidance of the party, more attention than had been the case throughout the 1920s. Primarily through his trade union work Midgley had become closely associated with prominent people in the British party, particularly Ellen Wilkinson who was also a full-time worker with NUDAW.

Midgley also continued to contribute regularly to *Forward* and he used its pages, in July 1932, to enter the debate over the question of ILP disaffiliation from the British Labour Party. Midgley was adamantly against disaffiliation and warned that the ILP was driving itself into 'the political wilderness'.[10] However, at a special conference in Bradford on 31 July 1932 the vote went for disaffiliation by 241 to 142. This caused confusion in Belfast with the ILP there unsure of whether to continue its activities in a frustrating kind of limbo, or simply to dissolve itself. It opted for the latter course but was reconstituted the following year as the Socialist Party (Northern Ireland) (SP(NI)). This latter group was to contain most of the far left members of the NILP to which it affiliated, and it came to act as a left-wing pressure group on the NILP throughout the 1930s as the ILP had done in relation to the British Labour Party before disaffiliation.

Although Midgley himself was a member of the SP(NI), it would not be long before he viewed it in a hostile light. Many of those who joined the SP(NI) were strongly anti-partitionist and lukewarm with regard to links between the NILP and the British Labour movement. For them true socialism in Ireland could only follow the political unity of the island. To Midgley this was to put the nationalist cart before the socialist horse, and it translated as impractical and romantic politics. In earlier years Midgley had at least sympathised with the ideal; by 1932 this was probably no longer the case.

The years 1931–3 saw Midgley make extensive preparations for the next Northern Ireland election. Having secured the backing of his trade union for the Dock Ward seat, Midgley set about canvassing support. In 1931 the NUDAW executive council decided to pay Midgley £150 a year towards the establishment of election machinery which was to cover all propaganda expenses, the engagement of such services as Midgley considered necessary, and the setting up of a ward committee. As his election agent, Midgley took on T. J. McCoubrie, the treasurer of the NILP at this time. A fair proportion of the allowance was used for propaganda purposes as Midgley poured out long, fact-filled and polemical addresses to the Dock electors.

Into these pamphlets and leaflets Midgley pressed the fruits of his knowledge; they overflowed with facts, statistics, and short statements about scientific innovations, historical events, and contemporary political, social and economic issues.[12] They were cogently argued and forcefully written. If Midgley's propaganda had a fault it was probably that it bombarded the reader too intensively with both facts and arguments. However, it did illustrate clearly the vigorous and exhaustive style of leadership that Midgley had begun to display in his efforts to get Labour's message across.

II

The programme of cuts implemented by the National coalition government in Britain led to a campaign of protest in many cities, protests which took the form of riots in places such as Birkenhead, Bristol and London.[13] These measures cut rates of unemployment benefit by 10 per cent and increased insurance contributions. They also subjected Transitional Benefit – which had been introduced as uncovenanted insurance benefit – to a family means test, and transferred administration of it to the Poor Law machinery. This brought many people – in Northern Ireland as well as the rest of the UK – into direct contact with the Poor Law for the first time.[14]

By British standards, however, those forced to rely on Poor Law Relief in Northern Ireland were very badly off. Belfast's Outdoor Relief rates were the lowest in the UK. In Manchester a man with a wife and one child received twenty-one shillings a week; in Liverpool twenty-three shillings; in Glasgow twenty-five and threepence; and in Bradford twenty-six shillings. The rate in Belfast was twelve shillings a week.[15] The situation was becoming quite desperate with thousands of people in Belfast living in conditions of acute distress.

An Outdoor Relief workers' movement was thus set up with the aim of bringing the Outdoor Relief rates into line with the rest of the UK. The movement's protest was also directed at the administration of the

system in Belfast by the Poor Law Guardians. The Guardians seem to
have been actuated by an outlook in which the poor had only themselves
to blame for their poverty and which led them to consider the problem of
relief payments in terms of how much money they could save the
ratepayers.[16]

The Unionist government began to heed the warning signals only
when the situation had so deteriorated that disparate sections of the
community such as clergymen and local businessmen joined in the
workers' chorus of protest. Prompt and effective action, however, was
hindered by the existence of a deep division in the Northern Ireland
state apparatus regarding social policy and government expenditure.
This division has been described as a conflict between a 'populist' group
led by the Prime Minister, Lord Craigavon, and the Minister of Home
Affairs, Sir Richard Dawson Bates, and an 'anti-populist' group led by
Hugh Pollock, the Minister of Finance, and the head of the civil service
in Northern Ireland, Sir Wilfrid Spender.[17] The 'anti-populists' were
very concerned to keep the state's financial expenditure under strict
control and to avoid the ignominy of 'begging expeditions' to the British
Treasury. The 'populists', on the other hand, were anxious to appease
their working class supporters whatever the cost, and to make good their
pledge to match British living standards. In the event the 'populists' won
the day and an extra £300,000 was paid out on relief schemes.[18]
However, this was not done without incurring the wrath of the 'anti-
populists', or in time to prevent trouble in the streets.

The episode illustrated clearly the political policy of Sir James Craig:
the policy he himself described as 'distributing bones' to government
supporters.[19] The Northern Ireland government proved itself
responsive to pressure groups such as local business interests, the
churches, and, perhaps most importantly, the Orange Order. The style
of government, especially under Craig, was informal and accessible, a
state of affairs which ensured that patronage would be common practice.[20] In some countries such informality and accessibility may have led
to good government; in Northern Ireland it produced much discrimination and policies distinguished by their narrowness of vision.

The Outdoor Relief workers went on strike on 3 October 1932. Their
protests went in tandem with those of single people who were not
entitled to any Outdoor Relief at all. Mass marches and demonstrations
were held and later that week minor outbreaks of disorder were reported
in some of Belfast's poorest areas. The workers were organised by a
committee heavily influenced by the Communist RWGs. Indeed

Tommy Geehan was secretary of the strike committee.

On the weekend of 8–9 October, mass meetings were held at which it was decided to hold a 'monster' demonstration on Tuesday the 11th. This meeting was prohibited by the government on the 10th and extra armed police were drafted into the city. However, at a meeting on the 10th, Geehan and other RWG speakers urged workers to defy the ban and proceed with the demonstration. On the 11th police attempted to prevent the march from getting under way, and there ensued fierce rioting in both Protestant and Catholic areas with workers of both religions united against the police. The result was two workers shot dead and scores of policemen and workers wounded and injured. As the trouble died down the Guardians announced an increase in the rates to twenty shillings per week for a man and wife; twenty-four shillings with one or two children; twenty-eight shillings with three or four children; and thirty-two shillings for five or more children.[21] These terms were accepted by the workers at a mass meeting on 14 October when Geehan declared the struggle a 'glorious victory'.

The Belfast riots must be seen in the context of the agitation which was taking place in Britain as a whole against unemployment and the Means Test. The economic depression had created conditions of near-starvation for many families in most major cities throughout Britain. Resistance among workers was widespread and gave rise to the establishment of the National Unemployed Workers' Movement (NUWM) which, like the RWGs in Belfast, was Communist-led.[22] The movement provided a medium through which workers' discontent could find expression in a way which the orthodox Labour movement, for the most part, did not seek to encourage. The idea of direct action such as a general strike was rejected by most Labour and trade union leaders who saw their primary concern as safeguarding the jobs of those workers in employment. There was thus a disparity of interests between the organised trade union rank-and-file workers, and the unemployed.

This was also the case in Belfast where Midgley had now come to be viewed as Labour's main spokesman. He expressed his attitude to the riots in Belfast in a lengthy article written for *Forward* in the wake of the trouble. The article[23] began with Midgley drawing attention to the problem of massive unemployment and condemning the Poor Law Guardians as 'callous' in their attitude to the poor. He then proceeded to outline the steps which the Labour movement had taken on behalf of the unemployed and Outdoor Relief workers beginning with a joint NILP and Belfast Trades Council conference in August 1932. At this conference it was decided to contest the Poor Law elections in June 1933, and to carry on a 'ceaseless propaganda campaign' with regard to Belfast having the lowest rates of relief in the UK. Midgley claimed that the Communists came to this conference and voiced their opposition to the policy of contesting the elections. Midgley was dismissive of their outlook: 'Of course they justified their attitudes (as usual) on the ground that they wanted something done immediately, implying, as they always do, that the Labour movement didn't want anything done immediately.'

The gravamen of Midgley's case against the Communists, indeed his indictment of their conduct, concerned their action in urging workers to march on 11 October despite the government ban and the influx of extra police. He stated:

Knowing Belfast as I do I have no hesitation in declaring that this was a stupid – a wilfully stupid – blunder on the part of certain people. No man who does not intend to face danger should incite innocent unthinking people to challenge armed forces; and this is precisely what happened in Belfast. Those who made the pretence of leading the helpless masses in defiance of authority – armed authority as it is in Belfast – were missing at the crucial hour. Some of them never emerged from their hiding places until the trouble had almost subsided.

Midgley went on to claim that the Communist leaders had held a meeting before the trouble started, and had decided to 'lie low'.

Regarding Labour's activities on the workers' behalf, Midgley wrote that Labour representatives went with the Lord Mayor of Belfast on 12 October to the Governor of Northern Ireland to ask him to pressurise the Guardians into granting the workers' demands. This the Governor did and he met again with the Labour delegation on the 14th when he announced that the Guardians were raising the scales of relief. Midgley thus claimed for the Labour representatives (including himself) an instrumental negotiating role in the resolution of the strike.

Midgley was sensitive to talk of the victory being won by the efforts of the RWGs: '. . . the truth is that had the workers half as much political intelligence as they have credulity for political knaves and adventurers they could have secured all they secured last week without the loss of a single life or one cracked skull.' In a similarly caustic vein, he went on: 'As I watched events in Belfast last week I recalled the old saying which I first heard in America: "when you feel the thud of the policeman's baton on your skull you hear the echo of the vote you cast at the last election." ' Obviously bitter that the Communists had made undeniable inroads into the working class, he turned his lash on the workers themselves:

. . . in their hour of need, brought about by their own political stupidity, they turn to counsels of despair and become an easy mark for those who, in the name of working class unity, rend the Labour movement into fragments – or try to; try to poison the minds of the workers against those who serve them best; and who act as if they were paid, not from Moscow, but from the Tory party.

A fortnight later in the RWG newspaper, *The Workers' Voice*, Tommy Geehan replied to Midgley, condemning him as a 'fakir' and a 'careerist'. He caricatured Midgley's attitude as 'starve another 9 months', and vilified the NILP as 'the most servile tool of the capitalist class enemy within the workers' ranks'. He did not attempt to challenge Midgley's charge that he and others deserted the workers on the day of the 'monster' demonstration.[24]

Midgley's attitude, as outlined, is understandable and defensible, if not in the final analysis wholly acceptable. As someone who, with others in the Labour movement, had spent the previous ten years or so working night and day on behalf of Belfast workers, it was only natural that he should feel somewhat piqued that a small band of people who had scant respect for such sacrifices should steal the limelight in this particular struggle. He could with justice say that he and others had served the working class best, and it was poor reward to have to watch them follow those whose main objective was to discredit the orthodox Labour movement.[25] The RWG leadership seems also to have shirked its responsibilities when the struggle spilled over into a violent confrontation. Certainly Geehan and the other leaders would have risked arrest by appearing at the 'monster' demonstration, but such a risk had not prevented them organising and speaking at earlier meetings. In any case it may be pertinent to ask if arrest and a prison sentence were too much to risk for those who purported to be dedicated to the class struggle.

Midgley was arguably justified in asserting that to urge the workers to proceed with their meeting on 11 October was a foolhardy act. It was obvious on the previous day, judging by the show of strength on the part of the police, that a violent confrontation was a real possibility and that the unarmed workers would come off worse. The disorders of the previous week had brought the weight of public opinion – if Midgley is to be believed[26] – down on the side of the workers' demands. In respect of the government, Sir Richard Dawson Bates, the Minister of Home Affairs, had earlier voiced his concern about the possibility of trouble,[27] while J. M. Andrews, Minister of Labour, had been scathing in his criticism of the Guardians.[28] Given the first week of troubles in October, and in view of the earlier disorders in other parts of Britain, it seems likely that the government would have taken action to resolve the situation. The RWGs argued that a direct confrontation with the State was required; the cost in terms of lives lost and injuries was evidently not considered too high in view of the victory achieved. It is impossible to say whether or not the events of 11 October were instrumental in bringing about that victory, but the observation might still be made that any loss of life is too high a price to pay when the situation is not without some hope of being peacefully resolved.

The Labour movement in Belfast was no less anxious than the Communists to see radical changes in relation to the Poor Law and the system of Outdoor Relief. If its political outlook was to be seen to be credible, however, it had to show that such changes could be effected peacefully. It had to prove to the workers that it was in their material interests to vote Labour and to thereby ensure that such things as the abuses of the Poor Law system would be eradicated. It had, in short, to turn its face against any accommodation with groups who held a diametrically opposed philosophy of how to bring about a better society. There could be no 'short cuts' without even more suffering and distress, and, in the view of the Labour movement, those who fed the workers such an illusion could not be co-operated with.

Midgley's response to the events, however, tends to suggest that he had allowed himself to become more concerned about Communist influences on workers than the successful resolution of the strike. It has to be made clear that the situation was an urgent one. There were many people on the verge of starvation who were not in the least consoled by the prospect of waiting until the Poor Law elections.[29] Midgley and Labour's strategy, in this case, seems to have been a little too resigned and tinged with a certain self-imposed powerlessness. Arguably their tactics could have been altered to intensify the pressure on the government and the Poor Law Guardians, and to stress the urgency of the situation without triggering off trouble on the streets. A one-day general strike, for example, could have been called, and could only have been called, by the leaders of the large trade unions with whom Midgley and the NILP worked closely at this time.

Put in historical perspective, the riots cannot but be seen as an isolated outburst of working class unity of purpose. They proved that both Protestant and Catholic workers suffered social and economic problems and that both felt suitably aggrieved and frustrated. Moreover they proved that both could participate in a united form of expression of these grievances. They did not, however, signal any change in respective attitudes to the national question, and they did not remove sectarianism from the forefront of Northern Ireland politics or from people's minds. The working class unity of October 1932 was brittle, and was soon to be exposed as such.

III

During 1933 Midgley continued his preparations for the Northern Ireland general election and maintained his flow of written propaganda for the Labour movement. On 26 August at the NILP conference he was re-elected Chairman of the party.

In his conference address[30] Midgley dwelt on the problem of unemployment, relating it to the structure of capitalism which in his view made it 'inevitable'. Economic problems would not, moreover, be solved by protectionist measures, or 'economic nationalism', said Midgley, since this 'could only result in the most degrading form of cut throat competition'. This was probably a veiled criticism of the protectionist economic outlook of de Valera who had come to power in the South in 1932. Midgley went on to warn that new technological advances would lead, increasingly, to the replacement in many jobs of men by machines. This did not mean that new inventions should be deplored, rather that the remedy was 'to make the discoveries of science and the inventions the property of the community instead of a small class'. The Labour movement, he said, wanted 'to scientifically regulate Production and Consumption'. His talk also ranged over international events and included an assessment of the new German Chancellor: 'In Germany we see an arrogant, cruel and imperialistic controller in power, who rules by ruthlessly crushing every phase of thought not in harmony with his own, by indulging in the most cowardly forms of race, religious, and political persecution.' He was no less trenchant or realistic with regard to matters on his own doorstep: 'The people of Ulster still drink at the rivers which have been poisoned at their source.'

Midgley seemed to be in full control of the party. The trade unions, for the most part, strongly supported his leadership,[31] and he had close friends and allies, such as John Campbell, T. J. McCoubrie, and W. J. Donaldson, in positions of importance in the party. Jack Beattie of course was the single Labour member in parliament, but his position within the party does not seem to have been a strong one – personal support was lacking, and his influence was consequently slight. With Midgley firmly backed by the trade unions and the mainstream of the party rank and file, Beattie had to look elsewhere for a personal following. The obvious source of support was the nationalist tendency of the party which soon realised that Midgley by now harboured scant sympathy for their ideals.

The party had already become very 'Midgley-centred' or 'Midgley-orientated'. Party literature invariably bore his authorship and party branches looked to him for guidance on all sorts of organisational matters. The minutes of the Armagh Labour Party (established September 1933) for the last four months of 1933 indicate just how central a figure Midgley was. His advice was sought on various matters ranging from how best to put a case before the town council to the advisability of having James Connolly's *Labour in Irish History* serialised in the local press.[32] Midgley's response to the latter is unfortunately unrecorded.

The Northern Ireland election was eventually called for 30 November 1933. Labour's preparations were far from satisfactory[33] with the exception of Midgley's contest in Dock. The only other candidates put forward were Beattie in Pottinger, and W. J. Donaldson in St. Anne's, a predominantly Protestant ward. While the party was certainly not financially healthy and while there were few 'winnable' seats around, it might still be said that the party, for this election, became in effect Midgley's personal vehicle. Most of its energies and resources were focused on the Dock contest. Given the relatively strong Labour party in Derry, it seems surprising that no seat was contested there.

The party fought the election on a social and economic programme which called for the alleviation of unemployment, better housing and the abolition of the Means Test. Other proposals put forward were: Old Age Pensions of sixty shillings per week at age 60; widows' pensions; full maintenance for the unemployed and their dependants; two weeks' holiday with pay; a forty-hour week; and the taxation of land values.[34]

In Dock Midgley launched a carefully prepared campaign against the parliamentary record of his Unionist opponent, Major Blakiston-Houston, and in promotion of his own record in the Belfast City Council. The constituency had an electorate of just over 11,000, but the substantial Catholic section of it (about 40% of the total) had ensured a fair number of local election defeats in the past for the Unionists. This time, afraid of Midgley's ability to win Protestant support, they hoped to win some of this Catholic vote. To do so they played up to the fact that Blakiston-Houston's wife was a devout Catholic, and the lady herself took a prominent part in the campaign, often to her embarrassment.[35]

Midgley betrayed his anxiety regarding this tactic in his election address, urging voters to show contempt for political tactics 'which seek to exploit the Church of God and the sacred feelings of men and women of every section of the community'.[36] In addition to this he distributed a special message to Catholic voters. This consisted of a quotation from Archbishop Downey – 'a Noble Spiritual Leader' – to the effect that he [Downey] was much impressed by the principles and deeds of the Labour movement, the purpose being to counter the 'unscrupulous propaganda' and 'deliberate misstatements' of the Unionists regarding the attitude of the Catholic Church towards Labour.[37] Finally, in another nod to the Catholic electorate, Midgley distributed a handbill delineating the 'misdeeds' of Blakiston-Houston, the most egregious of which was his attempt to have a divorce court set up in Northern Ireland.[38] It was all in the election game, and Midgley, desperate to enter parliament, was not above playing it.

Midgley enlisted formidable outside help during his campaign. Through NUDAW he acquired the services of John Jagger, Ellen Wilkinson, Harold Weate, Luke Hogan, William Robinson and Charlie Flynn, all able speakers and campaign workers who had had much election experience in England. It is doubtful, however, if they had ever experienced anything quite like the sectarianism of Belfast. Ellen Wilkinson expressed her horror at having 'drilled into her half a dozen prejudices about the Union jack, the Pope and the Battle of the Boyne'.[39] According to Midgley, the Unionist supporters cut up rough towards the end of the campaign, by which time meetings had to be confined to Catholic parts of the ward.[40]

The result was a clear victory for Midgley: 4,893 to 3,685. The Catholic voters had resisted the blandishments of Mrs Blakiston-Houston, and they gave Midgley a 'most touching' reception when he paraded their areas in triumph.[41] A scroll, 'signed on behalf of the voters of Sailortown', by five Catholic electors, was presented to Midgley to welcome him as their MP. It stated: 'It is not necessary for us to numerate your services to the working class . . . Sufficient to say that your life has been devoted to the cause of the working class. May God spare you to further this cause.'[42] In numerous Catholic homes in the warren of narrow streets Midgley's photograph graced the front window lit up by lamps fuelled with the best of oil.[43] The Catholic voters of Dock had 'sanctified' their new MP.

The election results in general reflected no apparent disenchantment with the Unionist Party among the majority of voters, despite the economic situation. The Unionists again managed to make the constitutional issue the most vital one in people's minds; they won thirty-six

seats, one less than in 1929. The Nationalists won nine, Independent
Unionists three, Republicans and Labour two apiece. Beattie was Labour's other success, retaining Pottinger after a close contest; Donaldson, however, was well beaten in St. Anne's.

It is worth stressing at this point that, their overall hegemony notwithstanding, the Unionist Party found Protestant working class wards in
Belfast difficult to control. Both the Independent Unionist mavericks,
John Nixon and Tommy Henderson, held the seats in 1933 which they
had won in 1929: Woodvale and Shankill respectively. Nixon was to
remain the MP for Woodvale until his death in 1949, while Henderson
did not relinquish his grip on the Shankill until 1953. In 1933 William
Wilton, a Protestant extremist who was closely associated with Nixon,
made a strong showing in Oldpark.[44] Moreover, both Midgley and
Beattie could not have won their respective seats without significant
Protestant working class support. While Protestant working class
Belfast never wavered in its support of the Union, it was less solid in
support of the Unionist Party, which could be made to suffer for the
rather aloof, comfortably-off image it presented.

IV

Midgley delivered his maiden speech in the Northern Ireland parliament on 19 December 1933. It was a confident and impressive debut.
The speech was long, and as full of facts, statistics and information as his
written propaganda. It ranged over a wide field of subjects: unemployment, education, the Unionist government's political philosophy,
industry, housing and the general problem of poverty. Midgley brought
the full fruits of his personal quest for knowledge to this speech and to
many others he was to make in the House in the years to come. On
unemployment he stated: '. . . I have made myself as familiar with the
problem as possibly any person in this house. I have studied Blue Books
and White Books, and all kinds of reports; I have gone to the libraries,
and I have burned the midnight oil.'[45] He ended with a call to the
government to adopt a 'bold constructive programme' to deal with
Northern Ireland's problems, and when he sat down he was warmly
congratulated by his old adversary Sir Robert Lynn, and by J. M.
Andrews who admired his 'eloquence and undoubted sincerity'.[46] It
was the first of many compliments he was to receive from his Unionist
opponents who obviously looked upon flattery as a way of taming the
House's 'firebrands'.

Midgley believed devoutly in the processes of parliamentary democracy, and on one occasion warned the government that if it did not listen to other points of view, people might turn to groups who were opposed to parliamentary institutions.[47] He sought to create a 'respectable' parliamentary image both for himself and the NILP, and was very sensitive to Unionist suggestions that he was a 'destroyer' or that he and the NILP were part of any 'conspiracy'.[48] Later he claimed that he had been 'assailed both from within and without the Labour movement, because I have rejected the principles of dictatorship'.[49]

However, Midgley's impetuous nature sometimes got the better of him. He frequently fell foul of the Speaker's rulings, and on more than one occasion was ordered from the House.[50] If his overall faith in parliamentary institutions was always steady, his regard for the workings of the Northern Ireland example was often low:

When I came here I came inspired with courage. I am not inspired now. This is a deadly institution . . . I speak more courageously and in a more inspired fashion and feel I am achieving much more good inside the Belfast City Council, with all its faults, than I can in this parliament. Every time you come forward with a new idea or try to develop a new problem and inculcate it into the minds of the members, you are met with the argument, 'it is outside our powers; it is a reserved service; do you expect us to do that on our own when other areas are not prepared to join us?' After you have been here for a while you become obsessed with the feeling that you can perform no useful function.[51]

This outburst came after only two months' experience of the workings of parliament. It was as if the obvious reality of Labour's political impotence had just fully struck him. The Unionists, entrenched in office with a comfortable majority, could – and invariably did – stifle any suggestion of change which came from outside their ranks. It is hard to resist the conclusion that the informal and open nature of government in Ulster, alluded to earlier, effectively rendered parliamentary procedures a charade. Debates had an unreal quality; members seemed simply to be going through the motions before a policy was inevitably ratified or rejected in the formal manner. Policy decisions were the result of pressure group interventions and their relation to the Unionist strategy for appeasing its supporters and their different – and sometimes conflicting – interests. Labour, in such a situation, could only persist in promoting its own alternative in the faint hope of checking Unionist politics to some degree, and of gradually converting more voters to their outlook. Such hopes were faint because the national question would continue to dominate Ulster politics while uncertainty surrounded it. For someone like Midgley who was desperate to achieve tangible changes, the situation was one of being politically manacled.

There were slight compensations, however. The House of Commons at Stormont[52] was another stage on which he could dazzle, and members of all parties were suitably mesmerised by his oratory. Many of his early speeches were undeniably self-indulgent in places, and liberally sprinkled with self-acclaim. Midgley was often criticised for being relentlessly egotistical, but vain as he could undoubtedly sound, these critics simply did not have an ear for the element of tongue-in-cheek self-mockery which was often present in Midgley's speeches. A good example is a remark relating to J. M. Andrews, the Minister of Labour: 'Like myself he is troubled with modesty occasionally, but it is only occasionally and when there are no elections.'[53] Clashes with opponents often brought out the acerbic in Midgley and sometimes made him disarmingly aggressive, but there was rarely any ill-temper or malice in these exchanges.

Midgley reserved some of his most magisterial oratory for the subject of sectarianism. With the deadening effect on policy debates of the Unionist stranglehold on government, the tone of debate in the House fell not infrequently to the depths of sectarian squabbling over such matters as provocative flags and emblems.[54] William Grant for the Unionists, and James Joseph McCarroll for the Nationalists, were particularly in their element here. Midgley complained bitterly about the amount of time devoted to sectarian affairs, and hit out equally at both sides.[55] This was not surprising, for, in addition to the history of Unionist hostility to him, he had, by the middle of 1934, felt the force of the Nationalists' wrath as well.

On 19 January 1934 Joe Devlin died. He had become a legendary figure in Irish politics, and his passing was widely mourned. Midgley joined in the tributes: 'Mr Devlin was a great man, and in his day and generation performed wonderful work for the masses of the Community regardless of their creed.'[56] Devlin's death vacated the Northern Ireland parliamentary seat of Belfast Central.

For months the seat lay vacant with the Nationalists at Stormont apparently reluctant to move the writ for a by-election. Matters at last seemed to be moving when the Nationalists announced that they would move the writ on 8 May. On 9 May they decided to defer the matter for another week, and, under orders from the NILP executive to move the writ if the Nationalists stalled further, Midgley duly did so. The consequent Nationalist anger focused exclusively on Midgley, for Beattie had decided to defy the party executive and had taken no part in the proceedings. The Nationalists' resentment at such 'unprecedented interference'[57] was fierce since they believed that both Midgley and Beattie owed their seats to votes which were given to them by the Catholic community in the absence of Nationalist candidates. Their reasoning was that because the votes had come from Catholics, they were really Nationalist votes; like the Unionists, the Nationalist politicians admitted of no non-sectarian voting behaviour. The NILP believed that the Nationalists were delaying the election to coincide with the Catholic Truth Society festival in Belfast in June, a charge hotly denied by the Nationalists. Midgley's attempt to move the writ was defeated by the Nationalists in the House; the Unionists abstained.

The Nationalists finally moved the writ the following week and the election date was set for 4 June. Their candidate was a well-known Belfast lawyer, T. J. Campbell, while Labour recalled William McMullen from Dublin in the hope of cashing in on his Connollyite credentials. An anti-partitionist Republican candidate, Harry Diamond, was also in the field, along with an Independent. The Unionists declined to contest what was an overwhelmingly Catholic ward.

The Nationalist campaign was virulently sectarian and anti-socialist. It stressed the Labour Party's hostility to the principle of denominational education and called on Catholic voters to 'protect their religion'. One supporter of Campbell voiced the opinion that a vote for McMullen was a vote for 'the Protestant Ascendancy'![58] Campbell turned his attention to Midgley more than once during the campaign. His bone of contention – besides the moving of the writ – was that Midgley had refused to accept a motion tabled by the Nationalists condemning sectarian speeches made by the Minister of Agriculture, Sir Basil Brooke. Midgley, said Campbell, had moved an amendment which 'evaded the real issue'.[59] Midgley's amendment had in fact related to what to him was the real issue: discrimination. His amendment had read:

That in the opinion of this House the employment of citizens in Northern Ireland should be on the basis of equality of opportunity and without discrimination as to religion or politics, this being the only basis on which full civil and religious liberty can be preserved.[60]

This hardly 'evaded the real issue' unless the real issue was to score sectarian points and revile Brooke personally.

Campbell won the seat but McMullen polled strongly for Labour[61] – a warning to the Nationalists that future contests in Catholic working class Belfast seats would be very hard fought affairs. Without Devlin the Nationalists in Belfast appeared very vulnerable, as indeed time would prove them to be. Their Belfast organisation was weak without Devlin's 'machine' political skills. The party's position in areas such as Derry City and Fermanagh and Tyrone was markedly stronger than in Belfast and tended to reflect a stronger tradition of abstentionism.

In the course of the Nationalist celebrations after Campbell's victory, one James Collins, of whom more will be heard, exalted that they 'had driven the socialist out', adding that soon they 'would drive the socialist out of Dock too'.[62] Little did Collins realise how direct a part he was to play in doing precisely that. Midgley's relations with the Nationalists, for a long time cool, now assumed a condition of mutual antagonism. At Stormont on 22 November 1934 he was involved in a bitter clash with Campbell, McCarroll and Richard Byrne, claiming that the Nationalists were trying to drive him out of public life.[63]

As Midgley's relations with the Nationalists deteriorated, so Beattie's prospered.[64] At the time of the writ controversy Beattie was hoping to be offered the job of secretary to the Irish National Teachers' Organisation (INTO) for which he had applied. The INTO was a Southern-based trade union with a strong anti-partitionist outlook, and in applying for the job Beattie was quite probably seeking to enhance his nationalist credentials within the NILP in opposition to the drift of the party under Midgley away from any kind of association with the united Ireland ideal. Beattie did not want to do anything to upset the Nationalists and so jeopardise his job application. This was the case he apparently put in his defence at an NILP executive committee meeting in June.[65] The committee was unimpressed and expelled him, a decision which annoyed those with an anti-partitionist outlook in the party. An attempt was made at the party conference in August to have the decision reconsidered, but it was easily defeated.[66] Midgley was now out on his own as leader of the NILP inside and outside of parliament. From the moment he had entered Stormont he and Beattie had co-existed rather than co-operated, with Beattie insistent on his status of senior parliamentarian, and Midgley on his as the chairman and recognised leader of the NILP. Neither would relent an inch when it came to a question of individual prestige and reputation. The problem was for now resolved. Midgley was the sole NILP member of parliament while Beattie sat with the designation 'Independent Labour'.

The NILP held two conferences in 1934, one in March and one in

August.[67] The former was specially convened to discuss ways of bettering the party's organisation. Again, G. R. Shepherd was in attendance, and promised financial assistance to the NILP in its attempt to build up a strong political machine.[68] To Midgley, this was the party's greatest need: 'The time has arrived when the people of Northern Ireland must emerge from political infancy and fashion a machine capable of challenging the reactionary political forces.'[69] Midgley's aim was to 'professionalise' the NILP, and to this end he was fostering closer ties with the British Labour Party.

In August Midgley devoted much of his Chairman's Address to the threat of fascism in Europe: 'the creed of the cruel, the bully, and the thug; and the last hope of a privileged class, that they may retain their privilege and despotic power through fascist dictatorship'. He called for the Labour movement to stand 'four square' in defence of 'political democracy', but also to fight for the 'economic democracy of socially owned wealth'.[70] Fascism was a subject on which he expounded in another of his pamphlets, *Important Facts for Old and Young*, published in July 1934. Detailing the effects of fascism in Italy, Germany and Austria he reached the conclusion that it was bound to lead to war.[71] Fascism in Britain was also examined and Oswald Mosley's anti-semitism excoriated.[72]

Midgley took great pains to spice his speeches and pamphlets with analyses of international events. He kept extremely well-informed of developments the world over, and was able to produce at random facts and statistics about various countries. His outlook was international in the truest sense, and in eschewing a parochial approach he was encouraging a healthy spirit within the party. His intentions were thus honourable, but unfortunately no amount of emphasis on international events could conceal, or make disappear, the party's fundamental difficulties.

V

In the wake of the Outdoor Relief riots of 1932 hard-line sectarian elements in Belfast attempted to ensure that there would be no repeat of the Protestant–Catholic unity which had been temporarily established. The Ulster Protestant League (UPL), an extremist Protestant organisation which had been set up in 1931, quickly condemned the riots and those Protestants who had been 'misled'.[73] The UPL was at this time small and rather insignificant, but during the next four years it was to grow in numbers and in influence. This probably owed much, initially, to the support it received from leading figures in the Unionist Party.[74] Prominent Unionists made sectarian speeches every bit as strident as the UPL in this period, the most infamous being that of Sir Basil Brooke on 12 July 1933 when he urged Protestants not to employ Catholics.[75]

Besides anti-Catholic pronouncements, the Unionists and the UPL also carried on an intense anti-Communist propaganda drive. The 'United Front' tactics of the Labour movement and the Communist Party of Ireland (CPI, formed 1933) on certain issues during 1934 and 1935,[76] enabled the Unionists and the UPL to brand the whole Labour movement as Communist. Both the NILP and the CPI headquarters in Belfast were attacked by Protestant mobs in June 1935. Labour was also tainted with Irish Republicanism, the outcome perhaps of the Republican Congress of April 1934 in which left-wing members of the NILP as well as the CPI and the left wing of the IRA had participated.

Fierce communal rioting finally erupted in Belfast in the summer of 1935. There had been isolated outbreaks of sectarian disorder in 1933 and 1934, but the real trouble started around the time of the Silver Jubilee celebrations of King George V in May 1935. In a report to the NUDAW Political General Secretary in June, T. J. McCoubrie, Midgley's election agent, complained that it had been impossible to hold meetings or distribute literature since the beginning of May when Protestant bands played party tunes in a Catholic area and started trouble. He went on to say: 'No doubt it will suit the government to have the workers divided again so that their attention may be diverted from the treatment which the Unemployment Assistance Board is handing out to them, by the way of allowances for their needs.'[77] In a later report he referred specifically to the UPL as being responsible for breaking up Labour meetings, and complained that the authorities had not given them proper protection.[78]

On 12 July 1935 the Orange Parade was fired on near Belfast city centre, an occurrence which triggered off the worst wave of sectarian trouble the city had witnessed since 1920–2. This parade – indeed all parades – had been banned by the Home Affairs minister Sir Richard Dawson Bates after an outbreak of trouble on 14 June. The 'twelfth' being a sacred day on the Ulster Protestant calendar, Orange Order pressure led him to revoke the ban for this occasion. The party who fired the shots remains a mystery. Protestants at the time took it to be the IRA; others have suggested that it may have been the work of hired gunmen acting on Unionist orders in order to provoke trouble. Whoever was responsible, trouble was certainly provoked. Rioting immediately followed and continued off and on for three weeks. By the time a tentative peace was restored, thirteen people had lost their lives, scores had been wounded and injured, and hundreds of families – mostly Catholic – had been driven from their homes. Most of the trouble took place in the Dock ward of the city, especially the York Street area. For some time before the riots the area had acquired a reputation for gangsterism and racketeering, with jobs – scarce as they were[79] – often obtained at the point of a gun.[80]

The area of course was Midgley's constituency, and the outbreak of the riots found him out of Belfast on holiday. It is not known exactly when he returned and what exactly he did in response to the situation when he found it. Some commentators have criticised what they have interpreted as his 'silence' concerning the riots,[81] and one of the most recent, Paddy Devlin, has also argued that:

Midgley was aware that he would always get the Catholic vote in the Dock area for it was virulently anti-Unionist and would probably support him at the polls in any case. To win the seat he had to have Protestant working class support. Rather than risk alienating that support which was shaky, he made no condemnation of the attacks on the Catholic residents of Dock.[82]

It has been further argued elsewhere that Midgley's 'silence' in 1935 was an important factor in his election defeat in Dock in 1938.[83]

The first point to make in reply is that Midgley did not keep silent in response to the riots, however much some may disparage what he in fact said. As Chairman of the NILP and the virtual director of its public statements, Midgley would in all likelihood have been instrumental in drawing up the notice which appeared in the Belfast press on 5 August in the aftermath of the riots. This stated that the NILP called upon the security forces to give 'adequate protection' to workers who had been threatened with violence if they returned to work, and that employers should take 'drastic action' against those provoking disorder. It went on to express 'grave concern' regarding people being ejected from their homes and the destruction of furniture, and criticised the government for 'abuse of power', as shown by 'the restrictions and denials of elementary civil liberties to sections of the community in Northern Ireland'. Finally, it appealed to all workers to dissociate themselves from those encouraging 'evil passions'.[84]

In an article which appeared in *Forward* on 10 August, Midgley gave his personal view of events. He claimed that the NILP and the Belfast Trades Council had sent a deputation to Dawson-Bates before the riots broke out, warning him of what might happen. At the time of the deputation, said Midgley, troubles were almost a 'nightly occurrence', a product in his view of the 'provocative activities' of Orange bands playing party tunes in Catholic areas, and of the activities of 'sectarian organisations [the UPL] arrogating to themselves the right to break up meetings, deny the right of free speech, and interfere in every possible way with the elementary rights of citizenship'. Midgley then went on to denounce both Unionist and Nationalist politicians for stirring up their respective supporters, and both the Unionist and Nationalist press for their partisan reportage. 'The atmosphere in Belfast', he stated, 'is akin to that which existed during the Great War. No lie or atrocity story is too foul or fiendish to ascribe to the "enemy", and of course, this creates the desire for reprisals and events move round in a vicious circle.' His conclusion was pessimistic – 'Belfast will continue to be the cockpit for rival sectarianists so long as our politics and parliamentary life are conducted along sectarian lines' – although he did refer to the 'welcome' unanimity of the Protestant clergy in denouncing the riots and in trying to safeguard the right of employment.[85]

Midgley was thus declaring a plague on both Unionist and Nationalist houses, and it is this 'fence-sitting' attitude which has drawn criticism from those who believe that he should have been more forceful in his condemnation of the Protestant mobs. Certainly the Catholic minority once again came off worse in terms of house burnings and workplace expulsions, and some stronger words with regard to the parts played by top members of the Unionist Party in fanning sectarian flames might reasonably have been expected from Midgley.

Of the fatalities, however, eight were Protestant and five were Catholic[86] so it cannot be said that this was a one-sided form of mass terror or persecution. The background to the trouble – as on earlier occasions – was arguably much more complex than one set of people being deliberately manipulated to attack another. Devlin[87] and Farrell,[88] to name the most explicit commentators, both convey the impression that the Catholic community in Belfast was so cowed and dispirited that it was set upon without provocation and routed without resistance. It could be argued that, on the contrary, the minority's spirit of defiance and self-confidence was a major factor in the occurrence of the riots. The early 1930s was a period in which the Catholic Church in Ireland, both North and South, displayed a crusading zeal. This was particularly evident in the massive celebrations which accompanied the Eucharistic Congress of 1932 and the Catholic Truth Society Festival in Belfast in 1934. This high church profile combined with a continuing Nationalist hostility to all things British was enough to cause even moderate Protestants some uneasiness. It is not to excuse the Protestant mobs of July 1935, or indeed of 1920–22, or to cover up in any way for the cynical way they might have been exploited by members of the Unionist Party, to say that animosities were probably as bitterly harboured on the Catholic side, and that these animosities were always plain for the Protestant community to see.

To support this contention some evidence from the *New Statesman and Nation* of the period can be adduced. This left-wing political weekly, in its first comment on the riots, put the blame squarely on Orange mobs.[89] The following week a reader going under the alias of 'North of Ireland' wrote to paint what to him or her was a truer picture. This correspondent made three points:

1. Bad feeling has persisted since the Jubilee celebrations during which Union Jacks were pulled down and burnt, and Jubilee badges snatched from school children.
2. The Orangemen on July 12th were proceeding in a perfectly orderly manner when they were fired upon. During the subsequent rioting a Protestant was killed. The funeral procession was fired upon. Then came reprisals.
3. With regard to the deaths – of the eight recorded to date (July 20th) six were Protestants. The following is on a gable wall in a Roman Catholic quarter of Belfast: 'Score Protestants 2 Catholics 6. You can loot, but we can shoot.'

'North of Ireland' went on: 'These periodic disturbances are carefully planned to break out at important occasions – a favourite time is just before the arrival of a royal visitor. The present ones have quite effectively destroyed the cross-channel tourist traffic.'[90] The same issue carried a report by the *New Stateman's* 'special correspondent in Belfast' who, while very critical of the government and the Orange Order, felt compelled to say at the outset: 'Irish political life in North and South is traditionally inflammable, and I have been too long familiar with these religious hatreds to risk apportioning blame for the actual outbreak of disturbance to one side or the other.'

Midgley's condemnation of the UPL and its followers have been noted. It is probably the case that the greater malice, given their virulent anti-Catholic outpourings, lay with this group. It is probably also true to say that measured over several months, the bulk of the provocation came from the Protestant side. The evidence, however, is rather shadowy, and it is impossible to pass definite judgements on people's motives and perceptions. Midgley knew all about Protestant prejudices and the Unionist manipulation of them, but he was also by now in a good position to appreciate the ways in which the Catholic community was badly served by its political leaders. Whatever the causes of the riots and whoever was to blame, it made sense to condemn murder and violence generally and unequivocally, and without reference to its sectarian colouring. As he wrote in *An Open Letter to the Electors of Dock Ward* in January 1936: 'No good purpose can be served by continually asking "who did this, or who did that?" or "who started this" and "who started the other?" Along such lines we will never find the pathway to peace, harmony and goodwill.'[91]

If the Catholic voters of Dock were displeased with Midgley, they had an opportunity of showing their displeasure at the local government elections in May of 1936. Midgley, however, was returned unopposed as Alderman for the ward which meant that he had won another seven years' tenure.[92] Had Catholic anger been as great as has been suggested, then it seems likely that a Nationalist candidate would have opposed Midgley. Equally, it cannot be deduced from the absence of a Nationalist candidate that there was no ill-feeling on the part of some Catholics.

The Council elections of May 1936 were notable for the appearance of 'Jubilee Protestant Defence Association' candidates, one of whom defeated the Unionist candidate to win a seat in Duncairn Ward.[93] This reflected the deep disaffection of some Protestants from the Unionist Party. Far from simply herding their supporters back into line after 1932, the Unionist government had created a climate of volatile sectarianism in which extreme Protestants were soon to denounce the Unionists as too 'soft'.[94] The strain of anti-populism within the government may not have won spectacular victories during this period, but it did manage to check the excessive populism which Craigavon and Bates threatened to indulge in.[95] As a result the government found itself astringently criticised over such matters as the perceived Catholic infiltration of the police force and the civil service. So convinced were many Protestants that the police was being overrun by Catholics, that Protestants mobs fought vicious battles with the RUC during the 1935 troubles as well as with the Catholics.[96] Some Unionist Party members may have tried to manipulate the UPL to their advantage, but as events turned out, the extremists got far too extreme for the comfort of the government. The Unionist government was not as secure at this juncture as Devlin, for example, has suggested.[97] The Unionists were confronted with two discontented minorities: the Catholics and the extreme Protestants. Their fundamentally sectarian political approach had bred more of the same to the detriment of the stability of the State.

The NILP could only lose by the events of July 1935. Midgley's strategy was the only feasible and honourable one for a party caught in the throes of a sectarian and nationalist conflict. The NILP had to make its appeal across the community divide and to attempt, however despairingly, to harness energies and passions to class rather than ethnic politics.

At the party conference in September 1935, Midgley retained his chairmanship and once again attempted to elevate people's preoccupations from the local streets to the international arena. 'We meet today under the shadow of war' was his opening remark.[98] This shadow was being cast from China and Abyssinia, not York Street. Fascism's spectre was growing more menacing in Europe. Prospects for the future, assessed from riot-torn Belfast, must have seemed grim.

Notes

1. *Ulster Year Book* 1938, HMSO, pp. xviii-xxii.
2. Ibid.
3. Farrell, op. cit. p. 124.
4. The best account of the Labour government's response to the crisis is R. Skidelsky, *Politicians and the Slump,* London, 1967.
5. *New Dawn* 21 November 1931.
6. M. Milotte op. cit. p. 273.
7. A. Clifford, 'Labour politics in Northern Ireland', Part 9, *Irish Communist,* August/September 1980 No. 176.
8. *Belfast Telegraph* 29 March 1932.
9. Ibid.
10. *Forward* 30 July 1932.
11. Executive Council Minutes 1931 No. 501, USDAW records.
12. See, for example, 'Things every elector should know', November 1932, *Midgley Papers.*
13. See C. Cook and J. Stevenson, *The Slump,* London, 1977 chapter 10.
14. See A. Clifford, *Poor Law in Ireland,* Belfast, 1983, p. 151.
15. P. Devlin, *Yes, We Have No Bananas,* Belfast, 1981, p. 121.
16. Ibid. *passim.*
17. See P. Bew, P. Gibbon and H. Patterson, *The State in Northern Ireland,* Manchester, 1979, chapter 3, and P. Bew and C. Norton, 'The Unionist state and the outdoor relief riots of 1932', *Economic and Social Review* 10, No. 3 1979, pp. 255–65.
18. Bew and Norton, op. cit.
19. Bew, Gibbon and Patterson op. cit. p. 79.

20. See P. Buckland, *The Factory of Grievances*, Dublin, 1979 pp. 16–18 and 59–68.
21. See Devlin op. cit. p. 132.
22. Both the NUWM and the RWGs were acting in accordance with the 'class against class' approach laid down by the Comintern back in 1928. This approach necessitated the breaking off of relations with reformist parties such as the British Labour Party and the NILP.
23. *Forward* 22 October 1932.
24. *The Workers' Voice* 5 November 1932.
25. See Tom Bell, *The Struggle of the Unemployed in Belfast October 1932*, Cork, n.d. Bell, a Communist, rejoiced in the belief that the RWGs disillusioned the workers with 'the reformists'.
26. 'In my lifetime there has never been such a manifestation of unanimity in support of a cause.' *Forward* 22 October 1932.
27. Bew and Norton op. cit.
28. Buckland op. cit. p. 158.
29. As it turned out Labour did badly in the Poor Law elections, winning only one seat. In the Belfast Corporation election of January 1933 they made no gains and lost a seat in Dock. See Farrell op. cit. pp. 131–2.
30. This speech was published as a pamphlet in October 1933 entitled 'The Labour movement and Ulster', *Midgley Papers*.
31. Interview with Tom Boyd 8 April 1980.
32. Minutes of Armagh Labour Party September/December 1933, Patrick Agnew papers, PRONI DI 676/1/1.
33. See Harbinson op. cit. pp. 64–7.
34. Ibid. p. 68.
35. As Midgley wrote after the election: 'It was quite a common thing to see the sectarian Unionists following their candidate singing ribald songs of a strong sectarian variety, and their candidate's wife sitting in the brake, or at the meetings, listening to the songs and the uncharitable epithets.' *New Dawn* 30 December 1933.
36. Election address, 30 November 1933, *Midgley Papers*.
37. Leaflet, 'Archbishop Downey and Labour', *Midgley Papers*.
38. Leaflet, 'Some votes and sayings of Major Blakiston-Houston in Parliament', *Midgley Papers*.
39. *Northern Whig* 28 November 1933.
40. *New Dawn* 30 December 1933.
41. Ibid.
42. Scroll contained in *Midgley Papers*. 'Sailortown' was one of the Catholic quarters of the ward down by the docks.
43. Information from Murtagh Morgan 12 June 1981.
44. The result was Sir A. W. Hungerford (Unionist) 5,427; William Wilton (Ind. Unionist) 4,155.
45. N. I. House of Commons Debate XVI, 77.
46. Ibid. 93–4.
47. Ibid. 1289–90.
48. Ibid. 523–4. Midgley was reacting to a speech made by Craig during which he delivered the threat to the Labour Party that they [the Unionists] would

'take the same steps that we took on former occasions' to protect Ulster's 'liberty, safety and honour', if Labour consorted with people 'we do not trust'. See *Northern Whig* 14 March 1934.

49. N.I. House of Commons Debates XVI, 581.

50. One such occasion during this early period in his parliamentary career was on 6 March 1934.

51. N.I. House of Commons Debates XVI, 1486.

52. The Northern Ireland House of Commons was simply referred to as 'Stormont' after the new Parliament Buildings had been opened near Stormont Castle in 1932.

53. N.I. House of Commons Debates XVI, 1496.

54. One particularly acrimonious debate centred on the question of whether the Coalisland Girl Guides should be allowed to unfurl the Union Jack in a Catholic area.

55. N.I. House of Commons Debates XVII, 137–55.

56. *Irish News* 19 January 1934.

57. Ibid. 30 May 1934.

58. Ibid. 1 June 1934.

59. Ibid.

60. N.I. House of Commons Debates XVI, 1121.

61. The full result was: Campbell 4,948; McMullen 3,784; Diamond 1,518; and W. McKeaveney 214.

62. *Irish News* 6 June 1934.

63. N.I. House of Commons Debates XVII, 142.

64. Midgley and Beattie were not on good personal terms by this time. The feud between them seems to have dated from the end of the 1920s. It was generally a matter of rival personal ambitions and concerned, in particular, trade union and financial wrangles. Beattie's anti-partitionist views were not obvious until the early 1930s when they appear to have surfaced in response to Midgley's gradual drift towards a more unionist position. Beattie had few of Midgley's leadership qualities – he was a poor speaker and wrote little or nothing for the Labour press – but he was a shrewd politician whose electoral record bore witness to his acumen.

65. Harbinson op. cit. p. 72. Beattie got the INTO job.

66. Ibid. pp. 72–3. The initial resolution for expulsion had been moved by two Catholic members of the party, John Campbell and John Glass.

67. Midgley was re-elected chairman, unopposed, at the August conference.

68. *Northern Whig* 12 March 1934.

69. Reported in the *Irish Workers' Voice* 17 March 1934.

70. Chairman's Address NILP Annual Conference 25 August 1934, *Midgley Papers.*

71. *Important Facts for Old and Young,* July 1934, *Midgley Papers.*

72. Ibid.

73. Devlin op. cit. p. 138.

74. Maj. Henry McCormick, the Unionist MP for St. Anne's in Belfast, was a leading figure in the UPL. The UPL used the Unionist Party HQ at Glengall Street in Belfast for their meetings.

75. Farrell op. cit. 137.

76. See Milotte op. cit. pp. 360–5. The 'United Front' agreements were always fragile, and in September 1935 at the NILP conference, the CPI's proposal to erect something more substantial was firmly rejected. Midgley dismissed the proposal as coming 'on orders from Moscow'. Milotte op. cit. p. 369.
77. Political General Secretary's Report 13 June 1935, USDAW records.
78. Ibid. 6 August 1936.
79. Northern Ireland's unemployment rate in 1935 was 25.3%. The shipbuilding firm, Workman and Clark, closed down early in the year with the loss of around 2000 jobs.
80. Interview with Malachy Gray 18 February 1981.
81. See, for example, Milotte op. cit. p. 368 and Farrell op. cit. p. 146.
82. Devlin op. cit. p. 143.
83. See Harbinson op. cit. p. 100 and Farrell op. cit. p. 146. See also next chapter.
84. *Belfast News-Letter* 5 August 1935, *Irish News* 5 August 1935. The party supported the Nationalists' call for an inquiry into the Unionist government's 'abuse of power'.
85. *Forward* 10 August 1935.
86. Farrell op. cit. p. 140.
87. Devlin op. cit. pp. 143–4.
88. Farrell op. cit. 136–42.
89. *New Statesman and Nation* 20 July 1935.
90. Ibid. 27 July 1935.
91. *An Open Letter to the Electors of Dock Ward, Midgley Papers.* This letter was reprinted from the January 1936 issue of *Labour Advocate*, a newspaper begun by Midgley himself in January 1935. The paper folded in March 1936.
92. *Belfast Telegraph* 7 May 1936.
93. Ibid. 16 May 1936.
94. See, for example, report of UPL meeting in *Irish News* 24 October 1936.
95. See Bew, Gibbon and Patterson op. cit. chapter 3.
96. *New Statesmen and Nation* 27 July 1935. Report by 'Special Correspondent'.
97. Devlin op. cit. p. 145.
98. *Belfast News-Letter*, 23 September 1935.

Chapter Six

Spain: The press, the pulpit and defeat
(1936–1938)

I

In February 1936, Midgley wrote an article for the Southern Irish weekly newspaper, *The Irish People.*[1] This piece set out – for a mainly Southern audience – Midgley's analysis of the problems facing Labour in the North and the strategy which he believed had to be adopted to overcome them. What this amounted to was essentially an appeal to Nationalists and Republicans to lay aside, for the time being, the question of partition and the reunification of Ireland.

Midgley first of all assailed the Nationalist politicians in Northern Ireland: 'The Nationalists have directed their appeals for support exclusively to the Catholic portion of the electorate, and thus committed themselves to a minority role in politics.' In Midgley's view this was a 'blunder' which played into the Unionists' hands: 'The cement that is holding the Ulster Unionist party so solidly together is sectarianism, and their opponents have made them a gift of it.' As far as the Republicans were concerned, Midgley applauded their attempts to keep clear of sectarianism, but considered futile their appeal to the electorate on the sole issue of Nationality. This had resulted in their obtaining negligible Protestant support: 'The Ulster Protestant will not, under present conditions be interested to the question of Irish nationalism. He is a Britisher in sentiment and outlook. During the whole of his lifetime he has lived in such an atmosphere.'

Midgley went on to articulate his frustrations with regard to the atrophied nature of the Northern Ireland parliamentary system. He reminded his readers that the Catholic proportion of the six-county population had actually decreased over the period 1901–26, and that even allowing for a dramatic future increase, there would be no likelihood of a pro-United Ireland majority for at least forty years. Midgley then claimed that although a 'large majority' of the electorate were dissatisfied with them, the Unionists held – and would continue to hold – the key to power: 'the exploitation of sectarianism and the border bogey'. In such a situation, therefore, it was Midgley's contention that the opposition parties had to change their tactics. The change he had in mind was the acceptance, on the part of Nationalists and Republicans, of the programme and outlook of the Labour Party. Besides the charter of social reforms he went on to outline, Midgley's demands in effect included the acceptance of the constitutional position of Northern Ireland within the United Kingdom.

The article did not specify it, but it was also Midgley's intention that an expanding Labour Party in Northern Ireland should work in close harmony with the British Labour Party, and in so doing build up an effective political machine with which to challenge the Unionist hegemony. For Midgley this electoral machine was the people's greatest need; an instrument to bring into being a strong non-sectarian party prepared to use the political machinery of the State and, by virtue of its strength, organisation and outlook, to render that machinery more meaningful.

In the final issue of his own monthly newspaper, *The Labour Advocate*, Midgley wrote of this ambition. The *Advocate* had run at a loss since Midgley launched it in January 1935, and, much dismayed and embittered, Midgley decided that publication would have to cease. He was embittered because of the lack of interest and support shown by the trade union movement in Northern Ireland. He blamed in particular the officials of the largest unions whom he accused of 'indifference' and of ignoring the paper's existence.[2]

Midgley saw the political potential which existed for a Labour Party strongly backed by the large trade union movement in Northern Ireland. In 1936, the total number of unions based in Britain or in Northern Ireland was seventy, with a total membership of 75,345.[3] The overwhelming mass of the unionised workforce – approximately ninety per cent[4] – belonged to British-based (National) trade unions. Since the unions were British-based, no organic arrangement existed between the NILP and the trade union movement in Northern Ireland. Some trade union branches were affiliated to the party, but since affiliation was on the basis of members paying a political levy on top of their trade union subscription, the affiliated membership was a fraction of the total. Thus the NILP did not receive from the trade unions in its area anything like the strong financial backing enjoyed by the British Labour Party from the trade unions throughout the rest of the UK.[5] Those unions affiliated to the NILP possessed a not insignificant voting strength, and eight places on the eighteen-strong party executive were reserved for trade union representatives.[6] In general, however, the unions did not play nearly as large a role in the NILP as their mainland counterparts did in the British Labour Party. Most trade union officials involved themselves politically only to the extent of participating in the formal mechanics of elections to party office, and lending modest assistance in parliamentary and local election campaigns. It was as if the officials felt constricted by the Unionist political attitudes of the vast majority of their members.

Midgley wanted to change this state of affairs and to integrate the trade unions fully into a well-oiled party machine. He faced formidable difficulties. In addition to being deprived of much potential trade union financial aid, the NILP could not escape the fact that it was a provincial party participating in the kind of provincial politics which nullified its appeal. In the last analysis important decisions affecting Northern Ireland workers were taken at Westminster. This pointed up the full extent of the 'limbo' in which the workers of Northern Ireland found themselves. Governed ultimately by Britain, and members, for the most part, of British trade unions, these workers could only participate effectively in the provincial politics of the Northern Ireland state which were of limited relevance to their material welfare. It was thus hardly surprising that Midgley found it difficult to stir up enthusiasm. In as far as Stormont really mattered, it derived its relevance in the eyes of most Northern Ireland workers as an institution embodying the will of the majority of the people to remain part of Britain. In such a situation Labour could not begin to compete with the Unionists.

On the other side of the sectarian divide, Midgley's strategy was also bound to come unstuck. Besides their opposition to any moves towards closer liaison with the British Labour movement, Nationalists and Republicans were not in the business of making the Northern Ireland parliament a more meaningful or reputable institution. The Nationalist members who attended Stormont did so out of a sense of duty to the minority community, not out of any desire to endorse the state. Midgley could not realistically hope to occasion the required revolution in their outlook. A few months after his overtures to the Nationalists, Midgley's strategic thoughts were in any case abruptly interrupted by an event which, in a short space of time, was to put paid to any such aspirations.

II

In July 1936 civil war erupted in Spain after a long period of political tension. The war was the outcome of a rebellion led by Army Generals

Franco and Mola against the Republican government which had been
elected to office in February. The rebellion was backed by Spain's
right-wing forces: monarchists, aristocrats, traditionalist Catholics, and
fascists. Their aim was to crush the Republic and its form of liberal
democracy which had precariously existed since 1931. The government
in Spain was of a Left Republican character but it had been brought to
power by a 'Popular Front' alliance which had claimed the votes of
socialists, communists and some anarcho-synicalists. The government
had won a narrow victory in February 1936, and the right-wing, far from
accepting defeat, had started almost immediately to plot its overthrow.

Viewed in a wide European context, the civil war seemed to many
outsiders to be a critical confrontation between democracy and the
growing force of Fascism. The Left in Europe certainly viewed it as such
and embraced the cause of the Republican government with intense
enthusiasm. Volunteers, orgainised in the International Brigade,
poured into Spain to fight for the government. The policy of both
Baldwin's British government and the government of the Irish Free
State under de Valera, was that of non-intervention. In this they joined
with France to form a Non-Intervention Committee. The rebel insurgents, however, were soon to obtain the vital assistance of Hitler's
Germany and Mussolini's Italy, both of which supplied arms and
aircraft. The Republicans received arms and aircraft from Soviet
Russia. The Nationalist rebels eventually wore down the Republican
resistance and their capture of Madrid at the end of March 1939 ended
the war and established Franco as dictator of Spain.

In Ireland, both North and South, the prevailing climate made
extremely difficult, not to say dangerous, the task of enlisting support for
the Spanish government's cause. In the South by the mid-30s there had
emerged a virulent anti-communist drive sanctioned by the Catholic
church and in some cases waged in practice by clerics. Communist and
other left-wing meetings were broken up, individual communists vio-
lently assaulted, and Connolly Hall in Dublin burnt to the ground. The
Fianna Fáil government led by Eamon de Valera had been in power
since 1932, and had already fashioned something of the isolationist and
insular mould into which the South would shortly settle. A strident
anti-British nationalism, a rigorous censorship over literature, economic protectionism, and a powerful and deeply conservative Catholic
church influence in many areas of social life, were perhaps the most
notable features of de Valera's Ireland.[7]

The Catholic church in Ireland took an unequivocal pro-Franco stand on the Spanish civil war, viewing the struggle as a Christian crusade against Communism and Godlessness. The church reacted with alarm to reports coming out of Spain concerning church-burnings and brutal killings of priests and nuns, and it viewed the Spanish government as a front for socialists and communists who were set on achieving the rout of the church and christianity in Spain, and the establishment of a materialist society. Some priests and bishops, most notably the Primate of Ireland, Cardinal MacRory, took an active role in organising financial aid for the rebellion in Spain. Some churchmen worked closely with the Irish Christian Front, a right-wing Catholic organisation led by Patrick Belton. The Christian Front echoed the quasi-fascist Blueshirt movement which had exploded onto the Irish political scene some four years earlier. This movement had been led by General Eoin O'Duffy who now, in response to events in Spain and some promptings on the part of Cardinal MacRory, enlisted some 700 men and set off in October to fight for Franco.[8] Despite the South's 'highly charged atmosphere of excessive piety',[9] however, some left-wing elements – including some communists – campaigned vigorously for the Spanish Republic, and by the end of 1936, around 2000 volunteers had joined the International Brigade as the James Connolly Battalion.[10]

In Northern Ireland, Catholic opinion was in large measure orchestrated by the church and the daily newspaper, the *Irish News*. The latter organ served up a diet of sectarianism and anti-Communist diatribes, and encouraged the Catholic community to view itself as an oppressed and much-wronged people. The Spanish civil war provoked a hysterical campaign in the *Irish News* against the 'Godless Reds' and, as will be made clear, the paper's message was dutifully endorsed by the great mass of its Catholic readership.

The Unionist government and press took its cue from Baldwin with regard to Spain. Non-intervention was viewed as an eminently sensible policy to pursue, given the dangers of a general European war. The Unionists showed little sympathy for the travails of the Catholic church in Spain, arguing that these had been brought upon itself, an opinion which predictably infuriated Catholics.[11] Neither, however, did the Republican government enjoy any favours from the Unionists who maintained their own propaganda campaign against socialism and communism.

Such then was the climate of hostility in which Midgley, from the outbreak of the civil war, attempted to rally local support for the cause of the Spanish Republic. He first of all took his fight to the columns of the *Irish News* in an effort to counter what he saw as invidious propaganda at odds with the facts of the situation in Spain.

On July 29 he had his first letter on the subject published, a reply to the paper's editorial – 'For Catholic Spain' – of the previous day. Midgley attacked the editorial as 'misleading, inaccurate and mischievous', before going on to argue that the Spanish government was 'purely Republican' in character and not socialist or communist. In response to the *Irish News's* claims about the persecution of the Catholic church, he replied that many of the rebels were using churches as forts from which 'to fire upon the working class troops'. As he was to do throughout the controversy, Midgley supported his contentions with reference to the Labour *Daily Herald,* a source which cut no ice with the *Irish News* or its readers. Some of these readers were sufficiently stirred to reply in defence of the rebels and to insist that the church was being persecuted. Their attitude spurred Midgley to polemical combat:

It is time that your readers faced up to the terrible alternatives which confront the Spanish people if the present rebellion succeeds. There is no shadow of doubt about it that the Spanish Generals, Franco and Mola who are leading the rebellion are receiving support directly and indirectly from Fascists and Nazis in Italy and Germany, and indeed, it seems all too clear that the Italian and German Governments are keenly interested in the defeat of the Spanish Government with the object of securing another nation in the bloc of Fascist nations.

Referring to what he believed would be a fascist dictatorship in the event of the rebels being successful, he concluded: 'If any reader of the *Irish News* believes that this likelihood is in keeping with religious liberty or necessary for the preservation of his religion, then God help his religion and his conception of spiritual freedom.'[12]

The readers of the *Irish News* joined battle. The controversy was to dominate the newspaper's correspondence columns for another two months, attaining remarkable degrees of intensity and, not infrequently, acrimony. It was also to have a profound effect on the development of Midgley's political career. Although the controversy surrounded the issue of the civil war in Spain, it soon spilled over into other areas and revealed much concerning the general outlook of the readers and the political standpoints taken at this juncture by Midgley himself. As it progressed it became clear that the mutual antagonisms aroused by the debate were no ephemeral phenomena. To both Midgley and his critics the Spanish civil war was an emotive issue the significant ramifications of which reached very close to home.

The readers who entered the controversy ranged in their opinions from outright admirers of fascism to Labour sympathisers who feared for the Catholic church in Spain. Some made belligerent noises about communist and masonic conspiracies, others argued reasonably. Some simply wrote to express unquestioning obedience to the church, others to carefully explain the church's hostility to communism. Midgley tended to make the mistake of classing them all as misguided bigots who were responding slavishly to their own prejudices and to the stance taken by their church. In the heat of the controversy, and in view of some malevolent abuse directed at him personally, he might have been excused for so reacting. However, it has to be said that Midgley's polemical style often echoed the belligerence of some of his critics, and as such it seemed to betray an insensitivity on Midgley's part towards the beliefs of his antagonists and perhaps also of many Catholics who did not share the church's views on Spain. This factor undoubtedly helped to give the controversy a bitterness which ensured that its significance would transcend the issue in contention.

Early in the debate, Midgley pointed out that trade unionists, socialists, communists and Jews were being persecuted under fascist regimes and asked if his critics only believed in complete liberty when it affected Catholics.[13] To one correspondent whose views were probably typical of the newspaper's readership, Midgley's stress on the nature of fascism was an avoidance of what to him and many Catholics was the real issue at stake: 'There is no use side-tracking the issue with horrors of Fascist Government; the issue is clear-cut: Christianity or Paganism. The suppression of religion never succeeds, nor will it succeed now.'[14]

Midgley's attempts to expose the nature of fascism and to relate this to the concept of civil and religious liberty thus fell on deaf ears. In contrast to Midgley, the question of fascism and the threat it posed to democracy was not viewed by the majority of correspondents as the central issue at stake in Spain. For them religion was what mattered and they resisted any attempt by Midgley to widen the debate beyond this subject. In this they displayed all the characteristics of the kind of 'siege mentality' they accused Unionists of possessing. Not only was the Catholic church under attack abroad, but would-be assailants also lurked in their midst. A 'trade unionist' wrote to warn his fellow workers of such as Midgley:

I would like to say that it is high time the Catholic men of this city, and especially the working-men, took heed of the doings of so-called Labour leaders. It is a regrettable fact that so few attend their trade union meeting regularly. There will be some of their money sent to help the enemy in Spain if they do not wake up.[15]

This attitude was shared by many other Catholic trade unionists who either left their unions, or protested vigorously, on account of trade union money being sent to help the Republican cause.[16]

Midgley soon realised that his defence of Republican Spain would probably exact a political price in Belfast. He had once more come up against the sectarian hurdle:

It seems an impossibility to carry on a newspaper correspondence in Belfast without being charged with being against the interest of one church or another. Sometimes it is from one side, sometimes from the other. In the present controversy my correspondents have suggested that I am deliberately defending a cause because it is opposed to the Church, and I have received anonymous letters threatening me with dire pains and penalties for my attitude on the Spanish question. In these letters I am called a bigot, and the writers have told me that never again will I be elected as a public representative in the city of Belfast.

After the obligatory defence of his public record on behalf of both Protestant and Catholic workers, Midgley struck the note of resentful defiance on which he conducted his part in the controversy from then on:

If . . . I am to be driven out of public life because I proclaim the faith within me and stand for what I believe to be true then I submit that the people who take up such an attitude are unutterable bigots, whether they call themselves Protestants or Catholics. If I am only to be permitted to serve the public on condition that I subordinate my individuality and smother my private convictions in regard to the rights of democracy throughout the world, then I should prefer not to be in public life at all.[17]

The prevailing mood of anti-communism among Catholics in Ireland at this time was an important factor in conditioning the response of the *Irish News* readers to Midgley's views. Midgley's dislike of communist activities in Northern Ireland has already been made clear, but in the case of Spain and the general struggle against fascism he was to work closely with leading Irish communists such as William McCullough.[18] At this time Midgley was less ill-disposed to the concept of communism as he understood it, than the tactics employed by those who called themselves communists. In reply to a correspondent's list of questions which requested his views on the nature of fascism and communism, Midgley offered the following reasons why he thought the former essentially evil and the latter essentially good:

It [fascism] is an expression of capitalism in extremis. It depends for its conti- nuance upon the negation of democratic Government and develops an ideology based upon racial, political and religious oppression . . . In addition, fascism makes its appeal to brute force and national egoism; it teaches the doctrine of glorifying war, and must inevitably lead to another world war.

Turning to communism, he argued:

In my opinion the principles of communism worked out to their logical conclusion must inevitably lead to good. In answering this question I must ask readers to differentiate between the principles of communism and the actions and words of those who sometimes profess to be communists, just as I warn my readers to differentiate between the principles of Christianity and the actions and words of those who profess to be Christians.

Communism for Midgley meant:

the communal ownership of the means whereby all the people must live, such as land, mines, factories, warehouses, workshops etc., as distinct from private possessions such as watches, fountain pens, cigarette cases, books and such things which people require for their daily culture and individual life. In my opinion real communism simply means the application of the Gospel of Jesus to human society.[19]

The christian socialism of his early boyhood ILP days thus continued to constitute the cornerstone of Midgley's political philosophy. But it was a school of thought with which the Catholic church had always been at odds, and there were few Belfast Catholics who would have been persuaded that it formed the essence of the doctrine of communism in the 1930s. Midgley's kind words for communism merely enabled many of his antagonists to complete the circle of a materialist, masonic and atheistic conspiracy against their church and way of life. Among the reader's rejoinders published by the *Irish News*, the one which perhaps said it all came from 'J.M.' who denounced communism as a 'diabolical pestilence' and urged 'the utmost vigilance of our faithful Catholic people and their incessant prayers'.[20]

The Spanish war was not surprisingly featured prominently in the speeches and discussions of the NILP conference on 29 August. In his Chairman's Address Midgley castigated the 'reactionary forces in Spain who, in their blind, insensate anger at the growing success of a democratically elected Government did not hesitate to plunge their country into the turmoil of Civil War'.[21] On Midgley's motion, a resolution was unanimously passed condemning the rebels and congratulating the government and workers upon their 'heroic resistance'. The resolution also appealed for donations to a fund set up for the purpose of equipping a medical unit for service in Spain.[22] Out of this a committee was formed – The Ulster Medical Aid for Spain Committee – and Midgley was appointed honorary secretary along with Sam Haslett, a prominent member of the NILP and Socialist Party (NI). Both men were to devote much of their time and energy to collecting for the fund and in enrolling volunteers to drive medical vehicles and administer medical aid to the Spanish Republican forces. During the discussion on the resolution, Midgley delivered a stinging attack on the *Irish News* claiming that it had sunk to the depths of 'journalistic villainy and depravity'.[23]

At the conference Midgley also secured the chairmanship of the party for another year and further underscored the trend he had set with regard to party policy away from anti-partitionism:

The Labour movement can offer the guarantee that there will be no defilement of religion at its hands, that political changes affecting territorial or religious issues will only be carried out at the behest of the people of Northern Ireland, and that civil and religious liberty will become a reality in the life of the country, instead of, as now, being merely a slogan used at elections by people who often degrade religion by using it to keep the masses of the people in poverty and destitution.[24]

Despite being camouflaged in rhetoric, Midgley's lack of sympathy with nationalist aspirations could be easily discerned, and Catholic opposition to him on the question was ensured.

A further contribution by Midgley to the *Irish News* on 7 September provoked another backlash from the paper's readers. Midgley claimed that he could refute with hard evidence stories published by the *Irish News* concerning alleged atrocities committed by the Republicans. He went on to add that the paper, by its blatant distortion of what was happening in Spain had convinced many Catholics that their church stood on the side of 'reaction, oppression and injustice'. The following day in its editorial, the *Irish News* retaliated, stating that Midgley's letter had reminded them 'of nothing so much as the typical Orange, anti-catholic propaganda of which we had such a spate last year'. Some of its readers had taken enough. 'A Catholic Layman' fumed at the space afforded by the newspaper to Midgley and his views: 'How dare you, Mr Editor, in the columns of your Catholic journal attempt to defend Catholic interests in opposition to the vapourings of a man who owes any little hold he has on public life to the votes of Catholic people!'[25]

By this time the Nationalist MP for Foyle (a Derry constituency) and editor of the nationalist daily the *Derry Journal*, James Joseph McCarroll, had entered the fray. The *Derry Journal* had taken a similarly uncompromising pro-Franco line on the Spanish civil war, and had singled out Midgley in its editorials for special censure. On 17 August, for example, it levelled the charge at Midgley that he had not devoted a quarter of the energy he was then expending 'on behalf of the Red-soaked Government of Madrid', on the Catholics of Dock who were 'subjected to a perennial antagonism and persecution'. The editorial invoked the riots of 1935, inferring that Midgley's concern for evicted and harassed Catholics had been minimal.

Midgley may have done well to ignore such spiteful attacks but it was not in his make-up to do so. He took the bait and sniped back at McCarroll:

> It may interest you to know that you and your co-religionists have been responsible for one of the worst developments in the history of the working class movement. By your association with the cause of reaction and oppression in Spain, and by your implied acceptance of fascism with all its cruelty and wrong and its bloody history throughout Europe, you have made many magnificent Protestants – men and women who built the Labour movement and suffered because of their stand for toleration – wonder whether Catholics are only interested in liberty as long as liberty is defined by their own church, or its interests affected. In my opinion you will regret this development.[26]

McCarroll's personal rancour against Midgley was also accommodated by the *Irish News*. In a letter published by this paper he delivered a torrent of personal abuse crowned by the comment: '. . . one wonders how you have managed so long to conceal whence your anti-Catholic instinct has really been derived'.[27] In reply Midgley dealt in a similar currency of vituperation. McCarroll's 'puny little sectarian whimperings and childish economic ideas' were in Midgley's opinion what constituted his 'rare, but not refreshing orations in the House [Stormont]'.[28] The rot of acrimony and intolerance had now set in on both sides. In taking a strong public stand against the Catholic church and the Catholic press, Midgley had been conveniently designated as 'Orange' and 'bigoted', labels which on the strength of the Spanish controversy alone he did not deserve. His antagonists were all too ready to see conspiracies and to summarily denounce all who professed different views to their own as conspirators or accomplices in a perceived campaign of persecution.[29] For his part, Midgley seems to have allowed his justifiable anger to prompt him into conducting the controversy in an increasingly provocative manner.

In a long letter in the *Irish News* of 11 September, later reproduced as a pamphlet *Spain: The Press, the Pulpit and the Truth*, Midgley countered a host of *Irish News* allegations and assertions about the civil war in Spain with detailed evidence. It was a propaganda feat as skilful and effective as any he had achieved before,[30] and illustrated clearly how widely he read about the war's developments, and how deeply he had delved into the background of certain questions at issue. For the most part the letter (pamphlet) was soberly argued with Midgley quite prepared to admit to some Republican atrocities and to the hostility which had been shown to the church in certain parts of Spain. In the last analysis, however, he held to the view that a 'rich and corrupt' church headed the reactionary forces in Spain and had been largely responsible for the country's retarded development and its illiteracy rate of almost fifty per cent. The letter had begun with Midgley – to his credit – attempting to inject a much-needed note of levity into the proceedings: 'I have been informed that the sale of your paper has gone up enormously since I began contributing on the subject of Spain. At the risk, therefore, of increasing your circulation still further, I must again proclaim the faith within me on this matter.' It concluded, however, with Midgley portraying himself, in melodramtic prose, as a martyr to his cause:

I realised when I wrote my first letter defending the Spanish Government, that I would lose many friends . . . that many of the electors would be stampeded by appeals to their religious feelings through a campaign of journalistic hatred, calumny, lies and slander, almost without precedent in the history of public life. Yet I decided to go ahead, and I do not regret it.

This was unlikely to move those people whose religion Midgley, in his final broadside, numbered among 'the powers of superstition and oppression'.

The latter rhetorical flourish was a fair example of Midgley's combative style. What he did not seem to fully appreciate was that, for many Catholic readers, such a comment transcended mere point-scoring polemics. One reader, 'Religion Before Politics', retorted angrily:

His [Midgley's] marathon letter . . . contained the word 'superstition' in connection with the Catholic church and I sincerely hope that Catholics will get the opportunity of demonstrating to him through the ballot box that they have no use for an individual who, by the language he makes use of, insults their holy religion.[31]

By so alienating many Catholics, Midgley had thrown his whole political future into jeopardy, depending as he did on the Catholic votes in Dock for his seat in parliament. By this time, however, there was no going back and Midgley was in no way inclined to do so.

On 26 October 1936 Midgley publicly debated the Spanish issue with Monsignor Arthur Ryan of the Catholic church. The debate took place in the Labour Hall and was conducted in a healthy spirit, Midgley and Ryan shaking hands before proceedings commenced.[32] Midgley went on the offensive against the church in Spain saying that it had associated itself with an 'intolerable tyranny' under which Spain had groaned for centuries. It had, he said, 'participated as landlord and capitalist in the economics of the country'. He then went on to repeat the point that the Spanish government elected in February 1936 had not been socialist or communist, and that only on 9 September had some socialists and communists been included in response to the civil war crisis. He accused the church of conspiring against the Republic from the time of the 1931 Constitution which sought to curb its power. In relation to the atrocities committed, Midgley claimed that many of these acts had been in response to the church's anti-government activities. He moved on to discuss the Rightist government which came to power in 1933 and which, asserted Midgley, restored ancient privileges and cracked down on the workers. In connection with the latter claim he referred to the General Strike of 5 October 1934 which had resulted in the murder of thousands and the imprisonment of over 30,000 workers, an outrage which had occasioned no response from such as Ryan. Finally, Midgley laid the blame for the horrors of the civil war squarely at the door of the insurgents whom he accused of creating a 'state of terrorism' in the months following the February election.

Ryan replied by claiming that the government had not won a majority of votes in February 1936 and that it thus had no claim to be democratic.[33] He defended the church's non-acceptance of the 1931 Constitution saying that it had led to the sequestering of its property and the outlawing of priests. In such a situation Ryan believed it was the right and duty of the people to overthrow the government 'by force if possible'. It was the outrages against the church, he argued, which had provoked the people to rebellion. He challenged Midgley's statements about the church as capitalist and landowner saying that the Spanish Liberal government of over one hundred years before had taken away its landed property. Ryan, however, refused to be drawn into a controversy over atrocities.

The debate was thus vigorously contested but it concluded amicably with Ryan paying tribute to Midgley's public record. He added that Midgley was not, in his opinion, a bigot and that he would be sorry to see his career in public life damaged on account of his stance on the Spanish issue.

However, relations between the two men were soon to be soured. Midgley addressed another meeting on 9 November in Dromore Town Hall during which he intensified his attacks on the Catholic church.[34] Ryan wrote to the *Irish News* to refute Midgley's assertions, and further

remarked that Midgley's style of argument had 'shaken his belief that he
was an impartial enquirer into Spanish affairs'. 'Every time he men-
tioned the Catholic church', said Ryan, 'he used some abusive epithet or
sneering innuendo'. Ryan was now of the view that Catholics should
ignore Midgley 'until he displays some of the elementary rules of fair
play'. In conclusion, Ryan expressed the kind of view indicative of the
Ulster Catholic mentality of the time: 'in the meantime Catholics are
confirmed in their position by suffering this barrage of abuse from the
"unholy alliance" of Socialists and Orangemen.'[35]

Midgley, as in the case of McCarroll's attacks, blazed an indignant
response which widened the chasm between himself and Ryan:

If to resent, repudiate and challenge the age-long dictation of clerics is bigotry,
then I am a bigot. But, if to strive for the upliftment of the masses (regardless of
race or creed) and endeavour to break the fetters which bind them to the
illusions and superstitions of the past, through which they are preyed upon by
those who use spiritual authority to perpetuate economic and intellectual
enslavement, is true toleration and justice, then I claim to be a bigot in the cause
of humanity, and not on behalf of a section.[36]

To Ryan such language was not argument: 'It is sublimated Billingsgate,
and I do not talk the language.'[37]

In addition to conducting a propaganda campaign for the Spanish
Republicans and organising medical aid and volunteers from Belfast,
Midgley was also deeply involved in another Spanish matter affecting
Belfast. From the outbreak of the civil war, a number of Spanish cargo
ships were impounded in Belfast harbour where they were to stay for the
war's duration. The ships' crews were government supporters and soon
made contact with Midgley and other sympathetic elements in the city.
Midgley took charge of the crews' welfare and saw that they were well
cared for. For his own part he put up Captain Luis Diaz and other
members of Diaz's crew in his own home until the end of the war in
1939. Diaz never forgot Midgley's gesture and continued to keep in
touch after he had left Belfast. He died in London in 1943. Midgley was
with him when he died and brought his body back to Belfast for burial.

According to Patrick Shea's recent autobiography, Midgley made
much of the Spanish sea captain's presence during this time:

He [Midgley] was frequently seen in their company in the constituency, he took
them to meetings, sometimes bringing them on to the platform to bear witness to
the sufferings of their fellow countrymen at the hands of a fascist military clique
waging war against democracy.

In addition to this, Shea recalls one occasion when the Spaniards witnessed a ferocious argument between Midgley and the local Dock Ward priest, Father McSparran, an argument during which the two men almost came to blows.[38] Thus the Spanish seamen did not totally miss out on the violence occasioned by their country's civil war!

III

Despite his sterling defence of the Spanish government, Midgley's hold on the NILP was still being subjected to a strong challenge from the left of the party. The left-wingers, most of whom were members of the Socialist Party (NI), were generally anti-partitionist in outlook and had been dissatisfied with Midgley's leadership for some time. They saw him – correctly – as out of sympathy with their Connollyite approach to the national question, and they considered his general political outlook insufficiently socialist in word and in deed. The SP(NI) had strong links with the Communist Party in Ireland, and several leading lights of both groups contributed to the newspaper the *Irish Democrat*.[39] This paper lasted from March 1937 until the end of the year and consistently attacked Midgley's leadership and the reformism of the NILP during this period. Although committed to a Republican victory in Spain, the paper seemed more keen to see the NILP purged of Midgley and his supporters and Midgley's activities regarding Spain were never alluded to.

At a special NILP conference in August 1937, held for the purpose of discussing electoral reform, Midgley's opponents co-ordinated their efforts. A resolution on Irish Unity was proposed by Armagh Labour Party and was promptly ruled out of order.[40] This provoked a chorus of protest from left-wingers and nationalists to which Midgley replied testily:

We believe that it would be inexpedient and bordering upon the realm of insanity for the Council to allow conference to be torn asunder by discussion of a matter which has no immediate relevance to the social outlook of the people. So long as I occupy any executive position I will not allow – nor will the executive allow – the Labour party to become the cockpit of elements which have for their object a further embittering of already too embittered passion and prejudices which are the heritages of a past based on suspicion and misunderstanding.

The conference eventually got down to the business it had been called to discuss, and ended by declaring its support for the system of Proportional Representation.[41]

The real confrontation was to occur at the proper annual conference of the party on 30 October. At this conference Midgley made his views

and his plans for the party abundantly clear. A few weeks earlier he had
attended and addressed the British Labour Party conference at Bourne-
mouth. There he had taken pains to remind his audience that organised
Labour in Northern Ireland existed entirely on the side of the British
Labour movement. He had urged the British party to ensure that
measures of social justice were extended to Northern Ireland and had
appealed to British Labour to:

treat us as part of your social concern, make us part of your business and join
with us in trying to remove the scales from the eyes of our people to the end that
we return the right kind of representatives, not only to the parliament of
Northern Ireland, but to the parliament of Great Britain.[42]

Midgley was therefore calling for the closest possible co-operation
between the NILP and the British Labour Party. He wanted to see the
latter active in helping the NILP in Ulster, but there is no evidence that
he favoured the British Labour Party actually organising in Northern
Ireland. A close relationship with British Labour was viewed by Midgley
as the basis for the development of a strong co-operative movement
linking the forces of Labour throughout the British Commonwealth.
The NILP conference's most important debate concerned this concept
of internationalism.

It was given expression in a resolution forwarded by the City Labour
Party, the old Dock Ward party reconstituted, and made up predominantly of supporters of Midgley. The resolution called for close co-
operation with the Labour movements 'thoughout the British
Commonwealth of Nations', and pledged 'to establish a new social order
based upon freedom, justice and security for all the peoples of the
Commonwealth, and using this as an instrument for the achievement of
internationalism'. The Armagh Labour Party moved an amendment
calling for the unity of Ireland and co-operation with the workers of the
Free State.[43] The battle lines were drawn.

During the debate Midgley nailed his colours firmly to the anti-
nationalist mast, and in view of his somewhat guarded expressions on
the subject before, it seems likely that the bitterness of the Spanish
controversy had forced his hand. He declared that he was not a nationalist and that the political environment which had trained the people of
Northern Ireland in Anglo-Saxon ideas for centuries, could not be
changed. He referred to his support in 'the old days' for the right of the
Irish people to manage themselves, but now he felt like asking what the
people of the South had got from nationalism. There was no desire, he
continued, on the part of the Northern people for unity; unity could be

achieved only by building up socialism in the North and South. Nationalism in the South, he averred, was not far removed from 'Hitlerism'. In
conclusion he declared that he would rather live under a British socialist
government than an Irish capitalist one.[44] The amendment was
defeated by 90 votes to 20 on a card vote, and the resolution on
internationalism carried by an overwhelming majority.[45]

Midgley also withstood the concerted attempt made by the Left, in
particular the SP(NI), to change the complexion of party leadership. He
easily defeated Sam Haslett in the election for the chair, and his ally
Albert Horatio McElroy secured the secretaryship over the the SP(NI)
nominee, Jack MacGougan.

The conference was a triumph for Midgley and a disaster for his
critics. He now felt empowered to press on in his quest to build a
powerful political machine in Northern Ireland. He believed he had
awakened the British Labour Party to its responsibilities to the people of
Northern Ireland,[46] and hoped that by being seen to be in close
association with the British party, Labour in Northern Ireland would
present a 'safer' image regarding the constitution to the majority of
Northern Ireland's electorate.

Midgley's pronouncements at the October conference confirmed
him in the 'Walkerist' tradition of Ulster Labour thinking. The reaction
from the 'Connollyist' school of thought was swift and damning. In the
Irish Democrat of 13 November 1937, Desmond Ryan addressed a
full-page article to Midgley, invoking in copious detail the Connolly–
Walker controversy of 1911. Ryan's article was hard-hitting but even so
it was a watered-down version of what he had orginally intended. On 6
November the editor of the paper, Sean Nolan, had written to Ryan
saying that he had altered the article's first two paragraphs, and adding
by way of explanation: 'We can't be over sharp on Midgeley [sic], bearing
in mind his attitude on Spain, when the rest of the Labour people just
funked it. And they still funk the issue.'[47] Nolan was referring to many
of those nationalist-minded Labour men both North and South who
had chosen to remain silent in regard to Spain rather than upset the
people from whom they hoped to obtain support. A good example in the
North was Jack Beattie who did not involve himself at all in the Spanish
controversy for fear of alienating the Catholic voters of Short Strand on
whom his seat in Stormont depended.

In addition to Ryan's article there was another anti-Midgley blast
from one Edward Anderson who carried his arguments over two issues
of the *Democrat*. Midgley's concept of internationalism was dismissed by

Anderson as a smokescreen obscuring the defence of British imperialism:

To declare oneself as an internationalist and at the same time to cling like the very devil to Anglo-Saxonism – imperialism – which is Orangeism in its most extreme form, is just shamefaced yellow liberal internationalism which runs away from imperialism in every country in the world.[48]

To Midgley such obsessively dogmatic anti-imperialism was indicative of a mind locked in the past, taking its thoughts uncritically from a man who wrote in response to different times, and impervious to the changing nature of the world. Midgley too had once shared Connolly's outlook: now he noted what unswerving nationalist fervour had led to both abroad and nearer home, in the Irish Free State. Like many others on the left during this period, especially in Britain, he identified nationalism closely with fascism. He had watched as fascist dictatorships had ridden to power on the back of chauvinistic nationalist sentiment in Germany and Italy. He had seen the rise of the Blueshirts in Southern Ireland and the development of a clerically influenced mood of virulent anti-communism. The high tide of imperialism had long since passed; Europe seemed now to be moving towards a momentous confrontation between the forces of fascism and democracy. Midgley believed that nationalism was a force invariably conducive to fascism and as such to be resisted. As Walker had viewed imperialism in 1911, Midgley now saw the British Commonwealth as a potential instrument of social progress.[49] More importantly in relation to his times, he considered it a bulwark in defence of democracy. Events in Spain, in Midgley's view, bore out the soundness of this perspective.

Spain and the unsavoury controversy arising from it, however, had added another dimension to Midgley's outlook: that of a deep hostility to the Roman Catholic church. He believed that the church had been responsible for many of Spain's problems and he came, via an analysis of the Spanish situation, to view the church's influence generally as a backward, reactionary force. This was certainly how he viewed its influence in the Irish Free State, and he may well have been further fortified in such an outlook by de Valera's 1937 Constitution which enshrined the special position of the Catholic church in that state. Opposition to the Catholic church thus became an integral part of Midgley's world view. Nationalism in Ireland was for Midgley 'Catholic Nationalism': an insular, clerical and reactionary movement. In contrast, the concept of a co-operative Commonwealth involving the nations of the British Commonwealth appeared outward-looking and progressive, and far more germane to the reality of a rapidly changing world and the increasing interdependence among nations.

At the NILP conference in October 1937, a leading member of the British Labour Party, its chairman George Dallas, had been present. Midgley, as previously stated, had tried to impress upon British Labour that it had a role to play in Northern Ireland politics. He seems to have impressed this successfully on Dallas, for between them they arranged a meeting between representatives of the NILP, the British Labour Party, and those trade unions having members in Northern Ireland. This meeting took place on 9 December 1937 at the Westminster House of Commons with Dallas in the chair and with Midgley and Sam Geddes (vice-chairman) representing the NILP.[50]

Geddes stated that affiliation fees received by the NILP from the British-based trade unions did not reach £200. On this point Midgley added that even if all moneys derived from the payment of political levies in Northern Ireland were retained in Northern Ireland, the NILP's dificulties would still not be solved. Of the total British-based union membership in Northern Ireland (62,556), only 23,847 were 'contracted-in' members whost total payment to the NILP – if it was all forthcoming – would only be £1,249. He thus pleaded with the national trade unions to make a determined effort to improve this situation. What the NILP desired was greater financial assistance from the national trade unions than they were then receiving, and the backing of the trade unions for a number of their parliamentary candidates to fight Northern Ireland constituencies. Geddes also asked for more help from the British Labour Party with speakers and organisation.

The trade union representatives present all expressed sympathy with the NILP's position and made promises of closer co-operation and increased assistance. Mr Marchbank of the National Union of Railwaymen moved that the NILP, backed by the British Labour Party, 'ask National Union for contributions to their election funds with special reference to the forthcoming elections for the north of Ireland'. He further moved that the question of candidates be dealt with by the NILP itself. The resolution was seconded and approved. Marchbank then went on to move that the National Executive Committee (NEC) of the British Labour Party 'be recommended to consider those constituencies in Northern Ireland which are represented at the Imperial parliament at Westminster'. This too was seconded and approved. The larger question of the formal relationship of the NILP and the constituencies in Northern Ireland to the British Labour Party was left over for further discussion.

Thus, by the end of 1937, Midgley seemed to be making good progress towards his objective of strengthening ties between the parties and involving the British Labour Party more actively in Northern Ireland politics. The second resolution seemed to suggest that the British Labour Party should seriously consider contesting Westminster seats in Northern Ireland, an important break with past thinking in the party which was always on the side of complete non-intervention in the affairs of Northern Ireland, however directly they had a bearing on the fortunes of the Labour Party. The first resolution must have satisfied Midgley and Geddes at the time, but unfortunately they were soon to find that they had made their move in this direction too late.

IV

For, to general suprise, Craigavon sprung an election on 12 January 1938. His reason for doing so was to give what he hoped would be a resounding Unionist reply to de Valera and his new Free State constitution. This constitution had come into operation in December 1937 and had claimed the whole of the island, including the six-county Northern state, as the national territory. The NILP had not anticipated an election until late into 1938 and it was now thrown into a panic in its efforts to raise money.

On 17 January a letter signed in the names of Midgley, Geddes, Robert Getgood (Treasurer) and Joseph Corrigan (Secretary) was sent out to the British Labour Party and trade union movement. The letter stated that the party wished to field eleven candidates and required £1,650 to cover deposits. This amount had to be raised by 29 January. The letter went on to appeal to the trade unions to make grants to finance the candidates.[51] The British Labour Party NEC also lent its weight in an attempt to obtain the necessary money from the unions. On 19 January it issued an appeal to the Labour movement generally, urging that the NILP be assisted. Its communication stated: 'The National Executive Committee desires to emphasise the duty of our movement to assist our Irish comrades in this fight which is being conducted under most difficult circumstances.'[52]

The money, alas, was unforthcoming. By 27 January Midgley had to admit that the response of the British trade unions had been poor, and that Northern Ireland workers had made 'paltry contributions' to the political fund. By this time the party had had to withdraw prospective candidates in Belfast, Derry, Coleraine and North Antrim. The Communist Party had offered their services on behalf of the Labour candidates but this offer had been declined.[53]

The party executive, and particularly Midgley, had also been embarrassed by the withdrawal over a week earlier of two prospective NILP candidates Cathal Bradley and P. J. McCann. Both men were staunch anti-partitionists and had been provisionally marked down to contest two seats – Belfast Central and South Armagh respectively – where they were likely to face Nationalist Party or Republican opposition. Splitting the anti-partitionist vote was something neither man could agree to do and thus they withdrew their names. A couple of days later it was reported that the East Belfast Labour Party – predominantly anti-partitionist in outlook – had decided to nominate Beattie as its candidate for Pottinger despite the fact that he had been expelled from the party. Later, during his campaign, Beattie enlisted the help of Frank Callaghan, an NILP member who had publicly dissociated himself from Midgley's stance on Spain during the height of the controversy in October 1936.[54] Midgley may have been forgiven for suspecting that anti-partitionists in the NILP were trying their best to discredit him at whatever cost to Labour Party fortunes. Certainly elements in the NILP seemed to be in open rebellion against Midgley and the executive at a time when an appearance of unity was most urgently required.

Midgley, however, had even more pressing problems to deal with in regard to his own contest in Dock. Soon after the announcement of the election it had been freely rumoured that the Nationalists were considering putting up a candidate to fight Dock against Midgley. At a Nationalist meeting on 17 January a Mr Robert Armstrong told his listeners: 'As a resident of Dock ward for 20 years he could assure them they would lose the opportunity of a lifetime if they failed to contest Dock ward. The Catholic voters of Belfast were determined that Alderman Midgley would never represent them again.'[55] The Spanish affair had been neither forgotten nor forgiven. On 24 January Midgley was quite candid about the possible threat to his seat: 'I have no illusions. If there is any Labour candidate who is uncertain about his seat, I am that candidate.'[56] A week later it was officially announced that James Collins would be the Nationalist candidate for Dock. The contest would now be a three-cornered one, the Unionists being represented by G. A. Clark, son of the wealthy shipping magnate.

As it turned out the NILP put forward seven candidates, one of whom, Patrick Agnew, was returned unopposed.[57] Besides Midgley, there were three candidates in Belfast seats: Tom Boyd in Victoria, John Glass in Falls, and Jack MacGougan in Oldpark. The latter two candidates were confirmed anti-partitionists. John Byrne contested South Down, a predominantly Catholic constituency, and A. Graham, the Protestant seat of South Tyrone. As was customary the party tried to fight the election as far as possible on social and economic issues with particular stress laid on unemployment.

As in the past, however, the Labour candidates were not permitted to concentrate on the party's chosen platform. From the start of the campaign, Midgley found it impossible to obtain a hearing in the Catholic parts of Dock Ward. He met with cries of 'Up Franco!' and 'Remember Spain!', and loud choruses of the Free State national anthem, 'The Soldier's Song'. The hostility grew more intense the more he tried to hold meetings, and eventually it gave war to ugly violence, Midgley's brake being rushed by the mob on one occasion. In a reversal of the events in the 1933 campaign, Midgley was forced to abandon meetings planned for Catholic quarters, and to take refuge in Protestant parts of the ward.[58]

Collins, during his campaign, recalled Midgley's part in the Spanish controversy and on one occasion quoted Monsignor Ryan's disparaging remarks about Midgley.[59] He also played up Midgley's anti-nationalist utterances at the NILP conference claiming that he had 'not only snubbed the cause of a United Ireland, but had also snubbed the Catholic church itself. They would be very poor Catholics indeed in this area if they stood for the insults which had been heaped upon them by Alderman Midgley.'[60]

Despite the ominous portents, Midgley nevertheless made a desperate bid to recoup some Catholic support in the late stages of his campaign. In a letter to the *Irish News* he replied to a claim by T. J. Campbell that the NILP and the British Labour Party were now offiically linked. Midgley wrote to deny this and, for good measure, added that the NILP and the Irish Labour Party still had a Standing Joint Committee which met alternately in Dublin and Belfast.[61] This of course was utterly at odds with the spirit of his policy to strengthen links with the British Labour Party and to distance the party from Irish nationalism. However, his desperate electoral predicament demanded desperate tactics. Midgley even invoked Connolly, albeit to indirectly attack those who mythologised him: 'I would rather see him [Connolly] living in Ireland than dead. I would rather see one live James Connolly living and working in Ireland for the oppressed than a thousand dead

James Connollys buried with the halo of martyrdom.'[62]

Midgley was also met with accusations that he had not defended the Catholics of Dock during the riots of 1935. He denied the charge, referring to his part in the deputation which tried to impress on Dawson Bates the gravity of the situation. He also claimed that he had attempted to induce an employer in Henry Street to take back Catholic workers, and referred to the letter which he had had printed and circulated at his own expense deploring what had taken place. In addition, Midgley claimed to have been part of the Expelled Workers' delegation which went to Britain in 1922 to raise money for those Catholic workers expelled from their jobs.[63]

Midgley's controversy with the Catholic community over Spain also cast its shadow over the other two contests where Labour candidates were attempting to win Catholic support. In Oldpark Jack MacGougan, who fought a strong anti-partitionist campaign, enlisted the aid of Cathal Bradley. As Bradley spoke he was interrupted by the shout: 'What about Midgley?' He replied that he was not concerned about Midgley: 'Harry Midgley was only one in the movement and if he had faults, they could not condemn the whole movement.'[64] Bradley was similarly heckled when he spoke for John Glass in Falls, and he eventually got round the difficulty of answering questions about Midgley by leading his audience in a chorus of 'The Soldier's Song'! For his part Glass claimed that he had gone forward on an anti-partitionist platform with the full consent of Midgley and the NILP executive.[65]

A turbulent campaign ended in disastrous defeat for Midgley. Clark won the seat with 3,578 votes, Collins came second with 2,891, and Midgley finished a poor third with only 1,923. Collins's intervention had had the desired result of ousting Midgley but only at the cost of handing back the seat to the Unionists. Only a few hundred Catholics could have voted for Midgley, and this clearly reflected the extent of the hostility he had aroused among the minority community. Midgley's unpopularity may have damaged the fortunes of Glass in Falls who lost out to the Nationalist Richard Byrne. The Nationalists, however, had always held this seat. In Oldpark, MacGougan, in the absence of a Nationalist and on the strength of his anti-partitionism, polled the large Catholic vote in the constituency; it was not enough, however, to defeat the Unionist. Tom Boyd was beaten into third place in Victoria and both Byrne and Graham were soundly defeated in their contests. Of little consolation to Midgley was Beattie's close victory in Pottinger, further enhancing his redoubtable election record. Overall the Unionists increased their

majority, winning thirty-nine seats. The Nationalists won eight, the
Independent Unionists two, and an Independent the remaining one.

Collins felt he had won a 'moral victory' but Midgley was predictably
defiant: 'I have preserved my soul, my independence and my character –
(cheers) – and I will never bow to any dictatorship, theological or
otherwise – (renewed cheers).'[66] The *Belfast Telegraph*, while cheered by
the Unionist success, expressed 'a tinge of regret that the House of
Commons is to be deprived of the personality of Alderman Midgley'.[67]
Midgley gave an interview to the *Telegraph* after the count during which
he announced that he would not fight Dock again:

I have given so much of my life to the working classes that I cannot, in the
interests of my health and my home life, allow myself to be continually sacrificed
to the peculiar whims and fluctuations of people swayed only by sectarian
impulses and who are likely to be carried away by such emotions at each
succeeding election.

He went on to denounce the parts played by both the Catholic church
and the Unionist party in securing his defeat, alleging that the one had
used and co-operated with the other.[68]

Midgley may have invited his fate, but his defeat was none the less
poor reward for over thirteen years' unflagging service to the constituency. The people of Dock Ward were to lose a man who had worked
tirelessly on their behalf, for a representative whose contributions at
Stormont, after his election, can be counted on the fingers of one hand.

V

Midgley's hardening attitude towards the Catholic church during the
Spanish controversy was so transparent in his writings and public
utterances that many Catholics were needlessly alienated both from him
and the cause he was espousing. The stridency of his language and the
blanket condemnations of various Catholics' points of view on the
Spanish issue seemed to suggest that he – like many of his antagonists –
had closed his mind to different opinions. The obvious political risk
which he knew he was running did not seem in the least to restrain him.
Such an observation leads one to ask if there was a latent streak of
anti-Catholicism in Midgley's make-up which found expression
through the medium of an ostensible fight on behalf of democracy and
against fascism. It has to be said that Midgley did not go as far out on a
political limb, or show so much concern, in relation to the activities of
the UPL and the rioting of 1935, as he did over Spain.

In the context of the NILP, Midgley's behaviour over Spain upset the precarious balance which existed within the party between unionist and nationalist forces. Those on the nationalist wing of the party accused him of being prepared to countenance the loss of Catholic support for the party in a way in which he was not prepared to do with regard to Protestant support. They saw his campaign on Spain as unnecessarily cavalier and reckless in form, and thus potentially disastrous in effect. In view of Midgley's disregard for party unity and electoral prospects over Spain, they felt entitled to similar licence for the expression of their strong anti-partitionist viewpoint. Hence the 'rebellion' of the most fervent anti-partionists in the party around the time of the 1938 election, and the exposure of serious internal divisions in the party over the very issue it sought to persuade the electorate to ignore.

Against this it first of all has to be borne in mind that, for Midgley, the Spanish civil war was no ordinary political issue. He and countless others on the left throughout Europe – many of them Catholics – saw the war as a possible turning point in modern history; a conflict which seemed to foreshadow a general European confrontation between fascism and democracy. Midgley believed that the issue was too important to shirk or even to soft-pedal. In his view it was above the normal run of NILP tactical considerations. Midgley may have argued agressively and shown impatience with his opponents but that had always been his way. He was an impetuous man who was always prone to take an impassioned stance on the issues of the day as he saw them. As usual, he threw himself into the propaganda war with no holds barred. In such a situation to counsel restraint and discretion was to ask too much of him. As was so often the case at Stormont and in the Belfast Corporation, opponents took offence where none was in all probability intended. Midgley revelled in a vigorously contested debate and the Spanish issue was no exception. That he was probably unaware of how deeply he was offending some people does not, however, exonerate him from the charge of insensitivity. This he was guilty of and he should have had the perceptiveness to grasp it.

Midgley may have possessed a residual sense of 'apartness' with regard to the Catholic community, a product, if such it was, of his own Belfast Protestant background. There were also factors, such as Midgley's involvement in Linfield FC,[69] which suggest that some of the Orangeism of such a social environment may have rubbed off on him long before 1936. There is, however, no concrete evidence for this, and even if there were there is a lot more evidence to argue that Midgley had never allowed himself to become slave to such emotions. If he was predisposed to take a hostile view of the Catholic church before the Spanish issue – and he might be said to have had cause for doing that – it cannot be deduced from this that he participated in the Spanish controversy more out of hostility to the Catholic church than belief in the Spanish Republican cause. To argue thus would be to hideously distort the picture portrayed by the vast bulk of the evidence which overwhelmingly points to a genuinely principled involvement on Midgley's part. Few people, outside those who fought in Spain, could have invested so much time and energy, and put so much at risk, as Midgley. This was quite apart from the personal domestic sacrifices he made in respect of the Spanish refugees.

Those nationalist Labour critics who blamed his 1938 defeat on what they saw as his provocative manner towards the Catholic church and on his alleged inactivity during the 1935 riots,[70] may well have been attempting to obscure their own coy attitude to the Spanish affair. For them the cause of Irish unity had to come first whatever the happenings elsewhere. As T. J. McCoubrie wrote in his report to NUDAW in September 1936:

We actually have members inside the movement resigning on account of our supporting the workers in Spain. These are the very people who cry out to the workers of the world about the fascism form of the northern government but when the workers of other countries are faced with fascist dictatorship they shout out about our supporting them. I suppose this could only be found in Ireland anyway.[71]

Midgley's critics now accused him of being an electoral liability to the NILP. Certainly there seemed little prospect of his acquiring significant Catholic support in the future. Such a state of affairs gave added impetus to their campaign to oust him from the party leadership. That Midgley's position as leader of a Labour party should come under increased attack from people claiming to be socialists, basically on account of the left-wing stance he had taken on the Spanish civil war, was ironic indeed. As McCoubrie said, it could only have happened in Ireland.

Notes

1. *The Irish People* 29 February 1936.
2. *Labour Advocate* March 1936.
3. *Ulster Year Book 1938*, HMSO, p. 163.

4. D. Bleakley, 'The Northern Ireland trade union movement', *Journal of the Social and Statistical Inquiry of Ireland* 19, 1953–54, 159–69.

5. It should be noted that, despite the fact that the British Labour Party did not organise in Northern Ireland and did not allow people in Northern Ireland to join, some trade unionists in the area 'contracted in' to pay the levy to the British party.

6. Bleakley estimated their voting strength in 1953 to be 17,000. In the 1930s the figure was probably a few thousand lower.

7. See T. Brown, *Ireland: A Social and Cultural History*, London, 1981, chapter 5.

8. See J. Bowyer Bell, 'Ireland and the Spanish civil war 1936–1939', *Studia Hibernica* 4, 1969, 137–63.

9. Ibid.

10. See M. O'Riordan, *Connolly Column*, Dublin, 1980.

11. Bowyer Bell op. cit.

12. *Irish News* 1 August 1936.

13. Ibid. 7 August 1936.

14. Ibid. 11 August 1936.

15. Ibid.

16. One Catholic worker wrote to the *Irish News* to suggest that Catholics form their own unions which would be run by Catholic chaplins. *Irish News* 25 September 1936.

17. *Irish News* 14 August 1936.

18. Midgley also worked closely and got on well with Paedar O'Donnell, a well-known Republican Socialist, with whom he addressed (frequently stormy) meetings on Spain in the North and in the Free State. Information from Paedar O'Donnell, 5 September 1981. See also Paedar O'Donnell, *Salud! An Irishman in Spain*, London, 1937, p. 244.

19. *Irish News* 18 August 1936.

20. Ibid. 22 August 1936.

21. Chairman's Address to the NILP Annual Conference 29 August 1936. Reproduced as a pamphlet, *A Bombshell of Facts on Home and Foreign Affairs*, *Midgley Papers*.

22. *Irish News* 31 August 1936.

23. Ibid.

24. *A Bombshell of Fact* op. cit.

25. *Irish News* 8 September 1936.

26. *Derry Journal* 31 August 1936.

27. *Irish News* 8 September 1936.

28. Ibid. 11 September 1936.

29. A good example of this attitude was a letter written by one Peter Grew, a prominent Midgley critic during this controversy. Grew warned Catholics not to trust people who claimed to be indifferent in regard to people's religious views. 'He who is not with me is against me', was Grew's advice. *Irish News* 17 September 1936.

30. The pamphlet, contained in *Midgley Papers*, was particularly well received by the same communists who had been so critical of Midgley in the past. They described it as 'brilliant' and helped distribute it in the Free State.

They also congratulated Midgley and the NILP on standing 'four square' for democracy in contrast to the Irish Labour party in the Free State. *The Worker* 26 September 1936.

31. *Irish News* 16 September 1936.
32. Ibid. 27 October 1936.
33. The election figures are still a matter of debate. Raymond Carr, *The Spanish Tragedy*, London, 1977 p. 47 says that 'nearly half' of Spain voted against the Popular Front while Hugh Thomas, *The Spanish Civil War*, London, 1961 p. 94 gives the combined centre and right vote a small numerical majority. The Popular Front won a majority of 63 seats.
34. *Irish News* 10 November 1936.
35. Ibid. 11 November 1936.
36. Ibid. 14 November 1936.
37. Ibid. 17 November 1936.
38. P. Shea op. cit. p. 163.
39. The *Democrat* was a combined effort on the part of Republican socialists and communists from both north and south of Ireland. Frank Ryan, the Republican socialist who was captured by Franco's troops in Spain, was the paper's first editor. See S. Cronin, *Frank Ryan*, Dublin, 1980, p. 104.
40. *Belfast News-Letter* 9 August 1937.
41. Ibid.
42. *The Labour Party, Annual Conference Report* 1937 p. 216. Midgley received a rather bland reply from Clement Attlee to the effect that close relations between the two parties was desirable.
43. Harbinson op. cit. p. 84.
44. Report of speech in *The Irish Democrat* 6 November 1937.
45. Harbinson op. cit. p. 85.
46. In his chairman's address Midgley said: 'The presence on our platform today of a distinguished and leading representative of the British Labour movement is, I take it, an indication of renewed determination on the part of the parent movement to hold out a helping hand to its offspring here in Northern Ireland . . .' The address was reproduced as a pamphlet, *Give Labour a Chance*, contained in *Midgley Papers*.
47. Letter from Nolan to Desmond Ryan 6 November 1937, Desmond Ryan Papers LA10/Q/6A, University College Dublin Archives.
48. *The Irish Democrat* 20 November 1937.
49. This had for some time been the general outlook in the British Labour Party. See *The Book of the Labour Party* III, London, n.d. – probably early 1920s, Chapter V, 'The British Commonwealth of Nations' by C. Delisle Burns. Burns concluded by saying that the Commonwealth should be seen 'not as a flag-waving, drum-beating enterprise, but as the co-operation of many peoples all consisting in the main of quite ordinary, peaceful, labouring folk' (p. 86).
50. Minutes of meeting in British Labour Party Archives, London, WG/NI/21. This is the source for the information which follows.
51. Labour Party archives WG/NI/311.
52. Ibid. WG/NI/31.
53. *Irish News* 27 January 1938.

54. Ibid. 29 January 1938.
55. Ibid. 18 January 1938.
56. *Belfast Telegraph* 24 January 1938.
57. This was for the seat of South Armagh from which McCann had withdrawn and which was then boycotted by the Nationalists.
58. *Irish News* 2, 3 and 4 February 1938.
59. Ibid. 5 February 1938.
60. Ibid. 2 February 1938.
61. Ibid. 7 February 1938.
62. Ibid. 8 February 1938.
63. Ibid. 5 February 1938.
64. Ibid. 8 February 1938.
65. Ibid. 11 February 1938.
66. *Belfast Telegraph* 11 February 1938.
67. Ibid.
68. Ibid. It was rumoured that the Unionists had helped to fund Collins's campaign.
69. Linfield were – and are – supported by large numbers of Orangemen throughout Northern Ireland. Sectarian trouble frequently marked matches played between Linfield and Belfast Celtic who were mainly supported by Catholics from West Belfast.
70. See, for example, *The Workers' Republic* July 1938.
71. Political General Secretary's Report 9 September 1936, USDAW Records.

Chapter Seven
NILP Showdown (1938–1942)

I

The period 1938–42 saw the most intensive efforts yet made by Midgley's opponents to remove him from the leadership of the NILP. The party at this time might be viewed as incorporating three distinct political tendencies. In effective control and in a probable numerical majority were those who were prepared – more or less enthusiastically – to accept Northern Ireland's constitutional position within the United Kingdom. This section of the party embraced the vast majority of those in the craft trade unions. Their outlook was reformist, and left-wing extremism was viewed with hostility. Midgley's personal base of support was concentrated in this section of the party. He enjoyed the confidence of a large number of people to whom he appeared as the party's only credible leader. However, there were some who, while sharing Midgley's general political outlook, were not uncritical supporters of his leadership. These people might have preferred someone who cut a less cavalier figure and who was not so prone to offend and alienate certain members of the party and some prospective sympathisers outside it.

The second largest group in the party was the left wing. Republican socialist in their philosophy, the vast majority of those on the left wanted to see the NILP adopt a firm anti-partitionist stance and to actively seek working class unity in both parts of Ireland. The left poured derision on the gradualism and constitutionalism of the NILP's leadership and wished to see the party's character undergo a revolutionary transition. Midgley was not surprisingly singled out as the main obstacle to the achievement of this objective. The most vociferous of those on the left were grouped in the Socialist Party (NI) which, according to one contemporary, had around 120 members at this time.[1] Another centre of extreme left activity was the Left Book Club in Belfast. This club was run by the Progressive Book Shop in Union Street, a venture Midgley had helped to get off the ground in the mid-30s with the shop's owner, Davie McLean. In Belfast's left-wing 'society' there was also a degree of overlap between the left of the NILP and those in the Communist Party of Ireland. Several Communists were in fact in the SP(NI) and the NILP during this period.

Finally, there also existed another group critical of Midgley's leadership. This section of the party – the smallest – was strongly nationalist in outlook and, for the most part, mildly socialist. Some people who can be accommodated in this category might indeed be said to have been on the right wing of the party while declaring strongly against partition and the leadership's apparent acceptance of it. Patrick Agnew and most of the membership of the Armagh Labour branch of which he was the leading figure, were typical of the kind of people who constituted this group. Only a firmer commitment to social change and a slightly less obsessive and narrow concern with the minority community set this group apart from those in the Nationalist Party.

Despite growing opposition within the party, Midgley determinedly pursued his Labour unionist strategy. In May 1938 the NILP executive held meetings with George Dallas and G. R. Shepherd (National Agent) of the British Labour Party. The purpose was to further bind the ties between the parties and to discuss the prospect of positive British Labour assistance to candidates fighting Northern Ireland's Westminster seats at a future general election.[2] Dallas said that no attempt would be made by the British party to interfere in Northern Ireland politics.[3] At a special NILP conference shortly afterwards the party executive announced that they intended to fight all eleven Westminster seats, an indication, perhaps, of how substantial the help promised by British Labour would appear to have been.[4] The conference also met to adopt a new constitution which, to the annoyance of the Connollyite Left and the nationalists, had 'the hallmark of the British Labour party stamped in every clause'.[5] The constitution also prohibited communists from attending party conferences as delegates.

At the party's October conference the new constitution was ratified. Stanley Hirst, an executive member of the British Labour Party, addressed the delegates and urged them to 'think in terms of the trade union and Labour movement and not particularly of a nationalist issue'.[6] Perhaps conscious of the way the wind was blowing, the Irish Labour Party declined to accept the invitation to send a fraternal delegate to the conference.[7] The left and the nationalists were frustrated in their attempts to question the decisions taken, and a Mr P. Devine of the Armagh party tore up his conference papers and walked out in protest.[8] Midgley once again concentrated on international issues in his chairman's address and reiterated his strong support for the Spanish government. He also relinquished the chairmanship, a decision he had taken a couple of months previously on the grounds that he had held the office 'a sufficiently long time'.[9] Robert Getgood took over, and Midgley was elected to the executive. Getgood was a Labour servant of long standing and, in terms of his general political outlook, close to Midgley and on the right of the party. The character of the party, therefore, remained much the same and Midgley was still regarded as '*de facto*' leader despite having stepped down as chairman and despite being without a seat in parliament.

The threat of war in Europe loomed closer in 1938 with Germany's invasion of Austria and Czechoslovakia. Against such a background, Midgley's efforts to make Labour in Ulster more keenly aware of international happenings and their possible implications, were laudable. In October 1938 he published a pamphlet *The Great Betrayal*[10] in which he summarised his views of the international scene and denounced the National government in Britain led by Neville Chamberlain. "During the past few weeks', he wrote, 'we have witnessed one of the greatest betrayals in human history, culminating in dismemberment of Czechoslovakia, and the virtual destruction of one of the finest democracies in the world.' For Midgley, the tragedy of Czechoslovakia was the latest in a long line of dismal retreats on the part of the National government: first there was the appeasement of Japan over her invasion of Manchuria, then the Italians after the invasion of Abyssinia, then the refusal to aid the Spanish government in the civil war, then another refusal to take action against Japan when China was invaded, and, finally, the steady process of capitulation to the demands of Hitler's Germany. It all added up, in Midgley's view, to a betrayal of democracy and a selfish desire on the part of the ruling class to protect its own economic interests. Midgley's alternative was not war; he, like so many in the British Labour Party, held fast to the concept of co-operation between nations as embodied by the League of Nations. The League could only be as strong and effective as the commitment to it shown by the participating nations, and it was on this count that Midgley levelled his charge against the National goverment. In contrast, he argued that British Labour governments, when in power, had given full support to the League and had set 'the highest moral example to all the other nations'. This they had done by giving full support to the principle that disputes between nations should be settled by international courts of law. Midgley also praised the 1929–31 government's attempt to arrange a Disarmament Conference for 1932.[11]

Midgley preferred to indulge in scathing attacks on the 'guilty men', as he saw them, than to confront the disarmament issue directly. He made it clear that he believed there had to be an end to the arms race; this, he argued, 'must be by international agreement and the negotiation of an international Disarmament Treaty'.[12] He at the same time pledged a future Labour government to 'maintain such armed forces as are necessary to defend the country and fulfil Great Britain's obligations under the League'. This provision for defence would, however, have to be examined 'in the light of the international situation and the new foreign policy which it would inaugurate'.[13]

When war came in September 1939, the Northern Ireland Labour movement's response was hesitant. Midgley himself had no doubts that the war had to be fought and won and he would dearly have liked to be able to count on the full support of the party he led. He knew, however, that this was impossible. Many in the party, including some on the right wing, were more anxious to ensure that conscription was not extended to Northern Ireland. They, and indeed the Unionist government, realised very well the fury such a measure would provoke among the Nationalist community. At Belfast's May Day rally in 1939 Midgley himself had come out against conscription. He had, however, added the qualification that his attitude would have been different had they in Northern Ireland had a government like that in New Zealand.[14]

The majority of the NILP's left wing, in common with the communists, viewed the war as another imperialist confrontation in which the workers should take no part. Fascism was of course denounced, but the prospect of Britain and Ireland ever being under Nazi denomination was not taken seriously. This was an analysis which the nationalists in the party were only too happy to go along with, especially in view of the policy of neutrality adopted by de Valera's government in the South. Midgley and other prominent party members such as William Leeburn of the ATGWU attempted to give the impression that Labour was backing the war effort. Midgley accepted a position on the Ulster Savings Committee set up by the government, and he did not balk at having to share platforms with government ministers in meetings held to promote the war effort. His efforts were predictably denounced in the left-wing press.[15]

At the NILP conference at the end of October, the war was not the primary concern of left-wing and nationalist delegates who again tried to force debates on the question of partition, and relations with the Labour movement in the South. They were once again frustrated and looked on sullenly as Midgley was elected chairman for the following year unopposed.[16] An amendment to a resolution urging the defeat of Nazi Germany which would have committed the party to an anti-war stance, was defeated by 18 to 10.[17]

In February 1940 the NILP held a special conference to discuss party organisation with a view to future elections. Midgley and Leeburn fought a rearguard action at the conference in defence of party policy. They believed that the party's difficulties derived from lack of resources, most notably, money. Many of the delegates did not accept this and advanced strident criticisms of the image presented by the party to the electorate. Mr H. Todd of the Belfast Trades Council put the point in the following way:

The sectarian issue rises up to the surface and we will have to face up to it. At the last election when I was speaking for some candidates I found that I had to alter the tone of my remarks in different constituencies, and in different parts of certain constituencies. I feel that none of us would have to do that if the party had a more suitable programme.[18]

Midgley was impatient with such criticism and replied to it abrasively and rather disingenuously:

I think that those people who are not in agreement with the policy of the party should not be attached to it, but should join an organisation which has a policy that they do agree with. Further, there is no necessity for any speaker to alter the tone of his remarks in any constituency, so long as he sticks to the Labour party policy.[19]

More than anyone else, Midgley knew the truth of Todd's remarks but he was determined to prevent a public split in the party over the national question. He was fully aware of the tensions created by the problem but he was anxious to keep conflict below the surface. He seems to have followed a strategy of, on the one hand, attempting to defuse potential trouble within the party, and, on the other, pressing ahead with his personal effort to give the party a 'dependable' constitutional image: a party which, despite dissenting voices from within, was 'safe' on the question of the border by virtue of its reciprocally close identification with the British Labour movement. It was a task which never really looked like being accomplished.

The conference revealed other weaknesses about the party. The delegate from North Antrim, Mr J. Donaghy, complained:

When I come to a conference in Belfast I get the impression that the Labour party is a city party, as we are always confronted with the problems of the city, and the provincial areas seem to be forgotten. In my opinion there is as much support for the Labour party in the country districts as there is in the city.

On the same theme the North West regional delegate, Mr J. Millar, said: 'I think that the Labour party policy should be stressed a little more in the agricultural areas.' The criticism was an eminently valid one and it was given further piquancy by John Glass, a West Belfast party member, who offered the following explanation as to why the provincial areas were neglected:

the difficulty in this question is that although there are a number of capable public speakers in the party they are very seldom invited to address a meeting. Some people seem to run away with the idea that there is only one suitable speaker and that is the chairman, Comrade Midgley.[20]

Glass's point was an important one. Not only was the NILP essentially a Belfast party; it had also become a 'Midgley-centred' party, a characteristic which had been in evidence even in the early 1930s. Midgley's personality dominated the party, not, perhaps, a surprising state of affairs in view of the strength of his personality and the relative dearth of able contenders for the role of leader. Midgley's energy, drive, oratorical power and organisational skill were ample justification for his dominance; he was, in short, the most outstanding figure in the party and one of the most able politicians in Northern Ireland. All this, however, cannot detract from the impression given at this time that the NILP suffered, as a party, from its dependence on one man. It was a state of affairs which Midgley arguably did little to discourage. He wanted to be in control, to direct party affairs from every angle, and he knew he was the most capable man to do it. He also became increasingly impatient and annoyed with criticism from within the party. This in turn seemed to instil in him a defensiveness which led him to trust fewer people and to afford his critics the minimum amount of influence and leeway. As a result tensions between Midgley and a large section of the party created an unhealthy atmosphere rife with suspicion and back-biting, and wholly lacking in a sense of unity and fraternity.

Midgley's hardening attitudes seem undoubtedly to have been related to the progress of the war. As Hitler stalked over Belgium, Holland and France, it became increasingly clear that only Britain stood between him and the extinction of democracy in Europe. Still the party bickering would not cease and still his critics sought to discredit him. The communists' paper, *Irish Workers' Weekly*, led the attacks,[21] but their views were to a large extent echoed on the left of the NILP. The communists and the left in the NILP accused Midgley of naivety in believing that the British constitution allowed for a peaceful transition to a socialist society. However, their own naivety, at this point in the war's development, was on a far greater scale. Their faith was pinned on a sudden united class action on the part of the workers against the British and Northern Ireland governments. This, the left believed, would inspire the German workers to move against, and destroy, Hitler and Naziism.

By July 1940 France was overwhelmed and the Nazi menace was at Britain's door. Midgley appealed to the Labour movement and to the workers of Northern Ireland to spare no effort in combating the threat.[22] On 27 September he broadcast an appeal on the BBC Home Service in Northern Ireland, saying that the British Commonwealth was 'the last great bulwark of democracy'.[23]

By this time there was a coalition government in Britain led by Winston Churchill and in which Labour was virtually an equal partner with the Conservatives. The Chamberlain government had fallen in May 1940 after a series of military setbacks had occasioned a widespread loss of confidence and a strong belief that changes had to be made. The public view of the Craigavon government's performance since the outbreak of the war was similarly critical. Northern Ireland's initial response to the demands of the war was sluggish, the 'king and country' rhetoric of the Unionist ministers notwithstanding. The British government had thought better of applying conscription to the province,[24] a fact which gave the impression that Northern Ireland was only half involved in the war. The North's seaports, however, were gratefully taken charge of by the navy. They were to be of vital importance in view of the South's neutrality and de Valera's refusal to allow the Allies access to those Southern ports Britain had handed back to Eire in a diplomatic agreement reached in 1938. In terms of manpower, however, Ulster's war effort seemed defective: unemployment still stood at 77,000 in 1940,[25] and a large question mark hung over the government's methods of mobilisation.[26] Government ministers met with fierce criticism even from within their own party, and in May 1940 Edmund Warnock, Parlimentary Secretary to the Minister of Home Affairs, resigned. He was followed a month later by Lieut.-Col. A. R. Gordon. The government's inability to absorb the pool of labour into war work was reflected in the number of workers sent to the mainland to join the effort there. Altogether, around 60,000 workers went to Britain from Northern Ireland during the war.[27]

The government's task was not made easier by the steady influx of immigrants from Eire. This development caused some alarm and indignation in Unionist circles, the belief being that these immigrants were in many cases lending support to the IRA. For its part, the IRA was not neglectful of the opportunities the wartime situation presented to them. After the failure of the bombing campaign in English cities in 1939, attention focused on Ulster. Operations, including bombings and shootings, were carried out in the period 1940–2, especially in the months of February and April 1940.[28] The IRA was a veritable 'Fifth Column' in that it had definite links with Germany and received some material aid from the Nazis.[29] The government responded with a ready willingness to use the internment powers granted to them by the Special Powers Act. The IRA campaign had virtually ceased by the end of 1942 by which time one of their number, Tom Williams, had been hanged for the murder of an RUC man.

Williams's fate was a matter of some anger and resentment among the minority community. Support for the war had not surprisingly been conspicuous by its absence in Catholic circles, an attitude apparently given clerical sanction by the public pronouncements of Cardinal McRory. McRory was fervently anti-British, if not actually pro-Nazi, and refused to co-operate with the Northern Ireland government in connection with the war effort.[30]

Midgley looked enviously across the water at the coalition administration galvanised by Churchill and Ernest Bevin, the latter a man of comparable energy, ability and outlook to himself. As Minister of Labour Bevin had quickly and successfully set about mobilising the nation's manpower to a far greater capacity than before. As this effort took place schemes for post-war social reconstruction were also in the air. The contrast with Northern Ireland was stark. Midgley desired to play a more influential role but his chances of doing so at this juncture looked slim. It did not seem to be on the government's mind to broaden the base of its administration.

One of the main factors militating against the possibility of a coalition government for Northern Ireland was the divided state of the Labour party. As long as the anti-partitionist forces were seen to be a significant force, so the NILP would always be considered 'unsafe' on the constitutional issue. Midgley realised this and, as the war progressed, it increasingly irritated him. His chance of leading Labour into a coalition government and of contributing his personal talents to the direction of the war effort seemed fated to founder on the rock of the party's internal squabbles.

These squabbles were again manifest at the party's conference in December 1940. Midgley's address was on the theme of winning the war and establishing an everlasting peace:

Broadly speaking we must recognise the spirit of all nations to equality of opportunity in the development of their culture and civilisation, and of access to the raw materials and resources of the world. In pursuit of this policy, however, we must now realise that in the world of today old-fashioned – or obsolete – nationalism, in addition to arrogant and aggressive imperialism, must give away to a recognition of the interdependence of states.[31]

Combined with a call for a 'social charter' and a 'holy war against poverty', Midgley's message was undeniably socialist in content. To his critics, however, this mattered little. They were not content to discuss matters of general political philosophy; they wanted debate on particular issues of concern to Northern Ireland such as the Special Powers Act, the question of workers being sent to England, and, of course, partition. These debates bristled with ill-temper and intolerance. The *Irish Workers' Weekly* reported that Midgley had never had to be on his feet so often 'in defence of his reformist class-collaboration outlook'. It further stated that Midgley had twice spoken at the conference of having to examine his conscience about staying in the movement if certain policies were opposed.[32]

The conference drew public attention to what Midgley had hoped might be concealed: the fierce opposition to himself and the strength of the anti-partitionist wing of the party. Armagh delegates demanded non-cooperation with the Northern Ireland government on matters of defence, a demand which carried much constituency party support, and was only defeated by the trade union block vote. The proposal for a campaign against the Special Powers Act – also formidably supported – was similarly thwarted.[33] Midgley was conspicuously unable to tie the conference down to discussion of the war effort. Despite another unopposed return to the chair, again by virtue of the votes of the large unions, it was not a good conference for him. He was still in the driving seat, but the party he led was hopelessly divided. Opposition to him personally was not confined to critical comment about policies; there was clearly a concerted campaign in motion to drive him out of the party leadership. Midgley, however, had fought off challenges to his position before and was in no mood to submit now. He still had his sights on lofty political plateaux. If a share in government was at this time improbable, a return to parliament was the least he could aspire to.

II

Lord Craigavon died on 24 November 1940. He was succeeded as Unionist leader and Prime Minister – to the surprise of some – by John Miller Andrews. Andrews had been Minister of Finance in Craigavon's government. His style of premiership was rather low key, due perhaps to the belief that he could not hope to cut the same kind of imperious and avuncular figure as Craigavon. Andrews was a quiet, diligent man dedicated to carrying on the kind of Unionist government he had been associated with since the state's establishment. Of the new Cabinet formed in January 1941, four ministers beside Andrews himself had all been in office since 1921. Sir Basil Brooke, Minister of Commerce, was the least experienced, having first tasted office in 1929. Almost immediately there were critical noises made about 'old men' who had been in power too long. The new administration, both in its composition and its style of government, did nothing to convince the public that the war effort was being tackled in a new spirit of urgency and purpose.

Andrews received fair indication of this as early as 27 March 1941 at a by-election in Craigavon's seat of North Down. In this contest the Official Unionist was defeated by an Independent Unionist. More dramatically, and tragically, the government experienced the wrath of the Belfast people in the wake of the German bombers' blitz of the city in April and May. The air raids claimed the lives of 942 and rendered many thousands homeless.[34] Midgley's own house in North Belfast was badly damaged and he and his family had to evacuate the area along with many neighbours. The inadequacy of the air-raid shelters, and the chronic shortage of them, were cruelly exposed. In addition to this, the government was unprepared for the consequent problems of rehousing the thousands of refugees who left Belfast for the countryside.

The NILP led the attacks on the Andrews government, while the German invasion of Soviet Russia on 22 June 1941 was the cue for an immediate about-turn on the part of the communists, in relation to the war. They now resolutely supported the prosecution of the war, and indeed became as vocal as the Unionists to this end. Midgley and his brand of Labourism were suddenly viewed in a less hostile light. Some people on the Republican left of the party also began to consider the winning of the war as the first priority, while maintaining their campaign against partition and the Special Powers Act. Thus the purely nationalist tendency in the party was for the moment somewhat isolated, and the campaign against Midgley lost some of its intensity. Many on the left as well as the right now advocated a coalition government in Northern Ireland as in Britain.

At the NILP conference in October 1941 at which he was confirmed as chairman, Midgley was given a less stormy passage than in previous years, and was better able to concentrate the minds of the conference on the war. His address to the conference was blunt and powerful. After praising the 'magnificent resistance' of Russia and recalling the British Commonwealth's stand in the dark days after the fall of France, Midgley went on to lash the Northern Ireland government for its lack of co-operation with the Labour movement: '. . . it is doubtful whether certain people moving in Government circles have changed their Nazi–Fascist spots since the days when they were closely associated with the enemies of the workers and working class movements on the Continent.' Midgley claimed the right of Labour to participate in the war effort, but added significantly:

To sustain our claim . . . we must leave no ambiguity in the minds of the people as to where we stand in relation to outstanding political issues . . . The Labour Party must not be used as political camouflage for the dissemination of creeds, philosophies and tactics peculiar to other organisations, whether Proletarian, Imperialist or Nationalist. Neither should the members of the Labour Party be led astray by the pursuit of Shibboleths.[35]

Midgley was thus concerned to leave little room for doubt in the minds of the public and the government that Labour could be trusted in its attitude both to the war and to the link with Britain. The anti-partitionist chorus of dissent was, for the moment, heard to little effect.

Midgley proceeded to reaffirm his commitment to the concept of a progressive and co-operative British Commonwealth of Nations. His model state was itself a Commonwealth member: New Zealand. Midgley was often to use the example of the New Zealand Labour government's achievements since 1935 to give empirical weight to what many considered a rather vague utopian theory. In Midgley's estimation – and in that of many in the British Labour movement in this period – New Zealand's system of social services and security ranked second to none. In his address to the 1941 conference, Midgley informed his audience that New Zealand workers were protected by a Legal Minimum Wage, that old-age pensions of thirty-shillings per week were paid at age 60, and that allowances for widows and orphans were the highest in the world. In articles written for the Labour press, Midgley went into comprehensive detail about these and many other aspects of conditions in New Zealand.[36] Because it was comparable in terms of population to Northern Ireland, Midgley took great inspiration from New Zealand, and believed that it had set a standard for the other Commonwealth nations.

The most notable occurrence at the NILP conference, however, was the announcement that the party intended to force a by-election contest in the Belfast constituency of Willowfield. The seat had been vacated by Sir Arthur Black, who had decided to take up the post of Recorder of Belfast. Midgley was to go forward as the Labour candidate with, it was intimated, the full backing of his trade union, NUDAW.[37] Midgley had not in fact received the backing of NUDAW when the announcement was made at the conference. As it happened NUDAW turned down his request.[38] However, Midgley was undaunted. He believed Willowfield to be too good an opportunity to miss and he was thus prepared to ignore the union's decision.

Willowfield did indeed present Labour with a realistic chance of undermining the government's position. It was largely a skilled working class constituency, and predominantly Protestant. If Labour was to have any chance of playing a significant future role in Northern Ireland politics these skilled workers had to be won to its cause. Given the relative trade union strength among these workers it made sense to perceive this section of the working class as the necessary backbone of support in a strong and thriving Labour party. If popular discontent with the government was all that the wartime mood indicated, then this contest might prove, or disprove, the point.

There were, however, the perennial factors which threatened to ensure that this contest would be nothing like those held anywhere else in Britain. The constituency had been solidly Unionist since it had been created in 1929 and had not been contested by Labour before. There were no hints from the past about how well, or badly, a Labour candidate would fare. That popular disgruntlement with the government's performance would alter the voting habits of a lifetime was highly questionable. There would be the inevitable Unionist appeals to loyalty and the usual scaremongering tactics about a vote for Labour being a vote against the border. Midgley's venture was, therefore, a personal risk which required courage. A defeat, following on from Dock in 1938, would severely damage his political reputation and render his hold on the party leadership very precarious. His critics could with justice say that he did not possess an ability to win sufficient electoral support from either side of the religious divide. A more promising prospective constituency might have been found for Midgley at some future time. But he was, as ever, in no mood to wait.

Midgley's opponent was a Mr F. J. Lavery. Lavery was an uninspiring candidate who did not seem to enjoy much personal popularity even among Unionists. His selection as candidate appears to have split the party, and Midgley later claimed that the voting had only been 60–40 in his favour.[39] The Unionist press was unimpressed with Lavery and attempted as much as possible to keep his personality in the background. Their editorial thrust concerned, not surprisingly, Midgley's attitude to the border. On this occasion, however, the Unionists' ability to score points in such a way was effectively blunted. Midgley's position on the issue was unequivocal and he could have left few in any doubt about his personal feelings, if not those of his party generally. On 21 November the *News-Letter* reported him as having said that 'there could not be, and must not be' any alteration of the constitutional position without the consent of the people. Midgley had then added that he had been in touch with British Labour cabinet ministers and had received the assurance that there was no desire to alter Northern Ireland's status.[40]

Midgley did not stop at verbal declarations of fidelity. His campaign was studded with symbolic gestures designed to convince the electorate that Labour was every bit as 'loyal and true' as the Unionists. At the end of one Midgley meeting the platform was asked whether there was any objection to the proceedings being closed with the National Anthem. The chairman, Mr Bob Thompson, replied that there was no objection. 'There were', he added, 'no stronger upholders of the constitution than the Labour party.' The anthem was duly sung.[41] Midgley himself took to wearing his Great War medals while campaigning, and one trade union advertisement in the press urged the voters to support 'the man with the medals'.[42]

Despite the efforts of such as Sir Basil Brooke and William Grant to cast doubt on Midgley and the NILP's commitment to the Union, the warning signs for the government were plain to see. In the Unionist press the election prompted a flood of correspondence. One letter to the *Northern Whig* signed 'Willowfield' expressed a common sentiment:

As a Unionist elector in the Willowfield Division I have no hesitation in saying that I intend to vote for Midgley. At the present time we are well represented by the Unionist party, and I believe a man of the dynamic force and personality of Midgley would act as a tonic in an assembly which is mostly composed of 'yes-men' who have shown neither initiative nor backbone. Midgley has a record of public service second to none, and it would have been a glorious gesture to give him the seat without a contest. He surely deserves it.[43]

The contest took place on 3 December. The following day the astonishing result was declared: Midgley 7,209; Lavery 2,435. Midgley's majority was 4,774 on a 60 per cent poll. Midgley's supporters chaired him from the City Hall with shouts of 'Gang way for the future Prime Minister.'[44] Labour's elation was unstinted while the Unionists affected equanimity. The Minister of Agriculture, Lord Glentoran, made the remarkable comment that the result was 'a moral victory for Unionist principles', since, 'the long quiet progressive government of the late Lord Craigavon convinced the majority of the people of the present generation that the Border question was not an issue . . .'[45]

The Unionist newspapers and their readers were more prepared to face the facts. The *Belfast News-Letter's* editorial on the election stated: 'To suggest that the result of the Willowfield by-election is other than a blow to the Ulster government would be merely to attempt to gloss over an unpleasant truth.'[46] For the *Northern Whig*, Willowfield was 'more than a nine-days' wonder: it is a warning'.[47] The *Belfast Telegraph* was similarly reproachful to the government's inclinations to bury its head in the sand. It was also far from unhappy about the result:

We believe Willowfield was won by Alderman Midgley because he was a strong candidate with an impressive record in civic and trade union affairs and a first rate platform man; because the Unionist party machine rates public intelligence too low when it expects the Border issue and any candidate to be sufficient at the present time to ensure an official victory.[48]

Readers' letters to the press echoed this latter viewpoint. Willowfield had struck a much-needed blow at government complacency. This, it was widely believed, would lead to beneficial changes both in the composition of the government and in the execution of its duties. Outside government circles, there were some Unionists such as Edmund Warnock who were probably of a similar mind. Midgley, after all, was someone who could be relied upon at Stormont to intensify the pressure on the government to step up the war effort.

The Willowfield result has to be seen in the wider context of British wartime politics. Paul Addison has suggested that 'a major upheaval' in British public opinion took place in the early years of the war.[49] There was a decided swing to the left and away from Establishment notions, a process which naturally harmed the Conservatives. There was substantial by-election evidence for this in Britain during the period 1940–2 when several improbable results were recorded. Indeed, as Addison argues, 'opinion may have been further to the Left in 1942 than it was to be in 1945'.[50] The apparent public endorsement of egalitarian radicalism suggested that the war was bringing about an unprecedented degree of social levelling in British society.

The evidence of Willowfield suggests that the Northern Ireland public mood underwent a similar shift. This development may be said to have been compounded by a lack of confidence in the government, both Craigavon's administration until November 1940, and that of Andrews succeeding it. The war news was not encouraging in the years 1940–1, and there was a widespread feeling that Northern Ireland was not pulling its weight. This was partly attributed to the fact that conscription had not been extended to the area, but also to general government shortcomings. Sir Wilfrid Spender was dismayed to learn on a visit to London that the Northern Ireland government did not enjoy a good reputation across the water. 'I am afraid', he wrote, 'it is due to the fact that Ministers seem to give the impression that they are more concerned with their own position than they are with helping on the war'.[51] This was a view which would probably have been shared by a great many people in Northern Ireland. In addition, the memories of German air raids – and the inadequacy of the government's preparations – were still fresh in people's minds at the time of the Willowfield contest.

The Unionists clearly blundered in their choice of candidate. Set against Midgley's gifts of oratory and personal dynamism, Lavery's appeal was anaemic. His campaign was pedestrian and too reliant on time-worn catch-cries. The Unionist 'heavy weights', moreover, did not add much credibility to, or even enliven, their candidate's cause.

Seen against such a background the Willowfield result becomes less remarkable. But it must be kept in mind that Midgley not only defeated the Unionist in a staunchly Unionist seat, he annihilated him. Midgley did not have the campaign resources of Lavery, and was fighting without trade union approval or financial backing. While the people's desire for change was probably as strong as on the British mainland, protest votes were not so lightly cast in Northern Ireland. Voting Unionist was considered by many thousands of electors as an article of faith which was broken at the cost of their birthright and national identity. This was the extent of Midgley's task in a great many cases. While he personally left no doubt as to his belief in the British link, he always carried the albatross of the anti-partitionist wing of his party. The press and Lavery's campaigners did not let him or the electorate forget this. It would thus have been a signal achievement to have won over just enough of these traditionally inveterate Unionists to scrape through. That he should have swung such support to his banner that his majority was positively crushing, was a personal triumph without comparison in his career. It was indisputably the biggest electoral upset in Northern Ireland politics since the state's formation.

III

Midgley returned to the Northern Ireland House of Commons on 9 December 1941. He joined a band of government critics which now numbered Unionist backbenchers in addition to Labour, Nationalist and Independent Unionist members. On 20 January 1942, in his first major speech since his return, Midgley moved a resolution calling for the reconstruction of the government. It was a merciless attack which created just the kind of adverse publicity for the government to give further momentum to the campaign for a new broader-based administration. Midgley accused the government of having no policy and of lagging behind Britain in implementing social reforms. He likened the government to a 'vast telephone exchange' with the Prime Minister sitting at the switchboard and cabinet members acting like 'communication plugs'. There was, he alleged, a complete lack of co-ordination. The industrial community, he added, was 'far from organised for total war'. Finally he went on to charge the government with presenting a poor image of Northern Ireland to the people of Britain. The apparent inability of the Northern Ireland government to put its case with regard to the national question frustrated Midgley. He concluded:

I believe Northern Ireland deserves to stand better. I believe the potentialities of Northern Ireland are great and have not been exploited to good purpose or for the advantage of the people. I believe in the days that lie ahead the government of this country can and will be improved.[52]

The speech was that of a man grooming himself for office. It was far from a mere succession of jibes at the government or a points-scoring opposition exercise. It was designed to expose areas of failure on the part of the government and to convince the House that he (Midgley) was as dismayed by these failures as he knew certain elements in the Unionist Party undoubtedly were. He wanted to sound at once critical and constructive; at once rabble-rousing and statesmanlike.

Two Unionists voted for Midgley's motion: Edmund Warnock and Lt. Col. Alexander Gordon. Warnock, however, went further. In a

speech which exposed the divisions in the Unionist Party he made a
powerful plea for the inclusion of Midgley in a new government. What it
could hardly have become Midgley himself to say, Warnock spelled out:

> The two greatest questions are manpower and production. The demand for
> production is absolutely un-precedented and in connection with that production
> the voice of Labour is of tremendous importance. If it would assist in getting
> Labour and Capital, employer and workman, to pull together with a stronger
> pull and if the inclusion of a Labour member in the government would help in
> that direction it should be done.[53]

The Labour member Warnock had in mind was not Beattie or Agnew.
The government survived the vote on the resolution comfortably
enough (23–8), but it knew that the pressures against it were mounting
and that the way ahead would be fraught with problems.

At least in essence, the criticism levelled at the Andrews government
by Midgley and others seems to have been justified. Northern Ireland
industrialists gave the impression of being more concerned with the
future of their enterprises after the war than the contribution they could
make to the war effort. Employers were generally able to look after their
own interests without pressure being exerted on them by the government to co-operate in answering the demands of war. Ernest Bevin
let it be known that he was most dismayed by some Northern Ireland
employers' unwillingness to release their skilled workers, and by the
Andrews government's weakness in response to the employers'
action.[54]

Amidst speculation and rumour over government changes, Midgley's
position in relation to the NILP became increasingly delicate. It seems
likely that Midgley would have accepted office if offered it by Andrews.
The only other Labour members at Stormont were Beattie (Independent) and Agnew (NILP). The former was more strongly anti-partitionist than pro-war, while the latter had no enthusiasm for the prosecution of the war at all. Midgley may have felt that – dominant as the
Unionists would remain in a 'coalition' – his inclusion would be the only
realistic way of involving Labour actively in the direction of the
Northern Ireland war effort. While he sought to expose the shortcomings of the Andrews government, he was not content to play a negative
role from the opposition benches. The exigencies of war had diminished, to some extent, the importance of party rivalries in Midgley's
outlook.

This was not the prevalent view within the NILP, either on the left or
right of the party. The Willowfield result had led many to believe that

the best hope for Labour now lay in a general election at the earliest possible date. Public dissatisfaction with the government was obvious and had to be capitalised on. If traditional Unionist voters in Willowfield had been moved to change their allegiance to Labour, how rosy the prospects now appeared for the NILP in a whole range of constituencies throughout the six counties. Had Midgley joined a reconstructed government led by Andrews, the bulk of opinion within the NILP would almost definitely have perceived Labour as having been 'bought off' at the most promising moment in its history. Midgley's inclusion would not have been viewed as sufficient Labour representation in the government.[55]

Midgley shared the party's desire for elections but not, it can be surmised, the belief that they would be held during wartime. Despite the differences in the character of the respective governments, the situation which obtained in Britain regarding a general election was almost bound to apply to Northern Ireland. The Westminster parliament had been prolonged by the Prolongation of Parliament Bill 1940 on a year-to-year basis. The question of an extension to the life of the Northern Ireland parliament would be a matter for consideration in 1943. There was of course the question of public confidence in the government, but it was probable that changes – if they were to be made – would take effect without recourse to a popular vote.

On 8 June it was announced that an NILP deputation headed by Midgley would visit London to request that nothing should be done to postpone the Ulster election. Midgley had raised this matter at Stormont on 2 June.[56] The deputation intended to consult the British war cabinet and representative sections of all British political parties.[57] Andrews was negotiating at this time with the British government to prolong the life of the parliament.

On 9 July Midgley made a peremptory statement on the matter at a meeting of the Belfast Corporation. From information he had received, he said, the Northern Ireland parliament had in fact had its life extended.[58] Midgley made this statement while another NILP deputation (consisting of Hugh Downey, William Leeburn and Milton Gordon) was in London holding talks on the issue with the parliamentary party and the NEC of the British Labour Party. The NILP secretary, Joseph Corrigan, told the press that neither the NILP nor this deputation knew anything definite about whether the parliament was to be prolonged. Midgley's statement came as complete surprise to them.[59]

The parliament's life was officially prolonged by an Act of the

Westminster parliament in November 1943, and the NILP's efforts do not seem to have put this decision in doubt at any time. It can be argued that after his own intervention in June, Midgley did not seem to hold out much hope of success. The fact that he made a statement before the second NILP deputation returned seems to suggest that he did not feel the matter worth pursuing. It was an example of Midgley's tendency – especially notable in this period – to give the impression of speaking for his party when in fact he was delivering a personal opinion. His pronouncements on the war – often made in Unionist company – were similarly taken by many to be made on behalf of the NILP. This proved decidedly irksome to many party officials and members, even to those who may have agreed with Midgley's views.

Anti-partitionist forces within the party were also far from quiescent. While welcoming the Willowfield result, they had been far from happy about Midgley's style of campaign. The attempts to wave the Union Jack as fervently as the Unionists had upset more than a few in the party. Midgley's clear objective was to identify the party closely with the British link, and both the left and the nationalists prepared to stem his progress. Such a development, they felt, could only alienate Catholic voters and lead the NILP to the redundant point where it was trying to outbid the Unionists in terms of loyalty. In what they considered a move to restore the balance in the party, Midgley's opponents thus began once again to make their presence felt.

In January 1942 two Nationalist Party councillors in Belfast, James Collins and Frank Hanna, resigned to join the NILP. Collins of course had been instrumental in bringing about Midgley's defeat in Dock in 1938, and past statements suggested that his conversion to socialism was somewhat sudden and unexpected. Both men cited dissatisfaction with the Nationalists' abstention policy as the main reason for their decision to join the NILP.[60] If Midgley and others in the party felt some disquiet about this development, then they kept it private. Both men were cordially welcomed.[61]

The presence of Collins and Hanna in the party undoubtedly gave it a greater appeal to Catholic electors, the desired aim of such leading individuals in the party as Jack MacGougan, Joseph Corrigan, Jack Dorricott, Patrick Agnew and John Boyle.[62] The culmination of this process was reached in the summer of 1942 when Jack Beattie was re-admitted to the party after eight years as an Independent. Despite the occasional speech in favour of a united war effort, Beattie had not tarnished his Irish nationalist credentials. He had not criticised Eire's neutrality and had taken a strong stand against conscription from the outbreak of the war.

In his history of the NILP, Harbinson argues that Beattie's re-admission was 'a most extraordinary move', especially in view of the complete lack of explanation given for the decision at the time.[63] What is also extraordinary is the apparent silence on the part of Midgley. Joseph Corrigan, in later correspondence with NUDAW, claimed that neither Midgley nor anyone else on the party executive had made an objection to the decision to re-admit Beattie.[64] Midgley may simply have been loath to precipitate a split in the party at the time of Beattie's re-entry. He may have taken the view that such a development would only have caused an unsavoury diversion from the war in which he would have been deeply entangled. He could not, however, have been unaware of the incident's implications. At Stormont now two out of three NILP members were declared opponents of partition and of the policy Midgley sought to implement on behalf of the party. Political opponents in rival parties, and the public in general, could not now be blamed for treating with scepticism any suggestion that the NILP took a firm stand on the constitution. In relation to Midgley's personal ambitions, the affair did his chances of securing office in the name of the NILP no good at all.

At the NILP conference on 31 October 1942 Midgley seemed to give notice that he was tired of political infighting in the midst of such a crucial period in world history. He declared:

For a variety of reasons fundamentals are rarely seriously considered in Northern Ireland. Indeed it seems as if we were destined to have our fondest hopes and cherished ideas thwarted because of the idiosyncracies and infantile political play-acting of those who learn nothing from history and who formulate their policies on centuries old events as if time stood still and the world had not changed.[65]

It is a fair bet that Midgley had his Labour critics as much in mind as the Unionist governing clique.

He went on to express his by now well-known commitment to the British Commonwealth and opposition to 'outworn Nationalism'. This in turn led him to excoriate the ' "Quislings", if not actual agents of Nazism in our midst', by which he clearly meant the IRA and those who sympathised with them. In so doing he dug in his heels; once again he had identified Labour with his own personal creed. His address ended emotionally with just a hint that it might be his swansong as party leader:

It has been my privilege to belong to the Labour movement – National and International – all my life, and I know that its highest ideals spring from the conviction that men the world over are brothers, and that we must work for the Brotherhood of the Nations on the basis of Justice, Honour, Truth and Love.[66]

Three weeks after the conference Midgley decided to risk an open confrontation. In an attempt to get official party backing for his views he issued a 'Declaration of Policy' at a meeting of the Willowfield Labour group in George's Street Hall on 20 November.[67] This declaration (see Appendix) committed the NILP to the constitutional position of Northern Ireland within the United Kingdom, and affirmed the party's belief in a socially progressive British Commonwealth of Nations.[68] Some time later Midgley stated that his intention in issuing the declaration was 'to stop the drift (within the party) towards Nationalism and Republicanism; a drift which became more evident by the re-entry and entry into the party of people who were in favour of having Northern Ireland absorbed into an All-Ireland Parliament'.[69]

On 25 November at Stormont Beattie seized his chance to publicly dissociate himself from Midgley's views. This he did in a powerful attack on the government over the issue of the prolongation of parliament. Incensed by Beattie's speech, Midgley promptly refused to speak in support of the amendment Beattie had tabled and which he had made the excuse for his fierce anti-partitionist outburst.[70]

In a statement to the press on 15 December 1942, Midgley claimed that in the wake of Beattie's speech, he attempted to have the party convene a special meeting to decide its policy on the constitutional question once and for all.[71] Midgley stated that the party did not take up his suggestion, but William Leeburn later said that the matter was raised at a meeting of the executive on 13 December and deferred.[72] At this meeting Midgley learnt of a decision reached on 4 December at a meeting of the Parliamentary Labour Party which he had been unable to attend.

The main business of this meeting had been to elect the leader, deputy leader and chief whip of the Parliamentary party. In attendance were Beattie and Agnew, and William Leeburn and Robert Thompson of the executive committee. Midgley was involved in an Education Committee meeting at the Belfast Corporation when the meeting commenced at 11 a.m., but according to the minutes, telephoned at 11.45 a.m. to say that he would be coming. Those in attendance waited until 12.30 p.m. at which time proceedings commenced without Midgley. The minutes of the meeting read:

It was decided that it would be necessary in order to bring about cohesion in the party, to elect from the existing M.P.'s a Leader, Deputy Leader, and Chief Whip, and the following decision was arrived at:

Leader: Mr J. Beattie, M.P.
Deputy Leader: Mr H. Midgley, M.P.
Chief Whip: Mr P. Agnew, M.P.

After what Thompson considered 'a good days work', the meeting closed at 12.45 p.m. without Midgley having made an appearance.[73]

On being informed of this decision on 13 December, Midgley intimated to the executive that he refused to accept it. The executive then convened a special meeting of the Parliamentary party for 15 December to allow Midgley's objections to be considered. At this meeting, according to a statement later made by the NILP executive, Midgley issued an ultimatum to the Parliamentary party: either he be elected Leader in the House of Commons or he would resign and make an announcement to the press.[74]

Midgley was reported to have demanded the leadership on the following grounds:

(a) That for almost 20 years he had been recognised as the virtual leader of the Labour party.
(b) That he was longer in the Labour party than any other member of the Parliamentary Labour party.
(c) That for eight years Mr J. Beattie had been expelled from the Labour party and that he had only been re-admitted to the party a few months ago.
(d) That he had faithfully served the Labour party during all those years, and had paid the penalty of his loyalty to the party on such issues as Spain and association with the British Commonwealth, at a time when Mr Beattie did not associate himself with such issues.
(e) That Mr Beattie had repeatedly made speeches in the northern Parliament which indicated, beyond all doubt, that he did not believe in the present political status of Northern Ireland.[75]

On the 15th, the Parliamentary party re-affirmed the decision of 4 December and referred the matter to the executive for a final verdict. On the 16th a special executive meeting was convened for 27 December. By this time, however, Midgley had issued a statement to the press to the effect that he was resigning from the party:

For some time past I have been deeply perturbed by the trend of events within the NILP. This has taken the form of pandering to elements more in sympathy with Nationalism and Republicanism than with the fundamental objectives of the Labour party, which are the social ownership of the means of life.

He added that 'to have accepted the deputy leadership would have implied an acceptance of Beattie's political outlook'.[76]

Midgley thus refused to wait for the executive's final decision on the dispute, a violation of the constitution which led to his formal expulsion from the party at the executive meeting held on 19 December. Midgley did not officially submit his resignation to the executive; he let his press statement suffice. The executive also expelled William Kennedy – Midgley's future son-in-law – for 'adopting disruptive methods'. The meeting emphasised that party policy was decided at the annual conference and not by individuals.[77] On the same day as Midgley announced his departure from the party, Leeburn made a statement to the effect that Midgley 'would not work in harness' and 'took it as a personal insult if his point of view on all things was not accepted'. Leeburn further stated that the NILP's only creed was socialism, not 'Toryism' or nationalism.[78] On the following day Beattie weighed in with a letter to the press accusing Midgley of attempting to 'split the resurgent forces of Labour', and advising him to join the Unionists rather than form a 'Midgley party'.[79] Beattie was to be disappointed. Midgley did not join the Unionists. On 19 December he formed the Commonwealth Labour Party with himself as chairman and leader.

Midgley's action lost him his trade union job. To its great annoyance, Midgley neglected to inform the union executive that he was leaving the NILP and forming his own party. Despite his protestations that events had happened with 'such startling suddenness',[80] the executive was not favourably disposed to Midgley. His disregard of the executive ruling over Willowfield had strained relations between them. The union files also show that Joseph Corrigan had been in touch with the British Labour Party's National Agent, G. R. Shepherd, who had promised the services of the party's 'good offices' to the NILP in the dispute.[81]

Midgley's departure from the NILP led to the disaffiliation of only one party branch: North Belfast. On 20 December this branch held a meeting to decide its future existence. A resolution to disaffiliate was carried by 35 votes to 16 after much wrangling over who should take the chair and how proceedings should be conducted.[82] No other party branch followed this example, although the Willowfield divisional party, while remaining in the NILP, expressed full confidence in Midgley.[83] There is no record, however, of the votes taken at other branch meetings, if indeed there were any.[84] Midgley claimed that 'quite a large section of Labour opinion' was behind him and that Milton Gordon of the Londonderry Labour Party had left the NILP along with him.[85] In January 1943, however, the NILP dismissed the defectors as 'a tiny handful of his [Midgley's] personal followers' and claimed that the party had not been split.[86]

The NILP was able to give the appearance of having survived the affair virtually united, but it is still an open question as to how many inside the party sympathised with Midgley but refused to follow him. Given the support he had enjoyed inside the party for so many years – no-one had been, or would be, elected chairman so often – it is fair to surmise that many were deeply saddened by his departure. Loyalty to the party and its constitution, however, was probably deemed a higher priority than regard for an individual. Midgley's decision was viewed by the NILP newspaper as the product of 'personal vanity' rather than political differences.[87] Many individual party members probably viewed the situation in this light. While the fiercest critic of the republican left the nationalist sections of the party had been expelled, the party remained very much in the hands of moderate men like Leeburn, Thompson, Getgood and the officials of the strongest craft trade unions. There was to be no extremist or nationalist take-over.[88]

IV

By the time of the controversy over the leadership of the Parliamentary party, Midgley and the NILP had reached an impasse. By his 'Declaration' of 20 November, Midgley forced the issue: either the party fell into line behind him or it made clear how it differed from him. For Midgley the time had come to declare unequivocally the party's policy regarding the constitution; majority opinion in the party, however, did not favour such a course. In Midgley's eyes the anti-partitionist sections of the party were gaining too much influence; to others, a balance was simply being struck between unionist and nationalist tendencies in an effort to keep the party's appeal as broad as possible. Midgley had to face the fact that even many of those who had supported his leadership through the years could see no benefit in adopting an enthusiastic unionist stance. Ironically enough they pointed to Midgley's own success at Willowfield as proof that Labour was on the march already and could make its appeal on non-sectarian, socialist grounds. With the Unionist Party trying unsuccessfully to conceal a serious split in its own ranks,[89] the prevailing opinion within the NILP was that unity should be preserved at all costs in this, Labour's hour of hope.

In its version of the Midgley dispute, the party executive emphasised that the Parliamentary party decisions had been made for a period of one year only.[90] The committee's concern to draw attention to this perhaps suggests that the factor played an important role in the thoughts of certain parties involved in the dispute. Leeburn and Thompson – both executive members – were party to the decision to elect Beattie leader in the House of Commons.[91] Neither was a nationalist nor was on the left of the movement. Both probably shared Midgley's view that Northern Ireland's future was bound up with Britain and that Ulster Labour could only benefit by the closest possible ties with the British Labour movement. Both men, however, desired the NILP to retain an appeal to both sections of the community and to avoid being given a sectarian label. After many years of having Midgley recognised as the party leader, they may have thought it was time for a change. They might also have been persuaded to this view by the overtly pro-British nature of Midgley's Willowfield campaign, and by Midgley's persistent tendency to deliver a personal viewpoint as if he spoke for the party. To elect Beattie leader would be to redress the balance at a time when Catholic support was in danger of being alienated. In a year's time – the party united behind a non-sectarian, progressive programme – Midgley's election to the Parliamentary party leadership would probably not be perceived as confirmation of the party's affirmative stand on the constitution. Leeburn's remarks after Midgley's departure also suggest that he harboured a desire to see Midgley work more closely with the party executive and not to adopt a stance above the movement. Leeburn and Thompson were very much 'party men' who disliked any display of maverick behaviour which indicated that an individual considered himself more important than the organisation. Midgley failed to realise how widespread within the party this kind of sentiment was. There are some who are prepared to follow leaders blindly, but there are always more who adopt a more guarded attitude, and whose support cannot be depended upon at all times.

Midgley's long period of personal dominance arguably induced in him a certain disregard for the party which he led. He became encouraged by his circle of admirers to look upon the party virtually as his personal property, his political vehicle. As noted earlier, this identification of the NILP in the personality of Midgley did the party more harm than good. There was not a wide enough delegation of party work and there does not seem to have been a strong enough spirit of co-operation and sense of purpose. Personality differences, conflicts over policy, a lack of communication and co-ordination between the Belfast organisation and those in other regions throughout Northern Ireland: all these factors seem to have debilitated the party throughout the years of Midgley's leadership. There were of course very sound reasons for such problems and it is highly unlikely that any other leader could have come up with effective solutions. Midgley's style of political leadership, however, could make him unnecessary enemies. His oratory often inspired and delighted but it could also offend. Midgley was all too prone to make personal attacks on his critics in public, attacks which fostered a climate of animosity in some sections of the movement. His impulsiveness led to more arguments within the party than were good for it.

The anti-partitionist forces in the NILP undoubtedly worked towards the end of removing Midgley from the party leadership. Their strength, however, was not sufficient in itself to bring about the events at the end of 1942. Their presence in the party and their activities were necessary preconditions for the split, but other factors determined it.

The first was Midgley's own impatience with the party's attitude to the National question. Had he been prepared to put up with its ambi-valence he would probably have remained leader and continued to tilt the balance within the party towards a unionist position. This, however, was not enough for him. The circumstances of the war – that is, Britain's heroic stand against the Nazis contrasted with Eire's neutrality – demanded, in Midgley's view, that a firm commitment be made. He saw Northern Ireland's post-war future as inextricably bound up with the process of social reconstruction promised in Britain. The social welfare proposals under discussion in Britain from the middle of 1942 which came to constitute the 'Beveridge Report', undoubtedly reinforced Midgley in his belief in the British link. It was unthinkable to him that Northern Ireland could sever this connection to embrace a society, demonstrably backward in terms of social and economic welfare, which had stood aside in the conflict between totalitarianism and democracy. In Midgley's view the NILP had to make a decision sometime; loss of support among Catholics in the short term was the price which had to be paid for a positive image to present to the electorate. The only way the constitutional issue was likely to recede from people's minds was if they had no doubts where the party stood in relation to it. As long as the party vacillated, its success would be uneven, ephemeral and insubstantial.

Northern Ireland's Unionist majority was a fact of life; the NILP could not hope to be more than a marginal political force if it continued to ignore it.

Midgley's success in Willowfield can be attributed to several factors, but without a clear personal commitment to the Union it is doubtful if he would have triumphed. Midgley realised that the Labour Party in Northern Ireland had to win large numbers of Protestant workers from the Unionist Party to have any chance of checking the latter's supremacy. Only on this foundation could the party hope to build up its strength. The prospects of winning back Catholic support lost by a declaration of support for the constitution were arguably fair. Many Catholics were unmistakably dissatisfied with the Nationalists' abstentionists tactics and cared more for good government than gestures of defiance towards the state. If the NILP showed itself to be a viable alternative, then Catholic eagerness to get rid of the Unionists would be likely to rebound to its advantage.

It was all of course hypothetical, and Northern Ireland politics would always be fraught with problems capable of upsetting the most meticulous strategical calculations. With the benefit of hindsight it has to be noted that an eventual declaration in support of the constitution by the NILP in 1949 did not, in fact, help its immediate fortunes. Circumstances, however, had somewhat changed by then.

Midgley had no desire to spend the rest of his political career reliving the frustration of the 1920s and 1930s. He advanced what to him seemed the only conditions for a possible way out of the limbo the NILP had existed in since the state's formation. Reality dictated that the party take the British road: a close working partnership with the British Labour Party on top of an unequivocal commitment to the constitution.

This led him into conflict, not only with the anti-partitionists, but with what might be called the mainstream of the party. The mainstream consisted of those with moderate socialist or labourist views who were prepared to accept the constitution themselves but who did not want the party to declare in favour of it for fear of losing its non-sectarian image. It was this section of the party about which Midgley probably made miscalculations. After receiving, for so long, general consent for his leadership and policies, Midgley perhaps believed that he enjoyed enough support within the party to carry him through a confrontation with the anti-partitionists. He failed to realise, however, the extent to which he was antagonising many of those in the party for whom his style of leadership, especially after the outbreak of war, was all too self-obsessed and cavalier. These people did not want any confrontation between nationalist and unionist tendencies in the party and resented Midgley's precipitative manoeuvres. It was this group, epitomised by Leeburn and Thompson, which was instrumental in denying Midgley his designs for the party and so prompting his resignation.

There is another angle from which the affair can be viewed. Midgley was almost certainly tired of the internal quarrels in the party and wanted to end them one way or another. In provoking a confrontation over the question of the constitution, however, he may not have been too distressed by the prospect of the party coming down against him. Some of those who took part in, or were close to, the events of this period, have later argued that Midgley manoeuvered himself out of the NILP, feeling that it had become a shackle to his own personal ambitions.[92] Others have felt that Midgley was extremely frustrated with the impotence of the NILP and that there came a point when he could take no more of the party's problems.[93]

Certainly Midgley was none too circumspect in his handling of events late in 1942. If he had had no political designs except to remain as leader of the NILP, then it is unlikely that he would have gone as far out on a limb as he did. His refusal to wait for the final decision of the executive on the matter also suggests that he was ready to leave. While it is probably unlikely that the executive would have overturned the Parliamentary party decision, it could surely not have been a foregone conclusion that it would ratify it. Midgley's position may have found some sympathy on the executive which had, after all, generally reflected his outlook during the period of his leadership. Midgley may even have felt beforehand that his efforts to change the party's direction stood little chance of success; that it was a last token gesture of his intentions for the party which he knew would not now come to fruition. Perhaps, above all, there was the consideration that his association with the NILP would preclude the possibility of government office.

Midgley did not feel that he owed the Labour movement anything. He had given it over twenty years of indefatigable service and had braved much personal animus and hardship in the course of these years. More than any other Labour politician, he had suffered the sectarian wrath of both sides in Belfast. His defeat in Dock in 1938, coming after years of frustration, was a blow which gutted him of much of his political romanticism.[94]

Midgley was also genuinely drifting away from the main body of opinion in the NILP. By the time of the split it was clear that only a

minority within the party was prepared to endorse his fervent belief in a
progressive British Commonwealth of Nations. Many preferred his
analysis of world affairs to that forwarded by inveterate nationalists, but
their enthusiasm was tepid. For years Midgley had taken pains to
present Northern Ireland's political problems in an international context; no party conference would pass without a comprehensive survey by
Midgley of world developments. This emphasis on international affairs
has been seen as 'an error of judgement', a miscalculation of the issues
which concerned the Northern Ireland people.[95] It is not necessary to
deny that local issues were closer to people's hearts to contest this
viewpoint; it needs only be asked what good a parochial approach would
have done the NILP. Tensions created by the national question were
always present in the party; it made little sense to constantly aggravate
them into open conflicts which would cripple party morale. Either the
question had to be faced and a final decision taken – as Midgley sought
in 1942 – or an uneasy truce had to be called with an emphasis laid
instead on social, economic and international issues. Midgley's analyses
of world events through the 1930s were knowledgeable, challenging
and, for the most part, correct. More than anyone else he raised the level
of debate within the party and widened the scope of its concerns and its
awareness. In the end Midgley had to concede that his efforts achieved
only limited success. The majority of those in the NILP, like the people
of Northern Ireland generally, were inward-looking to an obsessive
degree. It is to Midgley's credit that he strove so relentlessly to break, or
at least dent, this self-enclosed myopia.

   In the epochal light in which he viewed the war Midgley was again in a
minority. Few others seemed to grasp as completely the implications of a
Nazi victory as Midgley did. Few others understood as well the true
nature of Nazi rule in Germany and the conditions which had brought it
about. Few others seemed really to believe that the very future of
western civilisation was imperilled, and that local issues, however
fundamental they were to people's everyday lives, assumed virtual irre-
levancy against this threat. To Midgley it was all the culmination of a sad
chapter of developments throughout the 1930s, the most significant of
which for him was the Spanish civil war. He felt that his political stances
throughout the 30s had been vindicated. Now, at this most crucial hour,
he believed that he deserved the chance to exert effective influence.

   In forming the Commonwealth Labour Party, however, Midgley
continued to court the risks of political impotence. He had cut himself
off from any association with people antagonistic to the constitution, but

he had not sought admission to the one party which would have virtually guaranteed him power: the Unionists. By the end of 1942 opposition to the Andrews government was growing inside the Unionist party, but a coalition involving non-Unionists still looked unlikely to come about.

A mixture, therefore, of intrigue, personality clashes, policy differences and personal ambition occasioned the split between Midgley and the NILP in 1942. He had led the party through difficult years and the attendant problems had begun to wear him down. He had had enough of leading a divided party in a divided society which judged men by sectarian criteria. His leadership can be criticised on several counts, not least that his own temperament was unsuited to deal with some of the emotive problems he faced. Against this, however, he constructed a coherent policy for the party and provided energetic, imaginative and visionary guidance. His – and the NILP's – tragedy was that his personal qualities were never properly harnessed to the collective will and organisation of the party.

Notes

1. Interview with David Wylie 12 June 1981.
2. In 1939 Midgley tried – and failed – to get official NUDAW backing for the proposal that he be put forward as Labour candidate for East Belfast at the following British General Election. Political General Secretary's Report, 5 July 1939, USDAW Records.
3. *Belfast News-Letter* 20 May 1938.
4. Ibid. 23 May 1938.
5. *The Workers' Republic* June 1938.
6. *Belfast News-Letter* 31 October 1938.
7. Ibid.
8. Ibid.
9. Ibid. 30 August 1938.
10. Contained in *Midgley Papers*.
11. *The Great Betrayal* pp. 6–7.
12. Ibid. p. 14.
13. Loc. cit.
14. *Irish Workers' Weekly* 6 May 1938. On the second reading of the Military Training Bill on 4 May 1939 Chamberlain said that the bill would not apply to Northern Ireland (House of Commons Debates 346, 2103–5).
15. See, for example, *Irish Workers' Weekly* 2 December 1939.
16. Report of Annual Conference 28–29 October 1939, contained in box file on the NILP, 329.14 (416) British Labour Party Archives.
17. Ibid.
18. Report of Special Conference 10 February 1940, contained in NILP box file 329.14 (416).
19. Ibid.

20. Loc. cit.
21. See, for example, *Irish Workers' Weekly* 11 May 1940.
22. 'What Labour is Fighting For', *Northern Whig* 2 July 1940.
23. Harbinson, op. cit. pp. 105–6.
24. See note 14.
25. Farrell op. cit. p. 158. It should be noted, however, that unemployment in Britain still stood at 900,000 in January 1940.
26. The officially appointed historian of Northern Ireland's part in the war wrote that the government was 'slow at the outset to develop her civilian war effort'. J. W. Blake, *Northern Ireland in the Second World War*, Belfast, 1956, pp. 368–9.
27. Farrell op. cit. p. 158.
28. Blake op. cit. p. 171.
29. Farrell op. cit. pp. 154–5.
30. See, for example, correspondence reproduced in the Spender Diaries, D715/14 p. 63, PRONI.
31. Report of NILP conference 14 December 1940, NILP box file 329.14 (416).
32. *Irish Workers' Weekly* 4 and 11 January 1941.
33. Report of NILP conference 14 December 1940. With regard to the debate on the Special Powers Act, Midgley said: '. . . the Labour Party in NI had always felt that any Act that could be used for political repression was undemocratic. At the same time, the Executive believed that the present was a most unsuitable and inappropriate time to carry on a campaign like that suggested. It was ridiculous to try to embarrass the Labour Party in a time of war, when there were matters of greater importance to be attended to.'
34. Farrell op. cit. p. 159.
35. Chairman's Address to NILP Annual Conference 25 October 1941. Reprinted as a pamphlet, *Labour in Northern Ireland, Midgley Papers.*
36. See *Labour Progress* (newspaper of the NILP) April 1942 and May 1942.
37. *Belfast News-Letter* 27 October 1941.
38. Executive Council Minutes 1941 No. 751, USDAW Records.
39. *Belfast News-Letter* 25 November 1941.
40. Ibid. 21 November 1941. It is probable that Midgley had been in touch with Herbert Morrison with whom he had struck up a close friendship.
41. *Belfast News-Letter* 26 November 1941.
42. *Belfast Telegraph* 29 November 1941.
43. *Northern Whig* 23 November 1941.
44. *Belfast News-Letter* 5 December 1941.
45. Ibid.
46. Loc. cit.
47. *Northern Whig* 5 December 1941.
48. *Belfast Telegraph* 5 December 1941.
49. P. Addison, *The Road to 1945*, London, 1977 p. 15.
50. Ibid.
51. Spender Diaries D715/18, 12 January 1942, PRONI.
52. N.I. House of Commons Debates XXIV, 2562–88.

53. Ibid., 1615.
54. See Spender Diaries D715/18 24 January 1942, PRONI.
55. In *Labour Progress* June 1942, Hugh Downey (NILP Vice-Chairman) claimed that Midgley's resolution in favour of government reconstruction did not mean that he wanted to join the government.
56. N.I. House of Commons Debates XXV, 1408.
57. *Belfast News-Letter* 8 June 1942.
58. *Northern Whig* 10 July 1942.
59. Ibid. 11 July 1942.
60. *Belfast News-Letter* 7 January 1942.
61. See *Labour Progress* February 1942.
62. Interview with James Kelly 25 March 1982. Kelly was a journalist on the *Irish Independent* and a close confidant of Jack Beattie.
63. Harbinson op. cit. p. 114.
64. Corrigan to W. Robinson, Political General Secretary, 24 December 1942, Union File A(22), USDAW Records.
65. Chairman's Address NILP conference 31 October 1942. Reproduced as a pamphlet *The Pilgrimage of Hope, Midgley Papers*.
66. Ibid.
67. *Belfast Telegraph* 21 November 1942.
68. The declaration was reproduced in *Ulster for the Commonwealth* (1943), a pamphlet issued by the Commonwealth Labour Party. Contained in *Midgley Papers*.
69. *Ulster for the Commonwealth*.
70. See Harbinson op. cit. pp. 122–3, and the Spender Diaires D715/20, 27 November 1942, PRONI.
71. This statement was published in the *Belfast News-Letter* 17 December 1942.
72. See Harbinson op. cit. pp. 123–4.
73. Minutes of meeting of the Northern Ireland Parliamentary Labour Party 4 December 1942, *Papers of Mr Sam Napier*.
74. 'Official Statement by the Executive Committee of the NILP on the Expulsion of Alderman Harry Midgley J.P., M.P.', *Labour Progress* January 1943.
75. Ibid., and *Belfast News-Letter* 17 December 1942.
76. *Belfast News-Letter* 17 December 1942.
77. *Labour Progress* January 1943.
78. *Belfast News-Letter* 17 December 1942.
79. Harbinson op. cit. pp. 128–9.
80. Midgley to Joseph Hallsworth 31 December 1942, Union File A(22), USDAW Records.
81. Correspondence between Corrigan and Shepherd 17 and 26 February 1943, Union File A(22), USDAW Records.
82. Harbinson op. cit. pp. 129–30.
83. Ibid. p. 130.
84. Harbinson notes (p. 130) that West and Central Belfast branches both declared their support for the executive, and (p. 132) that Coleraine Labour Party met in January 1943 and voted unanimously in support of the

executive after it had been reported that the branch would follow Midgley out of the party.

85. Midgley to Joseph Hallsworth 24 December 1942, Union File A(22), USDAW Records.
86. *Labour Progress* January 1943.
87. Ibid.
88. The NILP stated that its main aim was to 'unite the people of all creeds in Northern Ireland', *Labour Progress* January 1943.
89. See next chapter.
90. *Labour Progress* January 1943.
91. Thompson told the writer in an interview (23 June 1981) that Beattie had been elected because he was the senior parliamentarian. This may well have been an important consideration, but it is very doubtful if it was the only one.
92. Interviews with William Logan 16 June 1981; Frank Hanna 6 March 1981; Bob Thompson 27 June 1981; Malachy Gray 18 February 1981; David Wylie 18 June 1981.
93. Interview with John de Courcy Ireland 6 June 1981; and Saidie Patterson 17 November 1980.
94. See his post-election article in *Forward* 5 February 1938.
95. Harbinson op. cit. p. 267.

Chapter Eight
Cabinet and Commonwealth (1942–1947)

I

Towards the end of 1942 the tide of war turned in favour of the Allies. For Ulster Prime Minister J. M. Andrews, however, there was little sense of euphoria. His government continued to come under heavy critical fire, and it soon became obvious that a deep split in the Unionist ranks was about to materialise.

Back in July 1942, Andrews had alluded to a new party 'being got up' which in his view represented an 'attempt to divide our Unionist party by a conspiracy'.[1] Andrews tried to ward off criticism by expedient moves. In July 1942 he rashly committed his government to a programme of post-war reconstruction which had been drawn up without the guidance or blessing of the British Treasury. The latter soon made clear its displeasure.[2] Andrews's expediency lost him the confidence of his civil servants whose chief, Sir Wilfrid Spender, saw in Sir Basil Brooke, then Minister of Commerce, a man who would govern more responsibly.[3]

Andrews and his 'old guard' still controlled the powerfully influential Ulster Unionist Council, but his position within the Unionist Party in parliament was becoming increasingly precarious. At a Parliamentary party meeting in January 1943 ten MPs voiced the need for changes in the government.[4] In February the government lost an Imperial by-election for the seat of West Belfast, the intervention of an Independent Unionist helping to secure victory for Jack Beattie and the NILP. More critical meetings of the Parliamentary party were held in March and April during which Andrews attempted to hold on to office. Brooke made the Prime Minister's position all the more difficult by resigning in March and refusing to form a government in conjunction with Andrews.[5]

Finally, on 28 April Andrews recognised his cause as being hopeless and resigned. Brooke replaced him and announced his cabinet on 6 May. The 'old guard' of Dawson Bates, Milne-Barbour and Lord Glentoran made way for a younger breed of Unionist. The government was not, however, completely drawn from the ranks of the Unionist Party. To the post of Minister of Public Security Brooke appointed the first non-Unionist to enter the Northern Ireland government: Harry Midgley.

II

In his memoirs some years later, Brooke wrote of his decision to bring Midgley into the government as a move which 'surprised some of my colleagues and shocked some others'. Brooke believed that the government in Northern Ireland should take on the appearance of a coalition, 'if only to forestall possible criticism of Stormont from across the water'. On many points Brooke and Midgley held opposing views but, as Brooke stressed in his memoirs, on the fundamental issue of the constitution they were in complete agreement. 'Many in the Unionist party', he wrote, 'were critical of the move, but in the end they agreed, some of them unwillingly.'[6]

It may have been the case that Brooke's difficulties in getting his colleagues to accept Midgley were smoothed over, initially, by his having them believe that Midgley intended to join the Unionist Party. At a meeting of the Unionist Parliamentary Party on 15 June, Col. S. B. Hall-Thompson asked Brooke if Midgley was joining the Unionist Party or not. Brooke replied that he had spoken to Midgley on the subject and that Midgley was going to join and would take an opportunity to state his position publicly.[7] This is a curious statement for Midgley did not in fact join the Unionist Party at this time. He remained Commonwealth Labour Party chairman throughout his time in government and, as will be detailed below, resigned at the end of the war in order to fight the ensuing election as a Commonwealth Labour candidate. There is no other evidence to be found that Midgley was about to join the Unionists at this time. All of his political pronouncements merely underlined the wide gulf which existed between him and the bulk of the Unionist Party, including Brooke, on social and economic questions. He was often to state later that he had been invited into the government because the Prime Minister had declared him sound on the issue of the union between Britain and Northern Ireland, and on the need to intensify the Province's war effort.[8] In addition, there is the evidence of Brooke's memoirs, alluded to above, which make clear that a 'coalition' government rather than another all-Unionist administration was desired by Brooke. In his anxiety to establish his new broader-based government, and to stifle objections from within his party, Brooke may have found it expedient to distort the truth about Midgley's proposed party allegiance. There is also the possibility that Midgley gave him cause to believe that he did in fact intend to join the Unionists in the near future. It is doubtful, however, that Midgley would have deliberately misled Brooke, by this time a personal friend, and so risked causing him political embarrassment.

It was freely rumoured in the Labour press that Midgley had accepted the Unionist whip soon after joining the government.[9] There is nothing to suggest, however, that this was more than a rumour. Midgley was certainly on good personal terms with Unionists such as Edmund Warnock who wished to see the party commit itself to the social security recommendations of the Beveridge Report. Had Midgley believed that Warnock's views were likely to prevail inside the Unionist Party, he may have considered moving into its ranks. Such a radicalisation of the Unionist party may have been what J. M. Andrews had in mind when he alluded to a new party 'being got up'. As will be discussed below, however, there was more reason for Midgley, at this juncture, to keep his distance from the Unionist Party.

The new government was given a guarded welcome in most Unionist quarters. The *Belfast News-Letter* and *Northern Whig* retained a lot of sympathy for the 'old guard', but the *Belfast Telegraph* approved heartily of the changes and, in particular, of the elevation of Midgley: 'Mr Harry Midgley's inclusion is timely recognition of a man who has the courage of his principles and whose ability has made him a conspicuous figure in public life for many years.'[10] The *Telegraph* applauded the new 'mix' in the cabinet with its younger flavour, and thought that it would be 'free from the lack of progressiveness which it is difficult for the public mind to dissociate from years of continuous office'.[11]

The Nationalist press was predictably hostile to the new Prime Minister whose sectarian speeches of the 1930s lingered odiously in the Catholic community's memory. The *Irish News* dismissed the notion of coalition government and described the cabinet as 'all-Unionist'.[12] The *Derry Journal* was more verbose:

As Mr Grant, who graduated to Stormont office through the 'Labour Unionist Association', has been retained, so Mr. Midgley has been brought in by the Unionist back door entrance which he styled 'the Commonwealth Labour Party' for a very specific purpose, namely to convey the impression in London where coalition Government is at present the thing, that six county Labour is represented in the new Stormont Government. The fact, however, that Mr. Grant's Association is a mere subsection of the Unionist Party and that Mr. Midgley for his part has been labouring under a deep sense of humiliation through his expulsion from the six county Labour Party, and that the thing he set up in opposition to it is still less representative of Labour in the six counties, shows how hollow is the pretence put forth in a Unionist write-up that 'Sir Basil Brooke has endeavoured to ensure direct representation of the industrial workers of varying political shades.' Forsooth![13]

The Northern Ireland Labour Party jeered at developments from the sidelines and, unsurprisingly, no-one jeered louder than Beattie. At Stormont on 11 May in the Vote of Confidence Debate he delivered an acerbic personal attack on Midgley in the course of a long tirade against the new government. He railed:

I want to say that one member of this new Government belonged to the Labour Party once upon a time, and I leave him to the workers. They know his quality. This much I will say; Quisling and the turn-coat are objects of contempt in all countries, but nowhere more so than in Northern Ireland. When the traitors of one party join with the traitors of another party they should form it into a limited company and call it 'Treachery Incorporated'.[14]

Beattie went on to have a field day with quotations and anecdotes concerning Midgley's past, pungently citing the declaration against partition which Midgley had signed during the 1921 election campaign.[15]

Midgley returned fire with equal venom. The House, he said, had listened to 'one of the most cowardly and contemptible performances that has been carried out in this Parliament . . .'[16] After alleging that Beattie had had the speech written for him, Midgley went on to defend his changed political outlook:

The position as I see it is that in a changing world . . . we cannot afford in 1943 to take up the identical attitude we adopted in 1923. The intervening 20 years have seen tremendous changes. The world is more interdependent today than ever it was before. We feel the repercussions of shocks in one part of the world more rapidly and completely than ever before. We have eliminated time and space by the development of radio and aviation, with the result that conditions throughout the world are very different today to what they were a generation ago. Furthermore, events have taken place in the last 20 years, not only in distant parts of the world, but at home, which have compelled many of us who thought from a certain political angle a generation ago to change our minds.[17]

The Communist Party, by now a Northern Ireland party in every sense, welcomed the change of government and gave Midgley a smoother ride than his erstwhile comrades in the NILP. Communist membership in Northern Ireland reached over 2,000 in 1943 as the party promoted a patriotic win-the-war image.[18]

While the new government's critics were more than justified in denying that it was a coalition in the proper sense of the term, it was none the less as near to it as any government could have come in the context of Northern Ireland politics at this time. The Unionists could not have taken the political risk of incorporating Nationalists into the government. The IRA threat, the attitude adopted by Cardinal MacRory, and the general indifference of the minority community to the war effort made co-operation at governmental level inconceivable. As always, the intransigence of one side reinforced that of the other. To most Unionists co-operation with Nationalists in any sphere of activity was unthinkable. The position of the NILP as a party was somewhat different. Its stance on the issue of the constitution was ambiguous and there were representatives of all shades of opinion on the war inside its ranks. After Midgley's departure, however, there was no-one in parliament representing the party who enthusiastically supported the war effort. Neither Beattie nor Agnew would have been likely to join a predominantly Unionist administration, conscious as they both were of the strong anti-partitionist support they depended upon. Only if the NILP had had men such as Getgood or Leeburn in parliament could it have made a plausible case for its inclusion in a coalition government. The inclusion of Independent Unionist members alone, if they had been willing,[19] would not have supplied the Labour credentials of someone like Midgley which were so necessary to give the government the appearance of being broadly based. In the circumstances of 1943 Midgley was the only political figure whose outlook was compatible with what the Unionists saw as the imperative questions of the day, and who was personally willing to become a member of the new government. As was made clear earlier, even Midgley's position was far from secure in the light of the reluctance displayed by many Unionists to accept him.

At the first meeting of the new cabinet Brooke expressed the desire that he and his ministers should work as a team,

unitedly resolved to maintain the existing constitutional position, to bring greater drive and energy into Northern Ireland's war effort, and to advance as far as possible the government's preparations for dealing with the problems of the post-war period.

Brooke warned that changes would be made if they were found to be necessary and that nobody's position, including his own, was a 'life appointment'.[20]

Midgley made a confident debut in cabinet, stressing along with the Minister of Home Affairs, William Lowry, KC, that the government should make clear that it had 'the fullest sympathy with the claims and aspirations of labour' and that they were prepared 'to fulfil their obligations in the letter and spirit to both workers and employers'. Although not technically within his formal brief, Midgley was concerned at the prevalence of strikes and labour unrest and offered the following suggestions in dealing with disputes:

(1) The machinery of negotiation and arbitration should be speeded up.
(2) Arrangements should be made for two or three tribunals to sit simultaneously.
(3) Decisions of the tribunal should be made retrospective and not merely come into effect from the next pay day.[21]

To Midgley it was vital that the government depart from the image presented by past Unionist administrations in regard to labour disputes: that of invariable sympathy with the management's side of the question and thinly veiled disregard for representations made by the trade union movement. He realised that the war had led to an increase in social and economic expectations and that, as in the case of the Great War, many people would demand material compensation for the sacrifices they had been called upon to make. To avoid a possible rupture in war production, workers had to be convinced that the government appreciated their efforts and that they would not go unrewarded. In this respect Midgley also urged that the government outline its policy in relation to unemployment:

He [Midgley] suggested that the figures should be analysed showing the extent of the 'hard core' of unemployables and the number who could not easily be absorbed into the war effort. He also suggested that some attempt should be made to anticipate the temporary suspension of workers arising out of the existence of bottlenecks and the changes in production. These pay-offs gave rise to considerable discontent and at least the reasons for them should be explained to the workers.[22]

Right from the start of his period in office, therefore, Midgley attempted to infuse the new administration with a spirit of respectful co-operation towards Labour and Labour representation. It was an effort which largely succeeded, for Brooke was nothing if not pragmatic and realised that the patriarchal high-handedness of past Unionist governments in response to the claims of Labour had no place in the new era being fashioned out of the war. Midgley also tried to impress on Brooke the need to clarify the government's policy for post-war reconstruction. In September 1943 he called for 'an authoritative statement' on the matter and urged the government to draw up national rather than local plans to deal with such issues as housing and mobility of labour.[23]

By the time of his entry into government, the war situation had so altered for the better that Midgley's duties as Public Security Minister were largely confined to ensuring that civil defence arrangements were in order and that civilian morale was maintained at a high level. He addressed numerous meetings and rallies of Civil Defence and War Savings groups throughout Northern Ireland, the lofty tone of his rhetoric supplying a touch of Churchillian grandeur in his efforts to ensure that the community spirit did not flag. In October 1943 he warned an audience in Coleraine that Germany was far from beaten and would become more dangerous as she headed for defeat;[24] he was determined that should another wave of bombing occur, Ulster would be better prepared, both materially and psychologically. He wanted nothing to distract attention from the effort such a state of preparedness required. Thus he spoke out regularly, and with increasing censoriousness, against strikes.[25] In cabinet he urged that the government take measures to ensure that certain owners of commercial buildings and factories provided code standard shelter for their employees. He alleged that the improvement in the war situation had made these people 'dilatory' in the fulfilment of their obligations. The issue brought Midgley into conflict with the Minister of Finance, J. Maynard Sinclair, who was concerned to save the money Midgley proposed to spend on shelters. The Minister of Labour, William Grant, supported Midgley by arguing that the provision of shelters would provide work for a number of unemployed men in the building trades. It was then agreed that the shelters be provided.[26]

Midgley enjoyed the esteem and confidence of Brooke, and the two men found much common ground outside the realm of political ideology. Both believed, for example, that Northern Ireland's image in Britain could be substantially improved, and that there was a need for the government to conduct a better system of public relations both in Ulster and outside it.[27] One of the most welcome developments for the government in this connection was the interest taken in Ulster affairs and the glowing tribute paid to the Province's loyalty by Herbert Morrison, Midgley's opposite number in the British government. As Minister of Home Security and Home Secretary, Morrison had to pay attention to Northern Ireland in terms both of civil defence and of its constitutional position. He visited the Province several times during the war and struck up a friendship with Brooke. Before the war he had come to know Midgley very well, and it seems likely that Midgley proved influential in persuading Morrison to the pro-Ulster viewpoint which he continued to hold after the war.[28] Midgley's presence in the government may also have been a factor in winning the support of the Secretary of State for Scotland, Tom Johnston, former editor of *Forward* and friend of Midgley's since the 1920s. Johnston, like Morrison, paid visits to Ulster and contrasted its loyalty favourably with the policy of neutrality pursued by Eire.

Midgley was even more concerned that the government should be seen to act positively in the realm of social problems. This concern focused, in late 1943, on the issue of wartime housing. During the inter-war period the housing problem in Northern Ireland had been badly neglected as central and local government authorities argued over responsibility.[29] The air raids of 1941 had rendered the situation quite desperate. The Minister of Home Affairs, William Lowry, attempted to get the British Treasury to underwrite an extensive house-building scheme, but at first could only receive the promise of materials for 250 houses to be built over a six-month period.[30] While sharing Lowry's dismay at the inadequacy of this offer, Midgley was anxious that the scheme should proceed straight away. For this the co-operation of the Belfast Corporation was necessary and it was not forthcoming. The corporation pointed out that Belfast had been denied grants for slum clearance during the inter-war period and that this entitled them to preferential treatment now. Lowry sympathised with this attitude but Midgely was impatient with it. On 25 October 1943 Midgley presented a memorandum to the cabinet on the subject. He argued that there was no time to waste on lengthy negotiations between the government and corporation and that early completion of the emergency scheme was imperative. In order to get round its difficulties, he advocated that the government undertake to build the houses or, alternatively, set up a Housing Trust to do it. This latter course was Midgley's personal preference.[31]

Lowry opposed Midgley's plan fearing that 'there would be opposition on the part of the Belfast Corporation and the general public to any proposal which encroached on the functions of local authorities'.[32] This view was shared by Sir Wilfrid Spender who feared that such intervention by the central government would set an undesirable precedent.[33]

By the end of November 1943, the Treasury had agreed to increase its offer to 750 houses and the scheme was able to proceed.[34] In view of this it might be argued that Midgley had decided prematurely in favour of measures which could only undermine the status of the corporation, a body on which he had served for over eighteen years.[35] He seemed, moreover, surprisingly willing to accept what was a palpably meagre offer. On the other hand, his anxiety that some action, however limited, should be taken to alleviate the distress which existed in the city, was understandable and commendable. There was, after all, still the opportunity to bargain for more houses while the ones promised were being built. The episode perhaps illustrates how keen Midgley was to exercise power in the cause of social benefit, now that he was in a position to actually do so. After years of having his schemes and suggestions defeated both in parliament and in the corporation, he was clearly determined to make the most of his new circumstances.

In September 1943 Sir Francis Floud, a British civil servant, came to Northern Ireland to investigate the workings of the government. He drew up a report which suggested how best the ministries' functions should be redistributed. Out of this it was decided to combine the functions of the Ministry of Public Security with those of Home Affairs, while creating a new Ministry of Health and Local Government. Public Security had been an emergency ministry and by 1944 there was little to justify its continuation. On 30 May 1944 at Stormont, Midgley made his last speech in this capacity:

I have valued my year of office as Minister of Public Security. It has given me an insight into the finest qualities of our people, and I look forward with confidence to the day when the goodwill and public spirit that they have shown so generously and so spontaneously under the stress of war shall be turned to the paths of peace and to the setting up of a new and finer civilisation in this Ulster of which we are so proud.[36]

It was widely predicted that Midgley would inherit the new Ministry of Health.[37] His year in office, however, had done little to soften the attitudes of those Unionists who resented his presence in the government. On 23 March 1944 Spender recorded in his diary that,

the Unionist members are not ready to accept Mr. Midgley as Minister of Health, and this will create very great difficulties for the Prime Minister in view of the fact that the Ministry of Public Security is obviously only of a temporary nature. If, therefore, he appoints a new Minister of Health, Mr. Midgley will almost certainly be compelled to retire.[38]

The Unionist members concerned probably considered the new ministry too potentially important in view of proposed post-war changes to be filled by a non-Unionist, and a professed socialist to boot. They undoubtedly desired Midgley's removal from the cabinet altogether, but in this they were not to get their way. Brooke, probably intent on preserving the government's 'coalition' appearance, allocated the new ministry to William Grant, and moved Midgley to the Ministry of Labour. The appointments dated from 1 June 1944.

III

While displaying a facility for practical politics in government, Midgley continued to express his idealism through the medium of the Commonwealth Labour Party (CLP).[39] He remained the party's chairman and leader throughout the war while in government, and contributed regularly to the party newspaper *Justice*. His commitment to the party was total. It was his invention and he was always in control of it. There was little criticism of his leadership, a fact which was hardly surprising given that the backbone of the party organisation comprised members of his family, and friends and admirers of long standing. His son, Harry Junior, edited *Justice* before leaving to serve in the armed forces, his daughter Marie was literature secretary, and his son-in-law William Kennedy was prominent as a speaker and organiser. In addition, his wife Eleanor served on the committee of the party's branch in North Belfast.

Some well-known names from Ulster's socialist past followed Midgley into the CLP. Bob McLung, a veteran campaigner from the early days of the Belfast ILP, became an agent of the party's Welfare Bureau; Alex Adams, NILP parliamentary candidate in the 1920s, took an active role in the party's Newtownards branch; and Hugh Gemmell, one of Ireland's most skilful socialist propagandists of the 1920s, taught a weekly course to party members on the art of public speaking. Gemmell's wife was an active member of the North Belfast branch.

The party gradually built up its strength until, by November 1943, it boasted branches in North, South and East Belfast, Bangor, Coleraine, Lisburn, Lurgan, Newtownards and Whitehouse.[40] Initially, Milton Gordon's Londonderry Labour Party had affiliated to the CLP, but in July 1943 Gordon severed his connection and his local party organisation followed suit. Gordon had been elected vice-chairman of the party at its inception but only attended two meetings of the executive before resigning.

The CLP believed that radical changes in Northern Ireland politics would be wrought by the war. In the first months of 1943 the party took encouragement from the internal troubles of the Unionist Party, believing that they would severely weaken the Unionists' grip on political life to the benefit of a party like the CLP. Harry Midgley Junior wrote:

It is plain to be seen that the days of the old party are numbered. The old catchcries no longer act with such great effect upon the citizens. The public has been taught through the experiences of the last few years of international conflict and co-operation and by necessary wartime internal reorganisation that many of the former conceptions of the manner in which the affairs of mankind should be controlled no longer hold water. They have also learned that some conceptions of society once considered Utopian are practical and possible.[41]

The CLP believed that its combination of resolute loyalty to the British link and a progressive social policy for post-war reconstruction would give it an appeal to the majority community in Northern Ireland which would eclipse that of a reactionary and divided Unionist Party and the nationalist-tainted NILP. As Midgley Junior put it:

The Commonwealth Labour party can be the saviour of Northern Ireland's future. It is the only political party in Ulster with a policy to fit the times. It recognises that both imperialism and nationalism are philosophies of the past.[42]

In the pamphlet *Ulster for the Commonwealth*, Midgley justified his party's adoption of the cause of the British Commonwealth with reference to four basic points. First, he stressed that the people of Northern Ireland were an 'English speaking community with our roots deeply buried in the history and traditions of many generations of English, Scots, Irish and – to a smaller extent – Welsh, who were our forebears'. This led him to repudiate the assumption of a 'pure and undefiled Gaelic origin in respect of our people'. Secondly, he claimed that the Northern Ireland state set up by the Government of Ireland Act 1920 had been accepted then by a majority of the Irish people, and was 'ardently believed in' by the majority of Ulster people. Thirdly, he argued that there could be no real unity throughout the whole of Ireland without the consent of the Ulster people: 'Unity under any other conditions would be artificial.' Lastly, he rejected arguments that the ending of partition would bring social and economic benefits to Northern Ireland. He held, on the contrary, that such a move would 'depress our standard of life, lower our social services, impoverish the mass of our people and destroy for many years to come the expectation (created by the possibility of the Beveridge Scheme) of an enlarged and expanded system of Social Security'.[43]

The CLP made much of the disparity in social benefits between

Northern Ireland and Eire and enthusiastically endorsed the proposals
outlined in the Beveridge Report (1942) which promised an even more
comprehensive and improved system of social security for Britain after
the war. *Justice* published several articles on the Beveridge proposals
including a résumé of the scheme as a whole by Midgley.[44] Midgley was
anxious to scotch suggestions that the scheme would be too costly, and
to emphasise the contrast between his party's unqualified support for
the proposals and the equivocation of the Unionists.[45] At Stormont in
March 1943 during a debate on Beveridge, Midgley declared on behalf
of the CLP: 'We believe in the Report not as end in itself, but a means to
an end. We believe it is the direction in which the social development of
mankind, and mankind's destiny will win through this terrific conflict.'[46]

A logical corollary to an endorsement of Beveridge was an acceptance
of the principle of social and economic planning. This indeed was the
policy of the CLP, but the party was explicit in its conception of such
planning as socialist in character. An article in *Justice* by 'Fusilier' in
June 1944 adumbrated the party's commitment to Beveridge, to a
system of comprehensive education, and to communal ownership and
control of industry. 'Fusilier' argued that the slogan 'Production for *use*
rather than production for *profit*!' was 'sound enough still', and ended by
proclaiming that they in the CLP had taken 'the banner of socialism
from unworthy hands'.[47] *Justice* also reproduced approvingly excerpts
from Sir Richard Acland's book *Our Struggle* which argued the case for
common ownership as 'the only way'.[48] Midgley himself stated the
party's position trenchantly:

... the Commonwealth Labour party is bound to emphasise that the power of
democracy in the future to maintain international peace is, in the long run,
inseparable from the growth, in each country, of the common ownership of the
main instruments of production and their co-ordinated planning for common
ends ... The private empires of privilege, whether in oil, munitions, or miner-
als, whether in power or the basic means of transport, are bound to frustrate the
fulfilment of democracy at home and the maintenance of peace abroad ... Only
the rapid socialisation of these instruments of production will enable us to move
to that plane of common action where co-operation for abundance instead of
division through scarcity is the chief motive in international effort.[49]

At the first annual conference in June 1944, the party passed
resolutions calling for the implementation of the Beveridge Report, the
establishment of a central economic planning bureau in Northern Ireland, a 'comprehensive housing programme', and 'equality of opportunity from the primary school to the university by the provision of publicly
controlled schools which all children may attend'. The latter resolution

also called for the raising of the school-leaving age to 16.[50] The CLP gave especial attention to education, again in an effort to distance itself from the Unionists. This it also sought to do by depicting the Unionist Party as hankering after a return to the conditions of pre-war years: wealth and privileges for the few, and social and economic misery for many.

The CLP thus attempted to corrode the Unionist supremacy in two ways: first of all by showing that the Unionists did not have a monopoly on loyalty to Britain and on commitment to the war effort; and secondly, that the Unionists were hidebound by a retrogressive social outlook which ill-equipped them to lead Ulster into the post-war world. Midgley did not stop making such political points at CLP meetings while serving in the government. Despite his admiration for Brooke,[51] and his concern not to cause any political controversy during the war, he was still careful to maintain his party's momentum. This further enraged those Unionists who had opposed his entry into the government.

The CLP found common ground with the Common Wealth Party in Britain. The latter was founded in July 1942, and won three wartime by-elections in the socialist cause.[52] It was led by Sir Richard Acland, a Christian Socialist whose earnest idealism fired large audiences at meetings throughout the country. Common Wealth reflected Acland's personal ideal of ethical socialism. It stood for the New Jerusalem of selflessness and classlessness. This kind of moral evangelism was echoed by the CLP in Northern Ireland. Like Acland, Midgley was fond of couching his message in terms of a spiritual revival,[53] while his son, Harry Junior, wrote floridly in *Justice* about the CLP's 'charter of upliftment', and the party's view of socialism as 'a burning faith – a moral conviction'.[54] In his address to the CLP party conference in 1945 Midgley claimed that, in submitting candidates for the local elections, the party was 'actuated by the supreme ideal of substituting social service and social consciousness for the sordid struggles of commercial rivalry and selfish individual gain'.[55]

Like the CLP, Common Wealth took much of its early inspiration from the Beveridge proposals and the new post-war order which they seemed to presage. As noted earlier, Acland's espousal of common ownership and his commitment to a full-blooded socialist society, were enthusiastically endorsed by the CLP. The two parties took well-established arguments for socialism and dressed them up in an evangelical rhetoric which, in the circumstances of wartime Britain and Northern Ireland, could make a stirring impact.

The CLP, however, by virtue of its pro-Britishness, could only hope to win converts among the majority Protestant community. Such questions of national identity did not trouble Common Wealth in Britain. While Common Wealth was free to deliberate on its concept of a new socialist order, the CLP in Northern Ireland spent much of its time and energies in convincing the Protestant population of its loyalty. The 'Commonwealth' tag in connection with the CLP owed more to the party's concern to present a pro-British image than to a conception of a new co-operative, socialist society. The circumstances in which the party came into existence in Northern Ireland ensured that Midgley would spend as much, if not more, of his time denouncing 'outworn nationalism', as he would excoriating the conservative views of certain Unionists. Common Wealth in Britain, moreover, did not hold the eulogistic view of the British Commonwealth of Nations as did Midgley and the CLP.

There were also important differences in the social composition of the respective parties. Acland appealed to the middle class and believed that the new managerial class would aid the revolution he sought.[56] The typical Common Wealth member has been described as 'a comfortably off schoolteacher living in one of the pleasanter suburbs of Liverpool, who had never been active in politics before, and quite likely would never be active in them again'.[57] In contrast, Midgley made his appeal to the skilled Protestant workers, the likes of whom had returned him at Willowfield in 1941. The skilled worker, dissatisfied with the Toryism of the Unionist party but fiercely loyal to the British connection, was the typical CLP member. Most of those who joined the CLP – at least in the early stages – had been involved in politics before, mostly in the NILP. This group constituted a personal following which Midgley had built up over his years as leader of the NILP. The CLP did, however, recruit a number of middle class, professional people who were probably more liberal than socialist in their outlook. Perhaps typical of these were Alex Mylchreest, a masseur, and Billy Lyttle, a dentist, both from Belfast.[58] Midgley was to find to his cost, however, that the Protestant middle class would not lightly forsake the Unionist Party.

Towards the end of the war Midgley identified the CLP with the internationalist message of Wendall Wilkie, an American statesman whose peregrinations around the globe in 1942 had moved him to write a book called *One World.* In it he stressed the growing interdependence of nations and called for international co-operation on a veritably global scale.[59] His thoughts were echoed by Henry Wallace, Vice-President of the USA, who urged that America take the initiative in bringing about a new world democracy after the war.[60] Midgley quoted both men copiously in his writings and public addresses. He used their pronouncements on international co-operation and political and economic democracy to fortify his contention that the day of nationalism and imperialism had passed.[61] Wallace and Wilkie both advocated extensive systems of international planning to make available to everyone the goods and resources they required. It was a theme Midgley often took up:

If we planned for peace along these and similar lines, we might preserve the peace of the world by eliminating the economic incentives which made for war. But if the nations went back to the mad competitive scramble for markets, and if, within each nation, individuals went back to the sordid struggle for profits regardless of the national well-being, then within another generation we would once again be faced with war.[62]

For Midgley and the CLP the concept of the British Commonwealth was not an end in itself. It was not a substitute nationalism. Rather it was looked upon as an instrument of international co-operation. 'The ramifications of the British Commonwealth', said Midgley in November 1943, 'can be extended, not for any acquisitive point of view, but from the point of view of giving the right of equal citizenship to any other part of the world based upon our British conception of citizenship.'[63] Such an interest in – and positive view of – the British Commonwealth was not, as has been noted, the hallmark of Acland's Common Wealth Party. Nor was it a notable feature of the British Labour Party's outlook. Before the war only 'a handful of dedicated enthusiasts'[64] in the latter party had shown concern for colonial and commonwealth affairs, although this situation was to change, to some extent, in the post-war period.[65]

Midgley also looked forward to the establishment of a Commonwealth Parliament, 'for the purpose of common protection and common resistance to aggression, and for the building up of world trade'.[66] Performing his feats of oratory on such an international stage must have been the stuff of his political dreams.

IV

By the time of his move to the Ministry of Labour, Midgley was becoming distinctly uneasy about the amount of Unionist antagonism to his presence in the government. He was sufficiently concerned to write for advice on the matter to Herbert Morrison. In a letter dated 29 May 1944, Midgley wrote:

For some time past a number of back-bench Conservatives (probably assisted or prompted privately by former Conservative front-benchers) have been trying to make the Prime Minister's position difficult because of my presence in the Government. The P.M. has given me his confidence and support right through, and my transfer to the Ministry of Labour is further evidence of this.

The latest form of antagonism to the P.M. is due to the fact that our Party, the Commonwealth Labour Party, has organised a number of open-air meetings throughout the area, so that our point of view may be presented to the people. Although I have consistently refrained from this form of campaign and have confined myself to addressing private meetings and conferences of our members, and devoting practically all my time to my Ministerial duties; nevertheless, the back-bench Conservatives – or Unionists – have now approached the P.M. with the claim that I am violating the principles of the coalition as observed in Great Britain. Briefly, their claim is that our Party should hold no public meetings in constituencies held by Unionist M.P.'s. They admit, of course, our right to hold meetings in any district where we have a branch, but only for the purpose of addressing members. This means that as I am the only Parliamentary Representative of the Commonwealth Labour Party our members would practically be confined to doing public work in one constituency. The Unionist back-benchers claim that this is the position in Great Britain, so I should esteem your observations on this matter.

Midgley went on to say that if the Unionists' viewpoint was upheld he would have to consider the advisability of resigning from the government.[67]

Morrison wrote back to say that he had made speeches in various parts of the country in Labour and non-Labour constituencies sometimes under the auspices of the Labour Party and sometimes of the Ministry of Information. He added that he had also addressed Labour Party Conferences covering a considerable number of constituencies represented by MPs from various political parties, his speeches being published. No objections, he said, had been taken to his conduct. Morrison went on to add, however, that there was a duty of those who were members of the Coalition government:

to avoid in our speeches attacks on our colleagues of other parties, and I should think on balance not to engage in direct party political propaganda – and electoral boosting as distinct from expressing in words the faith that is in us and the principles in which we believe, which I think we have the right to do.[68]

Morrison's reply, which he permitted Midgley to show Brooke, would clearly have helped to relieve Midgley of much anxiety. He could not, however, expect that the attacks on his position would cease. As Midgley pointed out in his letter to Morrison, these attacks were being made by backbenchers who were probably being encouraged by some of the 'old guard' Unionists who had been ousted from power. Such men included Lord Glentoran, J. Milne-Barbour, and the ex-Prime Minister, J. M. Andrews. These figures still carried a lot of weight behind the scenes and their brooding presence on the backbenches was an uncomfortable reminder to the government that its hold on office was less than unassailable.

A good example of how Midgley was given a rough time from the Unionist backbenches was the debate at Stormont in November 1944 over the government's Housing Bill. The bill incorporated the principle of nationalisation, if only to a very limited degree, by the provision of a Housing Trust. This, of course, was what Midgley had argued for a year earlier. The bill did not, however, allow the principle of nationalisation to apply to more than twenty-five per cent of the houses to be erected. This was still too much for Dr William Lyle, the Unionist member for Queen's University. Lyle was aghast that the government should have accepted the principle at all and alleged that it was introduced by 'the Commonwealth party'. He went on to say of Midgley:

With many of his views I am in complete agreement, but some of his views are abhorrent to me, especially this one of nationalisation. I hope that as he grows older, more mellow, more mature, and gets rather more common sense than he has at present he will drop those obnoxious views.[69]

Midgley was at this time 52 years of age.

A less patronising but far more blistering attack was made four months later at Stormont by another Unionist backbencher, Brian Maginness. This occurred during a debate on the Disabled Persons Bill which Midgley introduced. Maginness objected to Midgley's frequent references to the intentions of the Westminster parliament with regard to the bill. He thought it 'sheer impertinence' that Midgley should be standing in the Stormont parliament voicing the opinions of the Westminster parliament. After calling on Midgley 'to stand on his own feet', Maginness went on to raise further objections in the bill's clauses, his apparent intention being to cause Midgley as much embarrassment as possible.[70] Midgley was finally moved to retort: 'I have come to the conclusion that this is a jocular attempt on the part of the hon. and learned member for Iveagh to bring to light a new Country party, of which, I understand, he is chief commissar.'[71]

The exchange was an illuminating one. Besides displaying Unionist back-bench resentment of Midgley, Maginness's line of attack pointed up the strong 'devolutionist' attitudes which existed within the Unionist party at this time. There were a number of Unionists, alarmed at the prospect of a post-war Labour government in Britain, who – well before the end of the war – were coming out in favour of greater autonomy for the Northern Ireland parliament. Maginness's views expressed here foreshadowed the post-war debate within the Unionist Party between those who shared the desire for more independence and those who thought it imperative to keep 'step by step' with Britain. Midgley favoured the closest possible links with Britain in whose social progress he wished to see Northern Ireland firmly bound up. It is probably fair to say that he distrusted the Unionist Party in this respect, and feared that if it governed in the post-war era, it might soft-pedal the enactment of social welfare legislation. Traditionalist Conservative antipathy to all measures smacking of socialism was still an obvious strain in Ulster Unionism by the close of the war. Midgley's reference to a 'new Country party' was an oblique way of saying that he believed Maginness and those who shared his outlook wished to return to the pre-war politics of privilege and wealth. Midgley's Unionist critics, for their part, saw him as a malignant influence on the government, his socialist ideas already helping to shape its policy.

If the Unionist backbenchers had cause to fear the influence of Midgley's political outlook in the realm of social and economic questions, there was no reason for them to doubt his commitment to making secure the constitutional position of Northern Ireland. From around the middle of 1944 cabinet records show that the government was very concerned about the possibility of a large wave of immigration into Northern Ireland from Eire after the war. During the war residence permits were required for people to cross the border from Eire into Northern Ireland. It was beyond the powers of the government to administer the permits on the basis of discrimination according to the religion of the applicants, a fact which caused some members considerable disquiet. The Minister of Home Affairs, William Lowry, for example, expressed the fullest sympathy with the view that 'unless some steps were taken to ensure the Protestant ascendancy, the future of Northern Ireland was in jeopardy'.[72]

As Minister of Labour Midgley was alert to the possibility of exservicemen from Eire obtaining work in Northern Ireland after the war. He was worried that the markedly superior social welfare benefits which would be available in Northern Ireland after the war would lead to an influx of Southerners. On 9 September 1944 he presented a memorandum to the cabinet on the subject, the most notable passage of which read:

Recent legislation has made conditions in Northern Ireland still more attractive to persons from Eire and especially to Eire ex-servicemen, and the schemes for the social services will probably attract others. It seems likely, also, that some modified form of demobilization will take place at a comparatively early date, releasing more of these men to settle here and compete with our own ex-servicemen and civilians in a falling labour market. Many of them will gravitate to the disloyal element in our population and increase our political difficulties. In these circumstances, I suggest that further consideration should be given to our existing policy of granting residence permits to Eire ex-servicemen without regard to the labour situation.[73]

Midgley was of the view that the government's first duty lay in helping its own ex-servicemen and believed that many Eire men had enlisted in the armed forces 'owing to economic pressure and without any sense of loyalty to the Empire'. Many of these Eire men, said Midgley, would, if they came to Northern Ireland, 'adopt the views of their co-religionists and endanger our existence as a integral part of the United Kingdom'. Midgley also feared that employment in Northern Ireland after the war would not be as 'brisk' as in Britain and that there would consequently be an overcrowded labour market.[74] His warnings were heeded by the cabinet which decided on 15 September that 'Residence permits should in future only be granted to Eire ex-servicemen where the labour situation warranted it.'[75]

Southern infiltration continued to exercise the government's mind after the war, and the matter only rested when the Safeguarding of Employment Act was passed by Stormont in 1947. This act, which stipulated that permits were required to obtain work in Northern Ireland, was the product of negotiations between the British and Northern Ireland governments during 1945–7.

Another issue which concerned the cabinet in the period from late 1944 to early 1945 was that of education. The Butler Education Bill became law in England and Wales in August 1944. This bill gave generous government funding to denominational schools, both Roman Catholic and Church of England. Midgley emphatically stated in cabinet that he did not favour Northern Ireland doing the same.[76] He stood for a completely comprehensive, publicly funded and controlled system in line with socialist thinking in Britain and elsewhere. When the Minister of Education, Col. Samuel Hall-Thompson, drew up his proposals for educational reconstruction, Midgley took the opportunity to present the cabinet with his own blueprint of educational reform. He suggested firstly that the commencing age for all schoolchildren should be 5, and that the leaving age should be raised to 15 with legislative power taken to raise it to 16 at a later date. Secondly, he favoured the abolition of fees and the establishment of one system of secondary education for all. Thirdly, he came out firmly against Hall-Thompson's proposal to increase the capital grants for the building and reconstruction of voluntary schools from fifty to sixty-five per cent.[77] Hall-Thompson argued that raising the capital grants represented 'just treatment to the minority',[78] since most voluntary schools were Catholic. It was another sensitive issue and it was to be the source of much debate during the immediate post-war period.

As the war drew to a close, Northern Ireland braced itself for an election. Midgley's position in the government was now untenable. The CLP, along with the other parties, had been preparing for the election since April 1945.[79] Midgley knew that, sooner or later, he would have to resign. He did so on 29 May. There had been a suggestion that Midgley might have been able to stay in government, that the CLP would fight only Nationalist constituencies and so not endanger the 'coalition'.[80] This, however, would have meant the CLP virtually admitting electoral defeat before they started. The party's main political objective was to win the support of the Protestant working class from the clutches of the Unionist Party, and it would have made little sense to contest seats where they could not have made such an appeal. There was no question of the Unionists permitting a continuation of the 'coalition' government after the war given that it would have been solely for the benefit of Midgley. For his part, Midgley wanted to see the immediate implementation of the promised social reforms, and would probably have welcomed the chance to help steer the government along this course. He viewed with foreboding the 'traditionalist' element in the Unionist ranks, while full of admiration for Brooke and others such as Warnock who had made clear their commitment to the proposed social legislation. The demands of party politics, however, could not allow Midgley the best of both worlds: a government office and independence from the Unionists.   In his letter of resignation to Brooke, Midgley wrote:

In view of political developments which make it necessary that I should outline our Commonwealth policy to the electors I feel impelled to tender my resignation as Minister of Labour.

On purely personal grounds I do so with deep regret, for no-one could have served under a more considerate Chief, or one who was as tolerant and forebearing as you, and I shall not soon forget your kindly co-operation and sympathetic understanding when matters were in debate or dispute . . .

I can assure you, however, that although I feel constrained to part from you so that I may enjoy greater freedom to express our social policy without embarrassment to you, I will consider it my duty to associate myself – and my colleagues – with you in your maintenance of Ulster's constitutional position as an integral part of the United Kingdom.[81]

With that he departed for the hustings.

V

Midgley was defending Willowfield in the Commonwealth Labour interest, and the party had five other candidates in the field: William Kennedy in Belfast, Ballynafeigh; Norman Black in Belfast, Victoria; James Kennedy in Belfast, Windsor; Thomas Martin (a Unionist convert) in Armagh Central; and Albert Horatio McElroy in Newtownards.

Campaigning for himself and the other Belfast candidates, Midgley did not pull his punches with regard to the Unionists. He claimed that he had not joined the Unionists because there was a 'fundamental difference' between Unionist and CLP policies. He said:

The Unionist party stood for the perpetuation of old, vested interests, the unregulated, unplanned way of life with all its sorry and squalid struggle for existence, scramble for markets and the exploitation of man by man which resulted in poverty and insecurity at home and rivalry abroad.

The CLP, on the other hand, stood for 'a planned economy, based on the right of every citizen to enjoy the highest standard of life possible in a highly developed and scientific system of society'. Midgley listed the CLP's priorities as education, health and housing, social security and full employment. William Kennedy stated that the CLP stood for freedom for the small trader and shopkeeper but control for the large monopolies.[82]

At a meeting in Willowfield Unionist Hall, Brooke hit back by contending that the CLP policy was the thin edge of the wedge leading to the 'broad edge of communism'.[83] The 'border bogey' was not a viable electoral tactic to use against the CLP, so the 'communist' taint had to be increasingly employed. At another meeting Brooke described communism as 'the most fatal thing in the world'.[84]

Midgley was in a three-cornered fight with the Unionist, G.I. Finlay, and the NILP nominee, Bob McBrinn, a shop steward in the shipyard. Midgley concentrated on the Unionist challenge, however, and directed his propaganda at what he saw as their reactionary instincts for a return to a world left behind. At a meeting in the Albertbridge Hall he referred to Unionist 'wails and sobs' because their 'immemorial privileges were being curtailed in the interests of the nation'.[85] McBrinn tailored his campaign to the 'Unionist Labour' specifications demanded by the constituency: 'step by step with British Labour' his slogan ran.[86] Of this kind of appeal, however, Midgley had a virtual monopoly.

When the results of the poll were eventually declared on 10 July, Midgley emerged a clear winner, amassing 7,072 to Finlay's 4,488, and McBrinn's 1,082. The turn-out was just over seventy-five per cent. The other CLP candidates were not so fortunate: William Kennedy finished second to the Unionist but ahead of the NILP candidate; Black finished bottom of the poll behind the Unionist and NILP candidates; James Kennedy lost honourably to the Unionist; Martin was defeated by the Unionist; and McElroy, despite a strong showing, lost out to the Unionist.

Overall the Unionists won thirty-three seats, the Nationalists ten, Independent Unionists two, Independents two, NILP two, CLP one, Socialist Republican one, and Independent Labour one. On the face of it very little had significantly changed. In terms of votes cast, however, the picture was somewhat different. The NILP won 66,053 votes overall, despite only returning two MPs to Stormont.[87] The party fielded fifteen candidates and won the Belfast seats of Oldpark (Bob Getgood) and Dock (Hugh Downey). Beattie had been expelled again in 1944 and he and James Collins had set up the 'Federation of Labour'. Collins fought under this label in Falls but was defeated by Harry Diamond who had also set up a party: the Socialist Republican Party. The latter was anti-partitionist and anti-communist.[88] Beattie retained Pottinger as an 'Independent Labour' candidate. The Communist Party fielded three candidates and polled a very respectable aggregate vote of 12,456. The Commonwealth Labour aggregate total for six candidates was 28,079.

The opposition to the Unionists was thus very confused and fragmented, but the total vote of all parties and candidates of the Left came to 125,869 as against the Unionist total of 178,662. This was at the very least an indication that the war had had a radicalising effect on many people in Northern Ireland and that profound social changes were widely desired. By comparison, the aggregate vote of parties and candidates of the Left in the 1938 election had been a mere 24,255.[89] The Unionists had not been foolish enough to disown Beveridge. Their campaign was anti-socialist but not anti-social welfare and they promised that benefits in this regard would not elude Northern Ireland. This, coupled with the usual stress on the constitution, was more than enough to forestall the kind of seismic electoral shift which would have been required to end their hegemony.

Shortly after the Northern Ireland poll, attentions turned to the British General Election called for 5 July. On 18 June Midgley announced that he was standing in the constituency of South Belfast. No other seat was contested by the CLP and all efforts were directed to the end of returning Midgley to Westminster.

Once again it was a three-cornered fight, his opponents being Lt. Col. Connolly H. Gage (Unionist), and James Morrow (NILP). The constituency was the most redoubtable bastion of the Protestant middle class in Belfast, and was a Unionist stronghold. It comprised the largest concentration of professional and business people in the city, with a liberal sprinkling of skilled workers – mostly from Midgley's Willowfield ward – and a small Catholic population around the Markets area close to the city centre.[90] The odds against Midgley seemed daunting, but he had a strong base of support in Willowfield, and had reason to hope that many voters would change their allegiance in accordance with the promise of a new post-war era.

In his campaign Midgley strove hard to win the middle class votes he needed from Connolly H. Gage. The CLP, he proclaimed at one meeting, 'made its appeal to workers with hand and brain, to the professional classes who were looking for security and justice, and to those in the more comfortable walks of life anxious to open up better opportunities to the masses'.[91] It was a clever appeal, at once reassuring and challenging, and implicitly respectful. It was designed to counter the predictable 'red bogey' tactics of the Unionists, and to distinguish the CLP from the explicit class warfare of the NILP campaign.

Skilful as it was it didn't work. Connolly H. Gage won a comfortable victory with 24,282 votes to Midgley's 14,096 and Morrow's 8,166. The middle class had clung to Unionism with a solidity which was quite remarkable for the times. While the Labour Party in Britain romped home to a landslide victory with the help of a 'substantial section of the urban middle classes',[92] traditional loyalties proved more durable in Northern Ireland. Even with Morrow's votes Midgley would not have prevailed. A long-held ambition to perform on the Westminster political stage remained to be fulfilled.

Back at Stormont on the opposition benches once more, Midgley co-existed uneasily with Beattie, Harry Diamond and the Nationalist, NILP and Independent Unionist members. For much of the time he found himself arguing against those on the same side of the House as himself. There were frequent ill-tempered jousts with Beattie who was much given at this time to hiss such remarks as 'thirty pieces of silver' and 'Judas' at Midgley when he rose to speak.[93] Midgley was not adept at resisting provocation and in October 1945, following a sharp exchange over a point of order, his anger boiled over. He rushed at Beattie and struck him across the face before being restrained by William Grant and Harry Diamond. Midgley was ordered to withdraw but his rage was still not spent. Later in the day, at the end of a sitting, he resumed his altercation with Beattie and the two men burst back into the chamber in a renewed state of physical combat before being forcibly separated again. Midgley's conduct was condemned by the Speaker as 'grossly disorderly' and he made an unreserved apology to the House the following day.[94]

Midgley was a lonely figure at Stormont during the immediate post-war period. He had antagonised the Nationalists and the NILP to the point of no return, while his relations with the Independent Unionists had notably cooled due to his acceptance of government office during the war. His enmity with Beattie was, of course, unconcealed. On the other side of the House sat those Unionists who had been opposed to his government appointments and for whom Midgley was still a dangerous socialist. Midgley remained a maverick political personality but by this time a certain degree of ebullience and irrepressibility seemed to have gone out of him. It was not one of the happiest times of his life. His political career, from being in the ascendant of ministerial power, had overnight assumed an almost directionless uncertainty. As the Unionists entrenched themselves in office yet again it seemed that his chance of helping to shape Northern Ireland's future had passed. It was a far cry from tramping the corridors of power in London with British cabinet ministers and receiving write-ups in the British press like the following in the London *Evening News* in October 1944:

He [Midgley] is a wiry, dark-haired little man with bushy black brows, sharp, luminous eyes, a useful pair of fists, and a voice that I shall never forget.
It is just the sort of voice that I would ask the gods for if I proposed to fight an Irish election – penetrating, mellifluous, coaxing and scornful at will.
I fancy he could persuade a bird out of a tree with it. I predict that one day the Recording Angel will retire hurt when 'Mr. Midgley of Belfast' is announced.[95]

Midgley's health continued to trouble him, particularly during the 1943–5 period when he was in government. He was laid low with periodic illnesses which largely derived from the way in which he overtaxed himself. Government and CLP duties were onerous enough, but Midgley was also at this time a member of the Co-operative Society board of management,[96] and took an active interest in other institutions such as the Ulster Teachers' Union of which he became honorary vice-president, and Linfield football club of which he was chairman. This was all in addition to the demands of his domestic family life. The Midgely family was uprooted by the blitz in 1941, and later moved to Cedar Avenue, a little further north from their old home in Duncairn Gardens.

VI

Northern Ireland fully shared in the post-war reconstruction of British society. The Unionists had pledged at the election to accept whatever social welfare legislation was passed by the British government, and it was a pledge they kept. There was, however, considerable concern within the party. Labour's ascent to power in Britain aroused among many Unionists fears of socialist legislation being foisted upon a Northern Ireland electorate which had not voted for it. Most Unionists felt able to accept the welfare reforms which, after all, they had had time to get used to. It was the possibility of more extreme socialist measures such as widespread nationalisation which caused the alarm. The extension of the welfare programme to Northern Ireland meant that more money was paid from the British Treasury to the province, but along with this went tighter economic controls and a further limitation of the Northern Ireland government's autonomy.[97] Thus the Northern Ireland government's capacity to diverge from legislation passed in Britain was severely restricted.

For some Unionists the solution to the problem lay in achieving greater independence, or even Dominion status, for the Province. Although he stopped short of advocating the latter, Sir Roland Nugent, Minister of Commerce after the 1945 election, put this case most forcibly in cabinet. For Nugent Northern Ireland had to be treated differently given that it was less urbanised and industrialised than Britain. In return for greater independence, he was prepared to sacrifice Ulster's representation at Westminster.[98] Nugent was backed up by Brian Maginness (Minister of Labour) who had expressed his anti-integrationist views in debate at Stormont with Midgley. Nugent and Maginness faced opposition from Robert Moore (Minister of Agriculture) and William Grant (Minister of Health) who, mostly for economic reasons, opposed any loosening of the British link. The Prime Minister,

Brooke, who had also been filled with disquiet at the prospect of extreme socialist legislation being passed, finally came down in favour of the status quo in October 1947. He feared that any weakening of ties with Britain would not be popular with Protestant workers.[99] By this time initial Unionist panic regarding the Labour government had largely subsided, and Unionists were devoting more attention to countering the activities of the Anti-Partition League (APL).[100]

The APL had been set up in November 1945 to supply some organisational structure to Nationalist politics since, after the 1945 election, Nationalists had decided to abandon their abstentionist campaign and take their seats in both the Stormont and Westminster parliaments. The APL was complemented in Britain by the simultaneous development of the 'Friends of Ireland' group. The latter comprised a collection of mostly left-wing Labour MPs led by Ulster-born Geoffrey Bing. Their main objective was to bring to light what they saw as discrimination against the minority community in areas such as employment and housing, the flagrant denial of civil rights in the realm of the electoral franchise,[101] and the gerrymandering of electoral boundaries to the obvious advantage of the Unionist Party. The 'Friends of Ireland' also sought the unity of Ireland and acted as a pressure group to influence the Labour government to this end. In this latter respect their efforts came to little; Ulster's participation in the war and Eire's neutrality had changed the outlook of several leading Labour politicians and there was little sympathy, at least at cabinet level, for the anti-partitionist cause.

Despite only winning one seat at the 1945 election, the CLP continued to be optimistic about its future during the immediate post-war period. At the end of 1946 it claimed to have increased its membership over the course of that year by fifty per cent,[102] while in June 1946 *Justice* announced the establishment of three new branches in Portadown, Ballymena and Richhill.[103] In the local elections of 1946 the party won seats on the Belfast, Bangor, Ballymena, Newtownards and Richhill councils.[104] The Belfast success was that of Midgley himself in the Ormeau Ward in the south side of the city adjacent to his parliamentary constituency of Willowfield. The poll took place on 18 September 1946 and Midgley defeated the Unionist, H. R. Walsh, for the aldermanship by 5,710 votes to 3,987.[105] On his return to the Corporation Midgley took his place on the Improvement, Finance, Libraries, Museums and Arts, Markets, and Education committees.[106]

Midgley had made education the main priority in his local election campaign, and it came increasingly to the fore in CLP propaganda. He focused on the issue, for example, during his address to the CLP conference in November 1946. Midgley, by this time, had been involved in a protracted debate at Stormont over the government's Education Bill. He had criticised it extensively on a number of points, the most important being that of public control and public funding of schools. Midgley constantly stressed his belief in 'the complete democratisation and public control of education',[107] and vehemently criticised the proposal to increase capital grants to voluntary schools from fifty to sixty-five per cent. His point was that most voluntary – and all Catholic voluntary – schools would receive the increased grants without accepting the principle of some public control over their management. Midgley wanted the schools to be managed by the 'four and two' committees whereby there would be parental and civic representation as well as clerical on the voluntary school management committees. The Catholic church rejected this principle as being the first step towards complete state, and secular, control.[108]

Midgley was particularly explicit on the matter at the CLP conference in November 1946. After predicting that most Protestant voluntary schools would soon pass away leaving Catholic schools as the sole recipients of the grants, he averred: 'Those who persistently refuse to utilise public schools (with adequate spiritual safeguards and amenities for all denominations) should be told plainly that they must provide their own.' He went on:

The continual appeasement of those who reject Public Control and Democracy in Education can only lead to a demand (which, indeed, is already expressed) for one hundred per cent building grants for Voluntary (Denominational) schools. To concede this to one section simply means that it cannot – morally – be refused to others, and this, in turn, means that we may bid farewell to the ideal of a co-ordinated, publically controlled [sic], equalitarian system of education, for there cannot be the slightest doubt the perpetuation of the old Voluntary School system leads to children being kept apart in their most impressionable years, and thus reach the adult stage estranged and embittered. What hope can we have of building a happier country and a better world on such a basis?[109]

It was a powerful argument and one which was consistent with Midgley's views on education from his earliest days in politics. It was also, of course, the line which any party purporting to be socialist would have been expected to take. In Northern Ireland, however, Midgley's stance laid him open to accusations of anti-Catholic bigotry in much the same way as his defence of the Spanish Republic in 1936 had done. Again, many Catholics took offence at his mode of argument and his astringent criticisms of clerical teaching in schools. He faced virulent opposition to his ideas in Stormont from the Nationalists, one of whom, James McSparren, stubbornly announced that '. . . our concept of education has been expressed by the Pope in an encyclical'.[110]

By the time of the Education Bill controversy, however, Midgley had come to expect Nationalist opposition to him on just about everything he stood for. For his part, he had come to hold a rigidly polarised view of Protestant and Catholic community attitudes to political questions. He expressed this view in debate at Stormont in August 1945:

> There is only one Ireland, but there are two distinct races, two distinct psychologies, two different outlooks and two different perspectives. There are those people who believe they have the supreme and heaven sent duty of trying to breathe the breath of life into the dry bones of a dead nationalism that can serve no effective purpose, and who believe as a part of this policy that they ought to waste the time and belittle the intelligence of the community in trying to revive a language that has no value whatever from a world point of view. There is the other section of the Irish community who recognise world intelligence and who believe that their place as an economic unit is bound up with that of Great Britain, and that the best way of implementing all that is best in the human race is to strengthen and enlarge the British Commonwealth and so bring about a new world based on a proper foundation.[111]

This kind of statement, in its uncompromising self-righteousness, left no room for fruitful dialogue. Midgley had oversimplified matters to the point where, in his estimation, only Protestants held progressive views, and, by virtue of their national feelings, Catholics were reactionary. It is thus hardly surprising that so many Catholics interpreted Midgley's views on education as a manifestation of sectarianism.

Midgley had made his choice and for him there was no going back. He had learnt the hard way with the NILP that there was no room for ambiguity in Northern Ireland politics. He thus committed the CLP to winning Protestant support, and effectively ignored the minority. The CLP could not afford to try and be flexible in its appeal lest it resembled the NILP. All efforts were directed at undermining the Unionists' grip on the Protestant community. In early 1947 the CLP even appealed to the Orange Order to break its traditional association with the Unionist Party.[112] The more the CLP attempted such a task, however, the more it exposed itself to the charge of causing division in the ranks of the Protestant community, divisions which could be exploited by political opponents such as the APL or the 'Friends of Ireland' group. This was a charge to which Midgley was undoubtedly sensitive since, by now, he, as much as any Unionist, wanted the loyalty of Northern Ireland's majority to be properly appreciated in Britain in order to combat Nationalist propaganda. In August 1945 he had complained strongly at Stormont that Northern Ireland was not adequately represented in Britain from a propaganda point of view.[113]

The CLP's main justification for its existence was that it was a socialist as well as pro-British party and that its political ideology was far removed from the 'traditionalist Toryism' of the Unionist Party. By 1946–7, however, Midgley was beginning to sound decidedly less dogmatic on this point. In March 1946 at Stormont he spoke out against 'state control for the sake of state control' and advocated 'proper co-ordination between the State and properly developed private enterprise'.[114] In May 1947, also at Stormont, Midgley made a speech calling for all sections of the community to work for the common good and to create a 'better spirit in industry'. The speech also contained critical references to strikes called for 'frivolous reasons', and to people who were apparently disinclined to use the machinery of conciliation in industrial disputes.[115] The speech indicated that Midgley no longer viewed the world from a class perspective. He seemed to believe that such concepts were losing their relevance in a new egalitarian age. Even more significantly, in July 1947, he wrote an article for the *Belfast Telegraph*[116] in which he lashed out at Ulster's critics in Britain who, 'holding radical views, hate conservatism with such a fury that they are not prepared to consider Ulster's case simply because the Ulster people have, in the main, been Conservative'. In Midgley's view such people had fundamentally mistaken the nature of modern Conservatism:

... they assume that Conservatism is an unchanging philosophy whereas there is nothing truer than George Bernard Shaw's dictum that 'nothing stays put', and so it comes about that Conservatives of today often sponsor legislation that would have been considered revolutionary a few years ago. This is especially true of legislation in Ulster.

This was all a long way from Midgley's jibes about the Unionists being the party of privilege and reaction. It seems, however, that once the welfare state legislation had started to be implemented in Northern Ireland by the Unionists after the war, Midgley's outlook rapidly changed. His fears of an 'old style' Unionism reasserting itself against the new measures proved to be unfounded. During 1946–7 he found himself voting with the government for the introduction of such social measures as the Family Allowances Bill, the Housing Bill, and the National Insurance Bill. Only on education, as has been noted, did he diverge markedly from the government viewpoint. Before his eyes many of the reforms he had preached for over twenty-five years were materialising. Their fears of extreme socialism notwithstanding, the Unionists' approach to post-war social reconstruction echoed the consensus which had developed in this context in Britain.[117] In Midgley's view the Unionists had decided to move with the times. In addition, Midgley was no doctrinal socialist: he did not believe in nationalisation for the sake of it or in too much centralised government. His post-war outlook was sympathetic to the concept of a mixed economy: central planning along with a vigorous private enterprise sector. That such a wave of social reforms was being implemented also reinforced his faith in the virtues of parliamentary democracy as the best governmental means of effecting change and social progress. His outlook can perhaps simply be summed up as social democratic.

During the summer of 1947 Midgley suffered another lengthy bout of illness and had time to reflect on political developements and on his own career prospects. On Saturday 6 September at an executive committee meeting, he tendered his resignation as chairman of the CLP. His decision took the other committee members by surprise but they agreed that the party should carry on without him.[118] Three weeks later Midgley applied for, and received, the Unionist Party whip.[119]

The CLP went ahead with its annual conference on 27 September. The new chairman, William Brisbane, denied that the party was simply 'a Harry Midgley supporters' club', and expressed his regret at seeing 'such a personality in Labour politics lay down his fight that had been waged for almost thirty years in the interests of socialism'.[120] The CLP struggled on for a few more months before fading out of existence. The loss of Midgley combined with financial problems were too much for it to overcome. Some party members followed Midgley into the Unionists while others, notably Albert Horatio McElroy, joined the NILP.

The CLP had stood for some praiseworthy ideals and had championed the cause of social security legislation with more conviction than any other party in Northern Ireland. Such aspects of the party's platform, however, took on secondary importance beside the commitment to the constitution which determined the party's appeal, its tactics, its potential constituency of support, and, ultimately, its fate. In Britain, Acland's Common Wealth Party found that there was no room between the Labour and Communist parties for a viable third party of the Left. In Northern Ireland, the CLP discovered that there was no room, in the context of a political consensus regarding welfare legislation, for more than one party of loyalty and fidelity to Ulster's British heritage.

In retrospect Midgley's steady march towards the Unionist Party appears logical and unsurprising. It was, however, a journey fraught with political risk and governed by the unpredictable contingencies of a momentous historical period. Midgley's full-blooded support for the war was consistent with his view of international developments throughout the 1930s. That this support in practice brought him close to the Unionists was unavoidable given the Unionists' traditional pro-British reflexes. There was nothing inevitable, however, about Midgley's entry into the Northern Ireland government: had Andrews been more politically astute and as competent a minister as in his early career, the opportunity would probably not have arisen.

Midgley's change in outlook was also dependent on the Unionists changing theirs, and, whatever the internal arguments in the party, a new pragmatic acceptance of a socially-transformed post-war society did take place in the form of an endorsement of the welfare state. This was of enormous importance to Midgley: firstly, the glaring social injustices against which he had long fought looked like being overcome at last; while, secondly, such social progress distanced Britain even further from Southern Ireland whose neutral stance in the war was seen by Midgley as evidence of the fundamental inadequacies of Irish nationalism when put to a test of historic importance.

From the outset of a post-war era charged with new hope, Midgley was impelled to make his commitment to the British State and way of life all the more explicit in response to the anti-partitionist campaign which commenced at precisely this juncture. Suddenly, it seemed that a decision had to be made in consideration of this overriding issue. To Midgley, killing off the CLP was of small account when set beside the need to preserve and strengthen the Union.

Notes

1. N.I. House of Commons Debates XXV, 1810.
2. Bew, Gibbon and Patterson op. cit. pp. 104–5.
3. Ibid. pp. 106–7, and Spender Diaries PRONI D715/20 (1 November 1942 to 14 February 1943) and D715/21 (15 February 1943 to 16 May 1943).
4. Unionist Parliamentary Party minute book 19 Janaury 1943, PRONI D1327/10/1.
5. The Brookeborough Memoirs, the *Sunday News* 4 February 1968. Brooke insisted in his memoirs that he did not plot against Andrews and that he had no contact with the rebel backbenchers.
6. *Sunday News* 4 February 1968. According to the Reverend Ian Paisley, invitations to join the government were also extended to the Independent Unionist members, John Nixon and Tommy Henderson. Both refused

and, in Dr Paisley's opinion, were dismayed at Midgley's decision to accept. Interview with Dr Paisley 18 January 1983.

7. Unionist Parliamentary Party minute book 15 June 1943 PRONI 1327/10/1.
8. In an interview with the *Belfast Telegraph* after his appointment, Midgley said that Brooke had imposed 'no conditions whatever' on his joining the cabinet. *Belfast Telegraph* 6 May 1943.
9. *Labour Progress* July 1943.
10. *Belfast Telegraph* 6 May 1943.
11. Ibid.
12. *Irish News* 7 May 1943.
13. *Derry Journal* 14 May 1943.
14. N.I. House of Common Debates XXVI, 468.
15. Ibid., 478–9.
16. Ibid., 487.
17. Ibid., 491.
18. Milotte op. cit. p. 448.
19. See note 6.
20. CAB 4/541/10 PRONI.
21. Ibid.
22. Ibid.
23. CAB 4/556/8.
24. *Coleraine Chronicle* 9 October 1943.
25. See, for example, *Belfast Telegraph* 18 September 1943.
26. CAB 4/549/5 and CAB 4/549/7.
27. See Spender Diaries D715/22 (1 June 1943).
28. B. Donoughue and G. W. Jones, *Herbert Morrison: Portrait of a Politician*, London, 1973, pp. 307–8.
29. See Buckland, *Factory of Grievances* pp. 163–75, and D. Birrell and A. Murie, *Policy and Government in Northern Ireland*, Dublin, 1980, pp. 209–20.
30. CAB 4/557/3.
31. CAB 4/560/14.
32. CAB 4/560/17.
33. Spender Diaries D715/23 (Memo. dated 25 October 1943).
34. CAB 4/564/5.
35. Midgley resigned from the corporation when he took up his government post in May 1943. In his letter of resignation he referred to his work on the council as 'the happiest and most constructive part of my public career'. Belfast City Council, Minutes of Monthly Meeting 1 June 1943.
36. N.I. House of Commons Debates XXVII, 1355.
37. See, for example, *Belfast News-Letter* 27 March 1944.
38. Spender Diaries D715/24 (23 March 1944).
39. See G. S. Walker, 'The Commonwealth Labour Party in Northern Ireland, 1942–47', *Irish Historical Studies* 24 (May 1984) pp. 69–90.
40. *Justice* November 1943.
41. Ibid. February 1943.
42. Ibid.

43. *Ulster for the Commonwealth*, Belfast, 1943.
44. See *Justice* April 1944.
45. See, for example, N.I. House of Commons Debates XXVI, 21–2.
46. Ibid., 234.
47. *Justice* June 1944.
48. Ibid.
49. *Ulster for the Commonwealth*.
50. *Justice* July 1944.
51. While on a visit to London in February 1944, Midgley told a journalist that although he and Brooke were 'poles apart' on social and economic questions, he was a 'great admirer and devoted colleague' of his nevertheless. London *Evening Standard* 25 February 1944.
52. See Addison op. cit. p. 159.
53. See, for example, his New Year message in *Justice* January 1944.
54. *Justice* October 1943.
55. *Belfast Telegraph* 24 November 1945.
56. A. Calder, *The People's War*, London, 1971 pp. 632–4.
57. Ibid. p. 634.
58. See *Justice* June 1946.
59. W. Wilkie, *One World*, Edinburgh, 1943.
60. See *Justice* November 1944.
61. See, for example, Chairman's Address, Annual Conference of the CLP 24 June 1944, *Midgley Papers*.
62. *Newtownards Chronicle* 19 February 1944.
63. *Bangor Spectator* 10 November 1943.
64. Eirene White, 'What hope for a socialist Commonwealth?', in A Creech Jones (ed.) *New Fabian Colonial Essays*, London, 1959.
65. See Rita Hinden (ed.) *Fabian Colonial Essays*, London, 1945.
66. N.I. House of Commons Debates XXVIII, 535–6.
67. Midgley to Morrison 29 May 1944, *Midgley Papers*.
68. Morrison to Midgley 9 June 1944, *Midgley Papers*.
69. N.I. House of Commons Debates XXVII, 2193.
70. Ibid. XXVIII, 313 and 315–35.
71. Ibid. 330.
72. CAB 4/592/2.
73. CAB 4/597/7.
74. Ibid. See also Bew, Gibbon and Patterson op. cit. pp. 112–13.
75. CAB 4/597/17.
76. CAB 4/589/10.
77. CAB 4/606/4.
78. CAB 4/606/16.
79. See *Belfast Telegraph* 23 April 1945.
80. *Irish News* 24 April 1945.
81. *Northern Whig* 29 May 1945. Brooke replied praising Midgley's contribution to the government.
82. *Belfast Telegraph* 5 June 1945.
83. Ibid. 6 June 1945.
84. Ibid. 8 June 1945.
85. Ibid.

86. *Belfast Telegraph* 11 June 1945.
87. This and all other electoral statistics are from Elliot op. cit.
88. See letter from Harry Diamond to Desmond Ryan 4 March 1945, Desmond Ryan Papers, UCD Archives LA 10/09/1.
89. There were, however, only eight candidates of the left in 1938 as compared with twenty-nine in 1945.
90. The constituency comprised the Northern Ireland parliamentary election wards of Windsor, Willowfield, Ballynafeigh and Cromac.
91. *Belfast Telegraph* 4 July 1945.
92. Addison op. cit. p. 268.
93. Interview with James Kelly 25 March 1982.
94. *Northern Whig* 1 November 1945.
95. *London Evening News* 22 October 1944.
96. He was re-elected at the top of the poll to the management committee in January 1943. *Northern Whig* 21 January 1943.
97. See F. S. L. Lyons, *Ireland Since the Famine*, London, 1973, p. 739.
98. See D. W. Harkness, 'Difficulties of devolution: the post-war debate at Stormont', *Irish Jurist* xii (summer 1977) pp. 176–86. This is the source for what follows on the subject.
99. See Bew, Gibbon and Patterson op. cit. p. 123.
100. For an account of the APL see Farrell op. cit. chapter 8.
101. Northern Ireland did not follow the British example in implementing the 'one man one vote' principle for local government elections. The vast majority of those with property votes were Protestants and thus likely to be supporters of the Unionist Party. On the other hand many less-well-off Protestants, as well as Catholics, were disenfranchised.
102. *Belfast Telegraph* 2 December 1946.
103. *Justice* June 1946.
104. *Ulster Education and Democracy*, Belfast, 1946. Address by Midgley to the CLP conference 30 November 1946, *Midgley Papers*.
105. *Belfast News-Letter* 19 September 1946.
106. Midgley's council attendance from his election in 1946 to his resignation in 1949 was very irregular.
107. *Ulster Education and Democracy*.
108. See D. H. Akenson, *Education and Enmity: The Control of Schooling in Northern Ireland*, Newton Abbot, Devon, 1973, pp. 177–80.
109. *Ulster Education and Democracy*.
110. Quoted in Farrell op. cit. p. 180.
111. N.I. House of Commons Debates XXIX, 369.
112. *Commonwealth* February 1947. This newspaper was the CLP's successor to *Justice* which ceased publication at the end of 1946.
113. N.I. House of Commons Debates XXIX, 368.
114. Ibid. 295–6.
115. Ibid. XXXI, 212–13.
116. *Belfast Telegraph* 1 July 1947.
117. See Addison op. cit. *passim.*
118. *Belfast Telegraph* 8 September 1947.
119. *Northern Whig* 27 September 1947.
120. Ibid. 29 September 1947.

Chapter Nine

Unionist Evangelist (1947–1950)

I

In his letter of application to Brooke to receive the Unionist whip, Midgley made clear that attacks on Ulster's constitutional position had led him to believe in the need for Unionist unity: '. . . I have now reached the conclusion that there is no room for division among those in our community who are anxious to preserve the constitutional life and spiritual heritage of our people.' He then went on to add:

In taking this step I rejoice in the knowledge that many of the outstanding social and educational reforms which I helped to pioneer are now in operation. This fact, taken in conjunction with your declared policy of maintaining the highest British standards of social security and working conditions for all our people, is in harmony with my social objective.[1]

Brooke extended a cordial welcome to his former cabinet colleague and stated: 'I am fully conscious of your desire to lend all the weight at your command in support of our constitutional position, and I am glad to learn that you wish to join the Unionist party.'[2] On receiving the party whip, Midgley was also invited to join the Ulster Unionist Labour Association (South Belfast Branch) and was admitted, by a majority vote, to the Ormeau Unionist Association which comprised the two branches of Willowfield and Ballynafeigh.[3]

Midgley also became a member of the Orange Order,[4] and, subsequently, the more esoteric and even more secretive Royal Black Preceptory.[5] The former institution was one of the most important in Ulster political, social and cultural life.[6] Within the Unionist Party it constituted the best-organised body, and it made full use of the party's internal structure to wield profound influence over such matters as party policy and the selection of candidates.[7] The majority of Unionist MPs were Orangemen and it was generally accepted political wisdom in Northern Ireland that those with career aspirations in the Unionist Party were expected to be members of the Order. There were non-Orangemen who achieved cabinet rank, most notably Lt. Col. Samuel

Hall-Thompson who was at this time (1947) Minister of Education, and Midgley himself during the exceptional circumstances of wartime. These cases, however, were very much exceptions to the rule. The local Orange hall often provided the meeting place for the local Unionist Party branch, and both institutions frequently shared in the same social events and fund-raising activities. The Orange hall also became the centre of Unionist Party activity at election times, 'the engine room of the Unionist party machine ... well organised, highly efficient and exclusively Protestant'.[8]

In joining the Orange Order Midgley was undoubtedly looking after his own political career, but it would be wrong to conclude that he joined solely on these grounds. Some Unionists did join purely for such a purpose and did not identify with the Order's stress on Protestant religious tenets.[9] Midgley, however, had come to view the Ulster-British way of life in classical Orange fashion: that is, as a Protestant way of life, the substance of which derived from the principles of individual liberty won by the Reformation and consummated in the British constitution after the 'glorious revolution' of 1688–9. He thus looked upon the Orange Order as bulwark in defence of Ulster's British Protestant heritage, an egregious focus for the beliefs and values of a large section of the Ulster Protestant people.[10] In his attitude to the Order Midgley was unambivalent: he ignored its role in engendering social divisions, and overlooked the hatred and distrust of Catholics which it could inspire in some of its members.

Midgley was now intent on investing all his talents and energies in defence of the Ulster-British, and therefore Protestant, cause. His assumption of this new political role was in no way half-hearted or hesitant. The zeal of the convert gripped him as he styled himself a Unionist evangelist.

II

The time was ripe for Midgley to set himself such a mission. The propaganda campaign of the Anti-Partition League built up to a crescendo during the years 1947–9. The APL worked tirelessly throughout Northern Ireland and the South, and organised lecture tours by Nationalist politicians in Britain and America. Political developments in Eire in the same period fuelled the APL efforts and alarmed the Unionists. In 1946 a new party had been established: Clann na Poblachta (Family of the Republic), led by a former IRA chief of staff,

Sean MacBride. The new party sought to eclipse Fianna Fáil in terms of its republican appeal, and it consequently made the establishment of a republic in Ireland and the ending of partition the two main planks of its platform. It also adopted a more radical perspective with regard to the economy than Fianna Fáil, and urged the implementation of a social welfare scheme. In an effort to check the rise of the new grouping, de Valera called an election in February 1948. Fianna Fáil won sixty-eight seats and was by far the largest party, but the combined opposition total was seventy-eight. Clann na Poblachta won ten seats and agreed to participate in an improbable coalition of all the other parties including the Conservative Fine Gael. By the end of 1948 the new government had declared Eire a republic and had taken her formally out of the British Commonwealth.

De Valera responded to the election defeat by indentifying his party all the more strongly with Irish nationalist aspirations. After the election he undertook an extensive speaking tour of the USA, Australia and New Zealand in which he called on the British government to end partition. He reiterated this message on a British speaking tour in October 1948 when he also characterised Unionist Party rule in Northern Ireland as 'fascist', and hinted that the unity of Ireland might have to be brought about by force.[11] By 1949 both the Southern government and the Fianna Fáil opposition were working together in furtherance of the anti-partitionist campaign.

In the North the Unionists launched their own propaganda drive. In April 1948 Brooke hurried to London to reply to de Valera's American pronouncements and to attempt to counter the publicity they had been given by the British press. The Ulster Unionist Council published a series of pamphlets reasserting Ulster's loyalty and playing up her part in the war in contrast to Eire's neutrality.[12]

Midgley threw himself into this propaganda war in a fashion reminiscent of the rabid radical of his early political career. The oratory was just as eloquent and florid; the conviction just as burning and sincere. Once again he seems to have seen himself in a chosen role. In the 1920s he was a socialist pioneer who epitomised the evangelistic approach of the ILP in its attempts to usher in a 'new dawn'. Now, in the late 1940s, he acted as if he had been chosen to bear Ulster's standard in her most pressing hour of need. As Nationalist propaganda attacks intensified so Midgley's sense of crusading zeal became all the more pronounced.

On 5 January 1948 at Greenisland Unionist Hall, Midgley called for a 'spiritual awakening'.[13] Striking a personal note, he deliberated on the inspiration he received from listening to Handel's *Messiah*, and urged his fellow Unionists to steep themselves in music and literature so that 'their attitude and contributions to the sum total of human affairs would be positive and not merely negative'. In Midgley's view their political and religious creed 'placed no boundaries to the evolution of our minds or the majesty of our conceptions'. A spiritual awakening was needed since, for Midgley, 'material impulses and incentives' could not of themselves save mankind. A unification of body, mind and spirit, 'in the grandest symphony of all the ages for the regeneration of mankind', was the ideal he preached. In another rhetorical flourish he stressed that their outlook had to be based on 'the acceptance of a moral code in harmony with the purposes of the Divine Redeemer'. Tolstoy was invoked to make the point that 'the kingdom of God is within you'. Finally, in a passage which distinguished him from the bulk of his new colleagues in the Unionist Party, he declared: 'We must not degenerate into the condition of using our ancient watchwords and slogans (or allowing them to be used) as a veneer or camouflage behind which to defend or entrench interests which are the very antitheses of our spiritual grandeur.'

The speech was a remarkable one. Seldom, if ever, before, had a Unionist Party audience listened to such celestial rhetoric and been encouraged to steep themselves in the arts and to dwell deeply on the question of their spiritual health. Midgley was well aware of the dead weight of much of the Unionist creed, inward-pointing and defensive as it was. He wanted to fight the Ulster cause by galvanising Unionism into a vital, creative and outward-looking force which would not have to depend on the catchcries of the past to justify itself and maintain its position. There is again a suggestion that he continued to fear the recrudescence within the party of a section of opinion which hankered after the pre-war days of economic *laissez-faire* and social privileges. For Midgley the Unionist Party had to be visionary and had to be prepared to keep on adapting to change as it had done in the immediate post-war years. To him the best form of defence of Ulster's constitutional position was to take the initiative in building a new, prosperous Ulster closely linked as always to Britain. Midgley seems to have set himself the task of refurbishing the Unionist Party image single-handedly; of applying a progressive, philosophical gloss to what had come to be viewed, especially in Britain, as a stale, oligarchic outlook obsessed with the past. Midgley was not content to simply parrot 'not an inch' to his audience. He had adopted a cause and he was going to emblazon it with personal qualities such as had not before been synonymous with Unionism. Indeed he could be said to have attempted to imbue Ulster Unionism with the kind of soulful ethos which Patrick Pearse had sought to identify with Irish Nationalism.[14]

It was in such a vein that he addressed another Unionist gathering at Lisburn in April 1948.[15] At this meeting Midgley strongly denied that the Unionist Party was 'an old fashioned Tory' party, and said that it was 'not synonymous with the forces of reaction'. Unionist policy, he declared, was the preservation of the 'highest British standards of liberty, justice, wages, working conditions, educational opportunities and social security'. Resuming the evangelical tone of his Greenisland address, he went on to advocate an 'Ulster Day' when,

they should meet under the auspices of their various Protestant denominations . . . and dedicate themselves to the God of their fathers who had brought them out of the land of spiritual bondage into the light of a free, democratic and progressive way of life.

If, he suggested, it was decided to synchronise this day with the twelfth of July, then the latter celebration would take on 'a newer, deeper and grander spiritual significance through the wider realisation of the epoch making nature of the Battle of the Boyne'.

This speech clearly brought out the extent of Midgley's conversion to Unionism and Orangeism. He unequivocally identified the Ulster of which he was proud with the Protestant population. Implicit in the above declarations was the belief, made explicit on other occasions, that the Catholic community was in thrall to a form of spiritual and intellectual bondage which rendered it incapable of joining in, and contributing to, the way of life he cherished and celebrated. In Midgley's private papers there are several quotations regarding the Reformation and the revolution in the intellectual life of man occasioned by the development of printing.[16] In his scheme of things, Protestantism was the child of this revolution, a testimony to man's liberation from intellectual enslavement. Complementing, as he saw it, this belief was a view of Catholicism as a dogmatic, authoritarian creed still rooted in the pre-Reformation age. As was noted earlier, there was but a simple piece of deduction involved to arrive at the conclusion that, in modern Ireland, Protestantism represented the protector of every advance that had been won for the people, while Catholicism threatened to roll back the tide of progress.

Midgley seemed to view Catholicism as a monolith, the mass of Catholics blindly following the dictates of bishops and priests to the letter. At this stage of his political career it suited him to adopt such a view and to earn his Unionist 'spurs' with impeccably Orange-flavoured orations. It is pertinent to ask, however, if he was privately convinced. For many years in the Labour movement Midgley had been in close touch with the Catholic community and had enjoyed the friendship of many individual Catholics. Some of the latter had denounced the activities and outlook of the Catholic church as vehemently as Midgley. In addition Midgley had had personal experience of several election contests in Northern Ireland, including some of his own, in which a majority of Catholics had openly defied the wishes of the church and had voted for the Labour candidate instead of the Nationalist. Midgley's defeat in 1938, of course, was the election contest he would remember most clearly and for which he would never forgive the Catholics of Dock. On that occasion he had certainly been victimised by a mob which had responded slavishly to the Catholic church's pronouncements on Spain. Midgley, however, had undergone similar ordeals at the hands of Protestant mobs inflamed by the speeches of Unionist politicians and Orange leaders. In short, he had sufficient experience of both communities to know that the sweeping denunciations he took to making about the minority were as true a reflection of that community as Nationalist descriptions of 'duped Orangemen' were about the Protestant people.

Midgley was untiring in his efforts to make his mark as a Unionist. No attack on Ulster was to be left unanswered. Where in the past Unionists might have been slow to react to criticism, Midgley publicly leapt to Ulster's defence and made it known that he had done so. In May 1948 Brendan Harkin, Belfast delegate at the Electrical Trades Union conference at Great Yarmouth, stated that the Northern Ireland government was using the law of the country against the trade unions.[17] Midgley took the opportunity at a meeting in Strabane to denounce the statement as a 'damnable falsehood', and added that every piece of negotiating and conciliation machinery enjoyed by British workers was at the disposal of Northern Ireland workers.[18] A few days later he reacted just as swiftly to a statement made at the British Labour Party conference at Scarborough. At the conference a delegate by the name of Carleton described Northern Ireland as 'a police state as bad as, if not worse, than any other in Europe'.[19] Midgley immediately sent a telegram to the conference chairman, Manny Shinwell, which read: 'Emphatically repudiate statement regarding Northern Ireland made at your conference by delegate Carleton. One hundred thousand British trade unionists in Northern Ireland know that his assertions are fantastic and untrue.'[20] Midgley was thus determined to take the Unionists' fight into quarters where they had not hitherto deigned to join battle. His past experience of the Labour movement, both in Britain and Ireland, was of great benefit to the Unionists in this regard. Midgley's concern to impress upon British Labour opinion the views of the vast majority of Ulster's workers served to broaden the scope of Unionist political activities. He was now attempting on his own what the UULA had neglected to do for decades.

Midgley also carefully monitored the speeches and statements of Nationalist politicians in Northern Ireland. When he found that they had indulged in strong anti-Ulster or anti-British rhetoric, he took it upon himself to 'expose' this to the Ulster people as a whole.[21] Midgley was as good as his word. In Stormont and at meetings throughout Northern Ireland he proclaimed the Unionist viewpoint, denying anti-partitionist charges of discrimination and injustice, and lauding the freedoms and social benefits afforded to Ulster by means of her British heritage. He flayed 'Communist totalitarianism' as well as Irish Nationalism, saying that it was 'creeping over sections of Europe like a shattering paralysis'.[22] In September 1948 he went on tours of England and Canada to spread the word,[23] and to play his part in attempting to repair the damage which Unionists obviously felt had been done by anti-partitionist speakers. In October 1948 Midgley reflected the Unionist anger and anxiety caused by de Valera's British speaking tour. He described it as

one of the most malignant and mendacious attempts at political blackmail ever attempted by a politician whose vanity was so over-weening that he still regarded himself as leader of a people who had rejected his government at the last general election.[24]

While this propaganda war was being waged, sectarian tensions in Northern Ireland rose steeply and the political life of the Province grew more unstable. Against the background of the anti-partitionist barrage, and the British government's apparent reluctance once again to get too involved in Irish political affairs, the Unionists felt that a clear statement of the popular will in Northern Ireland had to be made. By declaring a republic, the Southern government had begged a response from the North. Brooke took up the gauntlet and called an election for 10 February 1949.

III

The election was held in an atmosphere charged with sectarian passion. Brooke announced quite bluntly that the Unionist government was going to the people on one question alone: 'whether this country is as determined as it was in the past to remain part of the United Kingdom'.[25] While all Northern Ireland elections had, in the final analysis, been referendums on the constitution, there had always been some effort made, in varying degrees by all parties, to win votes on other issues. This time nothing else mattered; effectively, it was a straight fight between Orange and Green.

The political parties of the new Irish Republic decided that it was their fight too. On 27 January 1949 an All-Party Anti-Partitionist conference was held in Dublin. De Valera attended for Fianna Fáil; Gen. Richard Mulcahy for Fine Gael; William Norton for Labour; and Sean MacBride for Clann na Poblachta. At this conference it was decided to set up a fund to help anti-partitionist candidates at the election, and collections were to be taken for it outside every Catholic church in the south on the following Sunday. The Unionists could not have been presented with a more lethal campaign weapon.

The contest was immediately dubbed the 'Chapel Gates Election' and the Unionist press carried photographs of the collections being taken outside the chapels.[26] The total sum accumulated has been estimated at £46,000.[27] Campaigning in East Down for the young Brian Faulkner, Midgley declared that 'the arrogant assertions and unsurpations of Mr Costello and his colleagues in Dublin constituted a challenge which no right-thinking and self-respecting loyalist could afford to ignore'.[28] Other Unionist candidates also exploited the episode which was used to justify Brooke's ringing clarion call: 'we are fighting for our existence'.[29]

In Willowfield Midgley faced the challenge of a familiar figure: William Leeburn of the NILP. It was a contest laden with irony, for, on 31 January 1949, the NILP conference voted, with Leeburn's support, to unequivocally endorse the constitutional position of Northern Ireland.[30] Such a declaration, of course, was what Midgley had urged in 1942 when he was opposed by Leeburn. The NILP had struggled on from that time, polling well in 1945 despite only securing two seats at Stormont, but still debilitatingly riven by the national question. In 1948 the party executive proposed to the British Labour Party that it affiliate as a regional council. This was too much for such individuals as the party chairman, Bob Getgood, and secretary Joseph Corrigan who both promptly resigned. While the British Labour Party stalled, more anti-partitionist members of the NILP left, and in January 1949 a Northern section of the Irish Labour Party was formed.[31] This left the NILP with nothing more to lose by declaring in favour of the border.

Midgley made the most of the NILP's muddle. In his election literature he reminded voters that Leeburn had been instrumental in Beattie becoming NILP leader in 1942. In addition, he represented the NILP's attempt to affiliate to the British Labour Party as a deliberate ploy to avoid a commitment on the constitution and to retain some anti-partitionist support: 'The Northern Ireland Labour party, is hopelessly divided, bemused, befogged, befooled and bewildered.'[32]

Elsewhere in Belfast emotions got somewhat out of hand during the campaign. Jack Beattie was stoned by a mob as he attempted to hold a meeting in a Protestant part of his constituency. He was thereafter confined to the Catholic Short Strand area. Beattie was standing as an Independent Labour candidate but he was avowedly anti-partitionist, as was James Donnelly, the Independent Labour candidate in Cromac. Donnelly also had his meetings broken up.[33] There was violence on both sides, however, and Unionist supporters were attacked by Nationalists in Dock.[34] Midgley appealed to Unionists to exercise 'patience and restraint',[35] but in view of the climate of tension in which the election was held he could hardly have been surprised that this advice was not always heeded. His contribution to such a climate had not been negligible. While he may have considered the following exhortation innocuous, some may have interpreted it as a battle order:

. . . we must enthuse, inspire and influence our relatives, friends and neighbours in every street, town, village and hamlet, so that from the break of day our people will march in companies and battalions to form one united army, marching with songs and victory on their lips, in their hearts a prayer for Deliverance from Tyranny and Wrong, and determined by their votes, to preserve their Free Institutions and Way of Life.[36]

The Unionists got the resounding vote in favour of the constitution that they had demanded. The obtained 234,202 votes and thirty-seven seats. The Anti-Partition League won nine seats and polled 101,445. The APL had put forward seventeen candidates. The NILP lost its two seats, as did Beattie his, to the Unionists, but two anti-partitionist Labour candidates were returned. Two Independents and two Independent Unionists made up the full complement of MPs. Midgley triumphed emphatically, polling 11,304 votes to Leeburn's derisory

1,611. The turn-out was high in Willowfield, as it was generally, and there was a poll of over seventy-seven per cent.[37] Midgley was suitably jubilant for, in holding the Willowfield seat, he had performed the unique feat, at least for British politics, of being returned for the same constituency under three different party labels: Labour, Commonwealth Labour, and Unionist.

In response to the South declaring itself a republic, the British government passed the Ireland Bill in June 1949. This measure guaranteed Northern Ireland's position within the United Kingdom and stipulated that it could not secede from the Union without the consent of the Stormont parliament. The Unionists had reason to believe that they had won the war of words.

IV

When the new Northern Ireland parliament met on 1 March 1949, Midgley seconded the King's speech. He used the occasion to expatiate on what he saw as Ulster's 'heritage of spiritual freedom'. It was another attempt by Midgley to stake a claim for political eminence:

We believe that within the ambit of the state with which we are proud to be associated, and within the structure of society in that state, there is room for every section of the community. Anything that is lacking in our community by way of compassion, any uncharitableness, or malice, or unkindness, or any deficiency is due to the inherent deficiencies in human nature and is a manifestation of the weakness of the flesh. They are not inherent in the social organism.[38]

Taking refuge in such rhetoric, Midgley was able to blind himself to the very real grievances suffered by the minority in Northern Ireland in such areas as jobs and housing. Once again he was neglecting to reflect on his years in the Labour movement when he championed the Catholics of Dock Ward who were particularly deprived in these respects. Again he seemed to be justifying his defence of Ulster society with reference to one fact: the Catholic community's hostility to the Northern Ireland state. The minority's refusal to share his pride in the Ulster-British way of life made it easy to lay the blame for all social ills at its door. Midgley simply reiterated the traditional Unionist attitude in Ulster's vicious circle: that while Catholics remained 'disloyal' and uncooperative they would be responsible for their own sufferings.

Much of the anti-partitionist propaganda was hyperbole, and Midgley and other Unionists were justified in pouring scorn on charges of fascism and on claims that Northern Ireland was a police state. The minority shared equally in the new social welfare schemes which elevated the standard of living of the average Catholic family in the North to an appreciably higher level than that of the average family in the South. If Catholics still constituted a disproportionately large section of the lowest paid occupational sector and of the unemployed, educational opportunities had improved sufficiently to give more Catholics access to the professions.[39] As far as the state's coercive powers were concerned, it must be kept in mind that the IRA had carried on a bombing and assassination campaign during the early years of the war, and continued to constitute a threat to the state after it had petered out. Events in the 1950s were to show that the Northern state could not afford to be complacent about security. Moreover, the Northern government's attempts to deal with the IRA in this period paled by comparison with the actions of the Southern government.[40]

In view of his sterling personal efforts on behalf of Ulster's cause, it seemed likely that a government post would once again come Midgley's way. In September 1949 it was rumoured that the Ministry of Health and Local Government was about to be split into two, and Midgley's name was linked with the proposed new Ministry of Local Government.[41] No such change was made but, in the following month, the Minister, William Grant, died. A cabinet reshuffle took place and Midgley was brought in as the new Minister of Labour and National Insurance. The appointment dated from 4 November 1949.[42]

Midgley scarcely had time to take stock of his new duties before a major controversy shook the Unionist Party. It centred on the government's education policy and the way in which the 1947 Act was being implemented by the Minister of Education, Lt. Col. Samuel Hall-Thompson. The 1947 Act had, as stated earlier, increased grants to voluntary schools, the majority of which were Catholic. This was opposed by a large section of Protestant opinion, including, of course, Midgley himself. For some Protestants, however, objections to the funding of Catholic schools were based on the fact that the 1947 Act had altered the education legislation of 1930 which had instituted compulsory bible instruction in schools which had been transferred to the state. The 1930 Act had been passed by the Unionists in response to Protestant church and Orange Order pressure over the 1923 Education Act which had attempted to introduce a system of secular education. As a member of the Belfast Corporation Education Committee, Midgley had been a fierce opponent of the 1930 Amending Legislation,[43] and had continued to oppose the principle of compulsory bible instruction.

After the 1947 Act had ended compulsion, many Protestants felt that they had transferred their schools in good faith and had been tricked out of receiving the kind of religious education they desired for their children. The Catholic school managers, on the other hand, provided strict Catholic teaching in their schools whose grants, of course, the government had agreed to raise to sixty-five per cent. The Orange Order once again threw its weight behind the Protestant churches' campaign,[44] and Hall-Thompson faced a storm of criticism which alerted Brooke to the potential danger the controversy held for the Unionist Party.

Midgley had made clear his opposition to the 1947 Education Act during the long debate which preceded its becoming law. From then on he had rarely wasted an opportunity to make life uncomfortable for Hall-Thompson, whether over the main issue of government grants to voluntary schools,[45] or smaller, subsidiary ones such as teachers' salaries[46] and intermediate school regulations.[47] In 1949 Hall-Thompson attempted to introduce a bill to enable the Ministry to pay the employers' proportion of teachers' National Insurance contributions in voluntary schools. Midgley led a revolt against the measure, at first from the back benches, and then in the cabinet. At a cabinet meeting on 18 November 1949 he stated that:

while from an administration standpoint he agreed it was appropriate that the employers' share of insurance contributions in respect of teachers should be treated similarly to their salaries, he was very unhappy about the tendency in this and previous legislation regarding the scale of assistance to voluntary schools, the bulk of which were under Roman Catholic management. He thought that the number of non-transferred Protestant schools would diminish so that in course of time practically the only voluntary schools would be those under Roman Catholic control. The government, by proceeding with the Bill, would be accepting a responsibility which later on would be a benefit for Roman Catholic schools alone.[48]

Opposition to Hall-Thompson's bill both within the Unionist Party and outside, coupled with the long-standing disagreement between the government and the Protestant churches, brought matters to a head. Brooke feared for the unity of the Unionist Party and felt that he had to head off a possible collision between supporters and opponents of the government's education policy. In the light of this Hall-Thompson was asked to make himself the government's sacrifice. After consultations with the Orange Order on 14 December,[49] Hall-Thompson duly resigned. His bill was to be introduced for a short period pending a final arrangement.[50]

In cabinet on 15 December, Brooke attempted to clarify the position:

The Prime Minister said that the difficulties which had been experienced in connection with the Bill arose mainly from the opposition of a section of the party to the existing provisions relating to voluntary schools. The hopes of the original planners that elementary schools would all come under local authority control had not been realised and the present system seemed to contain the seeds of continual trouble with the attendant risk of splitting the Unionist party and ultimately endangering the constitutional position of Northern Ireland. He had come to the conclusion, therefore, that it should be carefully re-examined in order to see whether some alternative could not be found which, while ensuring fair treatment for all creeds and classes, would be more universally acceptable. He was not, however, committed to an amendment of the law, as any fundamental change might prove to be impracticable.[51]

The cabinet minutes record that, in the discussion which followed, the weight of opinion came down in favour of the 1947 Act and against capitulation to the wishes of the 'extremists'. The sixty-five per cent grants principle was also upheld, the comment being that 'nothing should be said which might be interpreted as indicating a willingness to retreat from that position'. Finally, it was also urged that 'the announcement of the review should be related to the educational system and not to the 1947 Act'.[52] Midgley thus appears to have been in a minority in cabinet.

Brooke then went on to say that he would make clear the government's determination to proceed with the bill and that he was calling for a review of the educational system rather than of the 1947 Act. He also promised to indicate that the government's policy in respect of the sixty-five per cent grants would remain unchanged.[53]

While Brooke's intentions seemed clear from this, succeeding events somewhat belied his cabinet attitude. In Stormont on 16 December he simply promised that the government would review the whole educational system,[54] a promise which encouraged the Protestant protesters to believe that the changes they desired were on the way.[55] Secondly, to general astonishment and to the recipient's disquiet, he gave the vacant education portfolio to Midgley. The appointment dated from 12 January 1950.

It was a move which can probably only be explained in terms of Brooke's approach to government. He was a shrewd leader whose first priority was always the preservation of party unity. He had weathered one storm of criticism from within the party over education in 1946; then he stood by Hall-Thompson and managed to get the new act through a divided cabinet.[56] When he realised that the government's educational policy was liable to give rise to recurring internal quarrels, he decided that the guns of the troublemakers had to be spiked. In the context of the Hall-Thompson controversy, there seemed no better way of doing this than to replace him as Minister of Education with the man who had been his most outspoken opponent. In doing this Brooke sought to play off the factions against one another while discreetly continuing to steer the government in much the same educational direction. This probably explains Midgley's reluctance to take the post.[57] He could not help but be aware that the Prime Minister and the majority of his cabinet colleagues favoured a policy consistent with the terms of the 1947 Act to which he had made such strong objections. As he had clearly laid down in cabinet, Brooke was prepared to countenance no radical departure in policy, despite the ambiguous impression he chose to give to outside observers. Midgley was thus faced with the choice of taking over a ministry and administering a policy, large parts of which he did not believe in, or finding himself once again in the political wilderness of the back benches with little prospect of a return to government office. Not surprisingly, he brought himself to swallow his pride.

It has been speculated that Brooke may even have been trying to get rid of Midgley by pitching him into a ministry which had so recently been the graveyard of two reputations.[58] This is very doubtful, since it seems clear that Brooke was making a strong effort to solve the problems of party squabbling over education, rather than to create more of the same. He had also just brought Midgley back into the cabinet a month previously as Minister of Labour. Had he been afraid of Midgley's influence in cabinet he would assuredly have left him on the back benches. A more plausible thesis is that Brooke admired Midgley's talents and wanted to use them in government. The education issue, although important, was only one of many, and on the vast majority of the others he and Midgley were in full agreement. While Midgley might have caused friction in the party over education if he had been on the back benches or in another government department, as Minister of Education he would be obliged to implement government policy, however distasteful he found it.

As events turned out Brooke's ploy worked perfectly. His vague assurance that the government would endeavour to come up with an educational policy more amenable to all sections of the population stalled criticism and gave the Unionists time to heal their divisions. By the time Midgley came to declare to the House of Commons in March

1951 that no fundamental changes in the educational system were possible,[59] the chorus of protest had died to a whisper. It took the perspicacious Nationalist MP, Cahir Healy, to capture the significance of Midgley's declaration:

> If you dam a spring, as a rule you will very often find that it breaks out in very unexpected places, and if a rumour does not belie him, it does credit to the psychology exercised by the Prime Minister to be able to place one of the original sources of the educational trouble in the new gap of danger. The Minister, in his turn, has been able to persuade his late colleagues on the back bench – the planners if I may so describe them – to see that the present is a very inopportune time for raising new controversy out of religious prejudices.[60]

Brooke's manoeuvres had also presented Midgley with the biggest challenge of his political career. The 1947 Act was an ambitious piece of legislation which effectively sought to revolutionise education in Northern Ireland. Quite apart from being required to handle controversy, the new minister was faced with the daunting task of substantially realising the objectives of the act. Midgley's political reputation would stand or fall according to how well he responded to the challenge.

Notes

1. *Northern Whig* 27 September 1947.
2. Ibid.
3. Ibid. The fact that the vote was not unanimous indicates that there were some Unionists who could not forget Midgley's past.
4. L.O.L. 977, the Ulster Division Lodge.
5. See T. Gray, *The Orange Order*, London, 1972, pp. 209–18.
6. An account of the Order's history, objectives and ideology is set out by three of its more eminent members in M. W. Dewar, J. Brown and S. E. Long, *Orangeism: A New Historical Appreciation*, Belfast, 1967. For an outsider's view see Gray op. cit.
7. See J. F. Harbinson, *The Ulster Unionist Party 1882–1973*, Belfast, 1973, p. 90.
8. Ibid. p. 93.
9. A good example is that of Phelim O'Neill, Unionist M.P. at Stormont in the late 1950s and early 1960s. See Gray op. cit. p. 199.
10. Gray op. cit. p. 198 cites two estimates of the Order's strength: 100,000 in the six counties, and the same figures for the whole of Ireland. The estimate of '1 in 10' of the Protestant population of Northern Ireland is frequently offered in academic and non-academic work.
11. Passages of relevant speeches are quoted in British and Irish Communist Organisation *Irish Action*, Athol Books, Belfast, 1979, pp. 47–8.
12. See, for example *Ulster Unionists Are Telling the World* and *Twenty Questions for Mr. de Valera*, both published in 1948 by the Ulster Unionist Council.
13. Speech reported in full in *Carrickfergus Advertiser* 9 January 1948.

14. For an example of Pearsian rhetoric in this regard, see quotation in F. S. L. Lyons op. cit. p. 570.
15. Press release of speech, 8 April 1948, in *Midgley Papers*.
16. A good example is a quote from Agnes Strickland: 'The Reformation was cradled in the printing press, and established by no other instrument.'
17. *Northern Whig* 15 May 1948.
18. Ibid.
19. *Belfast Telegraph* 20 May 1948.
20. Ibid.
21. See, for example, N.I. House of Commons Debates XXXII, 598.
22. Press release of speech to Ormeau Unionist Association 16 March 1948, *Midgley Papers*.
23. See *Belfast News-Letter* 17 September 1948.
24. *Northern Whig* 12 October 1948.
25. Quoted in Farrell op. cit. p. 184.
26. See, for example, *Belfast Telegraph* 1 February 1949.
27. Farrell, op. cit. p. 194.
28. *Belfast Telegraph* 28 January 1948.
29. Ibid. 24 January 1949.
30. Farrell op. cit. p. 194.
31. Ibid. The British Labour Party was not enthusiastic in any case about the NILP's proposal.
32. *Ulster-British Championship, Midley v. Leeburn*, Midgley election leaflet, *Midgley Papers*.
33. Farrell op. cit. p. 186. Beattie received money from the anti-partitionist fund.
34. *Belfast Telegraph* 9 February 1949.
35. *Belfast News-Letter* 3 February 1949. Midgley accused the Nationalist press of 'exaggerating' the incidents which had taken place.
36. *Address to the Electors of Willowfield Division, Midgley Papers*.
37. This and all other statistical information is from Elliott op. cit.
38. N.I. House of Commons Debates XXXIII, 24.
39. See E. Aunger, 'Religion and occupational class in Northern Ireland', *Economic and Social Review* 7 (1975). See also the very useful comparison of Aunger's findings with the census figures of 1911 in Bew, Gibbon and Patterson op. cit. p. 167.
40. See J. Bowyer Bell, *The Secret Army: A History of the IRA 1916–1970*, London, 1972, chapters 9–12.
41. *Sunday Empire News* 11 September 1949.
42. *Northern Whig* 5 November 1949. Midgley promptly resigned from the Belfast City Council.
43. See Dewar *et al.* op. cit. p. 180.
44. The campaign of protest is chronicled in Rev. William Corkey, *Episode in the History of Protestant Ulster*, Belfast, n.d., and in Dewar *et al.* op. cit. pp. 174–85.
45. N.I. House of Commons Debates XXXIII, 733–4.
46. Ibid. XXXII, 1006.
47. Ibid. 980.

48. CAB 4/799/10.
49. In Stormont on 17 January 1950 Brooke denied that the consultations with the Orange Order had determined Hall-Thompson's resignation. N.I. House of Commons Debates XXXIII, 2368–70.
50. See Akenson op. cit. pp. 186–8. For an account by a contemporary civil servant in the Ministry of Education see Shea op. cit. pp. 161–2.
51. CAB 4/803/10.
52. Ibid.
53. Ibid.
54. N.I. House of Commons Debates XXXIII, 2276.
55. See Dewar *et al.* op. cit. p. 184.
56. See Birrell and Murie op. cit. p. 43.
57. 'On 7 March 1950', he said at Stormont, 'I went down to the Ministry of Education with a very heavy heart indeed . . . on the horizon everything seemed black and uneasy.' N.I. House of Commons Debates XXIV, 135–6.
58. See Shea op. cit. 162. Besides Hall-Thompson, the Reverend Robert Corkey had also been forced to resign from the Ministry in 1944.
59. N.I. House of Commons Debates XXXV, 345.
60. Ibid., 350.

Chapter Ten
Minister of Education (1950–1957)

Midgley made his first public speech as Minister of Education to the Mid-Down Unionist Association on 20 January 1950. Repudiating comments made by Nationalist MPs, he said that his appointment was not 'a danger signal indicating that the government intended to depart from all conceptions and standards of fair play and justice in regard to certain voluntary schools'.[1] At the Unionist party conference a few weeks later a motion was put forward demanding the gradual withdrawal of state aid from voluntary schools. The motion embarrassed Midgley who asked for its withdrawal, saying that it was 'ill-timed and impracticable'. He further appealed to the party to 'get away from heresy-hunting'. The motion was withdrawn.[2] Midgley had wasted no time in dissociating himself from the people he had led in the campaign against state aid to voluntary schools. The price of power in this instance was a public volte-face.

Implementing, or attempting to implement, the 1947 Act was a task fraught with in-built problems. The two main difficulties – the raising of the school leaving age and the establishment of a new system of secondary intermediate schools – were bound up with one another; '. . . the difficulty of achieving simultaneously these two ends was several times greater than the difficulty of achieving either end by itself'.[3] The 1947 Act had stated that the leaving age had to be raised to 15 by 1 April 1951. By this date, however, there was still an acute shortage of accommodation and of properly qualified teachers. On 26 April 1950 Midgley had to inform the Commons that only 11 intermediate schools out of a total requirement of 250 were in operation. Admitting that the 1947 Act was 'still largely a paper plan', he could only promise 'a most concerted attack' on the question of school-building.[4] By the end of the academic year in 1951, however, there was only one more intermediate school in operation.[5] As a consequence of this shortage of schools, Midgley was forced, in the Education (Amendment) Act of 1951, to postpone the raising of the school leaving age until 1 April 1953.

Midgley had actually wanted to press ahead with the raising of the leaving age despite the apparently insurmountable obstacles. In a memorandum to the cabinet date 5 May 1950, he listed the arguments for and against the issue,[6] and in cabinet on 9 May came down in favour with the following argument: 'Such a course [raising the age] would be an incentive to the education authorities to tackle the problems confronting them with determination and to achieve advances which otherwise might not be attempted for years to come.'[7] Opposition to him from within the cabinet, however, was unanimous, the general consensus being that the provision of additional schools and the supply of teachers should be Midgley's main priorities.[8]

The failure to realise the aims of the 1947 Act brought Midgley under heavy fire at Stormont during the first two years of his period in office. These were years of slow progress giving some members leave to wonder whether the 1947 Act was not, in practice, too ambitious a blueprint to attempt to impose on Northern Ireland. Criticism came from the ranks of the Unionist Party as well as from the opposition benches. In April 1950 the Unionist member for Carrick, Alexander Hunter, summed up the feelings of most of Midgley's critics in a despairing outburst:

The Education Act is rapidly becoming a mockery. Where are the high ideals of the White Paper and the Education Act itself, when only 11 intermediate schools are ready out of a total of 250, when there is talk of putting back the school leaving age, and when local education authorities are contemplating bringing back the six-year-old starting age instead of the five-year-old. All these things are beginning to depress us. Is it any wonder that teachers are scarce when one considers the remuneration paid to members of what should be the most noble profession on God's earth?[9]

Criticism such as this made Midgley's early days at the Education ministry a stringent test of nerve and resolve.

On top of this, there was also the larger question of the review of the whole educational system which had been promised by Brooke at the time of Midgley's appointment. As has been made clear, Brooke was not in favour of any substantial alterations to the 1947 Act. Midgley's scope for introducing changes would thus appear to have been extremely limited. He prepared two long memoranda for the cabinet, in March[10] and September 1950[11], which he subsequently summarised in a third memorandum dated 16 January 1951.[12] In the latter he proposed that the 1947 Act be amended by a provision that the sixty-five per cent grants to voluntary schools be continued for a specified period and that thereafter grants at this percentage be given only to those who accepted a 'four and two' committee, the remainder being reduced to fifty per cent grants. Midgley stated that he had also considered abolishing undenominational religious instruction in the county (state) schools and putting religious instruction under the control of the management committee of the schools. This, he said, 'would allay a great deal of irritation amongst . . . Protestant clergymen'. This proposal, however, was ruled out by the Attorney-General who declared it an indirect 'endowment' of Protestantism in the county schools.

Migdley's attempt to appease those who, like himself, were hostile to the scale of government funding to voluntary schools (mostly Roman Catholic), came to nothing. The cabinet did not endorse his proposal to place a time limit on the sixty-five per cent grant,[13] and he was forced to break the news to the back-bench rebels at a party meeting on 6 February 1951 that there would be no concessions to their opinions. According to the *Belfast News-Letter,* discussions at this meeting lasted four hours, an indication in the newspaper's view that the government's critics had not been completely mollified.[14] On 21 February Brooke announced at Stormont that there would be 'no changes of significance' in the government's education policy. Mixing his metaphors, he added: 'To put the thing in a nutshell, we cannot unscramble the egg.'[15]

Midgley was then left to introduce his Education (Amendment) Bill to the House on 8 March 1951. He accurately termed it a 'tidying-up Bill',[16] and his only morsel of comfort to its opponents was that it did not, in his view, represent 'finality'.[17] Of his critics, Professor F. T. Lloyd-Dodd (Unionist, Queen's University) was the most pointed in reminding Midgley of his former stance. Midgley had, he said, 'swallowed without a single qualm' all that he had said in 1946 about the Education Act.[18] Midgley replied that his views had not significantly changed but that he also appreciated that the law had been in operation for four years, and that it would be 'bad government and bad public policy to go back upon legislation upon which people had probably based their development schemes in regard to education for the next 5, 10, 15 or 25 years'.[19]

For Midgley the new bill was proof that the state education system had 'come to stay', and was 'gaining in momentum, influence and power';[20] there was also room, however, for the voluntary system, 'an inevitable and essential part of the educational system of Northern Ireland'.[21] The latter comment illustrates the extent to which Midgley had modified his views on the need for a comprehensive system of state education.[22] On the other hand he by no means enthusiastically endorsed the voluntary school set-up. In reply, on 22 November 1951, to Cahir Healy on whether or not he believed in the voluntary school system, Midgley said: 'I recognise the fact that it is there, but I do not go out of my way to add to it and extend it.'[23] Pragmatism had become his guiding principle. Put in a nutshell Midgley had some of the egg on his face and was trying to preserve as much credibility as he could in an awkward situation. Against a background of economic sluggishness[24] which retarded educational reconstruction, Midgley struggled to maintain the momentum of reform.

On 4 March 1953 he had the unhappy privilege of introducing another Education (Amendment) Bill by which the raising of the school leaving age was again postponed, this time to a date not later than 1 April 1957. Midgley admitted that the bill was 'unpalatable meat'[25] to which Harry Diamond scoffed that this was ' a deplorable admission of failure'.[26] Midgley defended himself by arguing that the problem of the shortage of schools was in many cases tied up with the difficulties of reforming the educational structures of areas whose local councils did not take easily to change.[27] As D. H. Akenson has written:

The Ministry of Education had a difficult task in overcoming the educational conservatism of the Northern Ireland populace, especially in rural areas. This rural conservatism more than any other factor explains why counties Armagh and Tyrone were without a single intermediate school for seven years after the act was passed and County Fermanagh for eight.[28]

Midgley made frequent appeals to local authorities to shoulder the burden of educational reform,[29] but winning their whole-hearted backing and co-operation was often an uphill battle.

By the end of the academic year 1952/3 however, Midgley had some achievements to his credit and had reason to believe that the tide had turned in his favour. By this time three more intermediate schools were almost completed, seventeen others were in the course of erection and some thirty were being planned. By 31 July 1953, twenty-three new primary, three new grammar, one technical and one new special school had been completed in addition to eighty major extension schemes (i.e. schemes costing more than £5,000 each) and 151 school meals projects. Thirty-four new primary and three new grammar schools were under construction along with forty-eight major extension schemes of all kinds. The number of new school places of all kinds provided between 1947 and 1953 reached a total of over 13,000. The number of students

engaged in teacher training courses in the year 1952/3 was 1,251, over
twice the figure for 1948/9. The problem of the teacher shortage was, by
1953, well on the way to being resolved. The size of primary school
classes had also been reduced, and the number of grammar school and
university scholarships awarded greatly increased.[30] Midgley had also
promised to strive for the establishment of a college of music,[31] a project
dear to his heart given his love of music and his frequent attendance at
concerts and recitals throughout Northern Ireland.

By the end of September 1953 Midgley felt sufficiently satisfied with
Ulster's educational progress to claim that, in the period from 1949, it
was 'unequalled' anywhere in Britain or the Commonwealth.[32] It was a
large claim, somewhat at variance with the fact that the new system was
only just beginning to get off the ground. However, it was once again
election time in Ulster, and Midgley never was one to hide his light
under a bushel.

II

During his years as Minister of Education Midgley was no stranger to
political controversy outwith his department. Of all the members of the
Northern Ireland government during the 1950s he was the most consistently outspoken. Harry Midgley neither mellowed in temperament nor
lost his passion for what he stood for; he grew old imperceptibly.

In the Northern Ireland general election of October 1953, he
retained his Willowfield seat by defeating his NILP challenger, Norman
Searight, by 6,539 votes to 2,966. His majority had thus been consider-
ably reduced but the poll was a low 59.5 per cent.[33] It was, in fact, a very
quiet election with low polls the norm throughout the Province. The
sectarian temperature had somewhat cooled despite the continuing
propaganda efforts of the Nationalists and several disturbances during
the coronation celebrations of Queen Elizabeth II. The Unionists won
38 seats, one more than in 1949 notwithstanding the fact that their total
vote was just over half the figure for that election. Nationalist, Anti-Partition, Republican and Irish Labour representatives accounted for
eleven seats. The Unionists again saw off the NILP challenge in all
contests, and the new parliament thus had the same complexion as the
previous one. Perhaps the only result of note was the defeat of Col.
Hall-Thompson, former Minister of Education, by the leader of the
National Union of Protestants (NUP), Norman Porter, in the Belfast
constituency of Clifton.[34] Porter, a lay preacher, had based his appeal on

his opposition to government funds for voluntary schools while Hall-Thompson had defended the principles of his 1947 Education Act. Porter was to carry on his fight at Stormont where he was to beard Midgley regularly over the issue, and to remind him of his former stance on the matter before he became minister.

Midgley's speeches and writings of the 1950s frequently endeared him to the 'hard-line' wing of the Unionist Party who applauded his blunt and forthright pronouncements about the minority in Northern Ireland, and the government in the South. While some Unionists in this period, most notably Brian Maginness and Morris May, lent a liberal inflexion to the party's overall voice, Midgley's contribution served as the most striking evidence that traditional concerns still held sway.

In terms of a general political outlook encompassing social and economic developments, Midgley could still, in this period, be considered a 'left of centre' politician. He retained, for example, his membership of two trade unions – NUDAW and the Amalgamated Society of Woodworkers (ASW) – and was most proud to do so. He believed that profound, even revolutionary, changes had been effected in British society in a humane and peaceful manner, and he believed that these beneficial gains had to be consolidated and made imperishable. For Midgley this meant resistance to the extremist politics of Left and Right. In an election speech on behalf of a Unionist candidate on 30 October 1952, he said:

We cannot return to the bad old cruelties and injustices of early capitalism, and it is to be devoutly hoped that we shall not drift or be forced into a cruel regimental system of state collectivism which would be the prelude to a soulless communist materialism.[35]

Midgley's world view and general political philosophy were, however, of secondary importance in regard to the impact he made on Ulster politics at this time. The long-running 'cold war' between the governments of North and South in Ireland did not in the least ebb during the 1950s, and Midgley was one of its most active 'participants'. His efforts, moreover, did not go unnoticed either by Nationalist politicians and propagandists on one side, or by Protestant extremists on the other.

The views of the latter group were articulated through the columns of the *Ulster Protestant,* a newspaper which combined a fierce anti-Catholicism with a detachment – often critical – from the Unionist Party. The paper afforded much space to Norman Porter's NUP but denied that it was this organisation's official organ.[36] Midgley contributed articles to the *Ulster Protestant* and had several of his most controversial speeches reproduced in full. In contrast to the scorn heaped upon those Unionists deemed to be 'appeasers' of the minority, the *Ulster Protestant* had nothing but admiration for Midgley.

In March 1951 the paper carried a full report of an address delivered by Midgley to the Duncairn Unionist Association. Midgley's message on this occasion was the stuff of many an *Ulster Protestant* editorial. He said:

The broad, outstanding fact is that Protestantism has been almost extirpated in Eire . . . Not only can Northern Ireland Protestants observe the dwindling of the Protestant population in Eire, they cannot help but be aware of the fact that there is a steady tendency to set aside, or ignore, British legal decisions in the interest of the Roman Catholic faith when any case involving the custody of children comes before the Eire courts.[37]

Midgley's attacks on the role of the Catholic church in the Irish Republic not surprisingly intensified with the outbreak of controversy in the South surrounding Dr Noel Browne's Mother and Child scheme.[38] Browne was Minister of Health in the coalition government and, in March 1951, he drew up a health services scheme for mothers and children. The Catholic hierarchy immediately expressed its disapproval of the scheme on the grounds that it was a danger to Catholic moral teaching and that it represented an increase in state power. Browne's scheme was dropped as a result of the hierarchy's opposition and Browne himself resigned in April 1951. Protestant suspicions that political power in the South was vested in the church rather than parliament seemed amply justified.

The day following Browne's resignation, Midgley told Willowfield Unionists: 'There is no doubt that the Roman Catholic hierarchy has entered the political arena and that it is becoming more and more aggressive in extending the frontiers of Roman Catholic authority into the fields of medicine and education.'[39] For Midgley, the episode vindicated all he had been saying about Catholic church power in Ireland. However, his triumphalist response served primarily to bolster Unionist self-righteousness and to furnish more reasons for Protestants to be distrustful and intransigent in relation to the Catholic community. Midgley's 'soap box' technique had long been part of his political style and had lent colour and flair to his personality. It could also have the effect, however, of selling him short as a man capable of providing responsible leadership. Midgley had the intelligence to offer constructive criticisms, and the strength of personality to encourage the same from the people he addressed without recourse to belligerence or bigotry. It is to be regretted that on the vast majority of occasions in this stage of his career he took the easier option and played his own part in fortifying the cultural and political barriers which stood resolutely between Ulster's Protestant and Catholic communities.

Midgley's outspokenness was such that he became something of an irritant and an embarrassment to the government. His contributions to the *Ulster Protestant* could hardly have endeared him to those Unionists who were the butt of some strong criticism from that organ. A good example was Brian Maginness, Minister of Home Affairs from 1949 to 1953, and then Minister of Finance.[40] Brooke himself was never singled out for criticism but he was unavoidably implicated in the paper's allegations of government 'appeasement' of the minority. Indeed, Brooke had to suffer interruptions during his 12th of July speech at Finaghy Field in 1954 when protesters calling themselves 'the Orange and Protestant Committee' made loud objections about government policies, including the funding of voluntary schools.[41] As was shown clearly in regard to educational policy, Brooke had set his face against any appeasement of this vocal Protestant extremist minority. Northern Ireland needed outside investment and new industries very badly, and at least an appearance of communal harmony was thus much desired by the government.

At Stormont in November 1955, the Nationalist MP, Joe Stewart, claimed that he had had a meeting with an English Tory who also happened to be a Catholic. This Tory had expressed astonishment over Midgley's attacks on the Catholic hierarchy. Stewart asked rhetorically: 'Is that helpful in trying to bring British industrialists over here?'[42]

On 5 February 1955 the Southern newspaper the *Irish Press* published an interesting editorial attack on Midgley who, around this time, had been particularly critical of the Catholic church's educational policy. The editorial began with the observation that Midgley was not noted 'for a tactful manner or a disciplined tongue', which was eminently fair comment; it then went on to accuse Midgley of upholding an educational system which 'heavily penalises them [Catholics] for keeping their own educational establishments', which was not. In conclusion, it offered the following contention:

Mr. Midgley, in speaking of the ecclesiastical leaders with contempt, is pandering to the meanest level of intelligence among the Orangemen. 'The Bishops, get at the Bishops!' is an old cry from the Lodges. By reviving it Mr. Midgley hopes to snatch a few notes from the Norman Porters and other anti-Catholic crusaders to the right of him.[43]

If the *Irish Press* was right to claim that Midgley was actively seeking support from Protestant extremists – and his writings and speeches of the 1950s suggest that he was – the question arises as to whether or not Midgley had designs on ousting Brooke and riding to power on the back of a populist Protestant surge. The question is an impossible one to answer with any certainty,[44] but there are points to be made in connection with the matter.

The first is that Midgley was undoubtedly looked upon as a champion of Protestant interests by such people as Norman Porter with whom he was on very good personal terms. In March 1956 Porter stated at Stormont:

My quarrel with the Minister [Midgley] is that he has not yet been able to carry into effect his own personal views in the Cabinet of which he forms a part. I hope the day is not far distant when the Prime Minister, who was with him at that recent meeting in Dungannon, will be converted to the principles which I have so often heard the Minister of Education pronounce . . .[45]

This statement, perhaps significantly, was reproduced in the *Ulster Protestant.*[46]

The meeting in Dungannon alluded to by Porter took place late in February 1956 when Midgley was reported to have urged Protestant landowners not to sell lands which would be used for the building of Catholic schools.[47] Joe Stewart, the Nationalist MP claimed at Stormont on 7 March that a prominent Unionist had expressed his disgust to him at Midgley's speech. According to Stewart, it was this Unionist's view that Brooke had made an 'excellent and reasonable speech' at the meeting but that Midgley 'tore the whole back out of the Prime Minister's speech with a vicious attack on the Catholic church'.[48]

Moreover, it was also the case that Midgley's only route to the leadership of the Unionist Party lay in a 'revolt from below'. The party bosses were people of many years' loyalty and service who remembered all too clearly Midgley's NILP and Commonwealth Labour past. In 1953 after the death of J. Maynard Sinclair, Midgley was passed over for the vacant post of Minister of Finance which would have put him in line to succeed Brooke as leader of the party. Midgley may thus have felt that only by distancing himself from Brooke and taking opportunities such as the Dungannon meeting to embarrass him, could he win enough popular support to panic the party into making a change. The Unionist Party always watched carefully for signs of Protestant disaffection. Such signs had been apparent in 1942–3 and had played an important role in unseating J. M. Andrews. The criticisms of the government in the early and mid-50s constituted no such threat to Brooke, but it was not beyond doubt that dissent would continue to be confined to a small minority, especially if economic hardship was to befall the Province.

Midgley at no time made any attempt to modify his rhetoric. One of his last public speaking engagements took place at Portadown on 13 February 1957. On 15 February the *Portadown Times* reported him as saying that 'all the minority are traitors and have consistently been traitors to the Government of Northern Ireland'. His remarks caused a furore at Stormont where Harry Diamond raised the matter at question time on 28 February. Midgley claimed that the *Portadown Times* report was misleading and that he had only been making the point that the general attitudes of the Protestant minority in the South and the Catholic minority in the North to the respective states were strikingly different. Midgley further claimed that he had been told by the Mayor of Portadown that the local newspaper was regarded as 'suspect' by many people in the town because of the activities of a journalist whose sympathies did not lie with the government.[49] It was more publicity of an unwelcome kind for Brooke who might have been forgiven for suspecting political manoeuvring on Midgley's part.

Midgley also distinguished himself from other Unionist politicians by publicly philosophising about world trends and man's future. He dwelt repeatedly on communism and – interestingly – linked his critique of this political system to his broadsides against Catholicism. Midgley appears to have been much influenced by the attacks on communism made in the post-war period by some former party members. He frequently referred to the book *The God That Failed* (1950), a collection of critical pieces by ex-communists including Arthur Koestler whose work Midgley particularly admired. He was also influenced by George Orwell's *Animal Farm* and *1984*.

Above all, he was deeply impressed by Paul Blanshard's *Communism, Democracy and Catholic Power* which, according to his diary, he was 'studying' in January 1953.[50] In 1953 Blanshard came to Ireland to research a book which was published later that year: *The Irish and Catholic Power*. This book was a scholarly attempt to show that the Irish Catholic church had such a tight grip on the country's social, political and cultural life that the Irish Republic was in effect a theocratic state.[51] Midgley became personally friendly with Blanshard and promoted his book enthusiastically, as did several other prominent Unionists.[52] Midgley seems to have made an equally strong impression on the

American author, for, in his chapter on Northern Ireland, Blanshard wrote:

The Unionist government had in its colourful Minister of Education, Harry Midgley, one of the most outspoken critics of Catholic educational policy in Ireland. A veteran Labour leader and opponent of Franco's Spain, he does not hesitate to cross swords with any priests. He has the sagacity to attack the weakest feature of the Catholic system – the theological coercion used by the Church in maintaining that system. He contends that thousands of Catholic parents would like to send their children to schools with the children of other faiths in order that they should learn tolerance and co-operation, but that the Catholic hierarchy prevents this 'rapproachement'.[53]

Midgley reviled communism's 'soulless materialism' and portrayed its political threat as 'poisonous and deadly Totalitarianism'.[54] He proclaimed his faith in 'the Christian conception of life and ordered progress' against those whom he accused of subordinating all human rights to the glorification of a 'super state'.[55] With all this no Catholic bishop or priest could have quarrelled. For Midgley, however, Catholicism had all too much in common with communism.

On 30 August 1952 at Summerisland he argued that communism was far more likely to emerge in Catholic rather than Protestant countries. 'It seems', he said, 'a striking and significant fact that tyranny begets tyranny, and populations which have been subject to the spiritual form more readily assimilate the materialist form, hence the quick transition from clerically controlled states to communist states.'[56] For Midgley, Protestantism's guarantee of democracy and civil and individual liberties created a climate in which no tyrannical or authoritarian system could take root. This was a view echoed by the *Ulster Protestant* which, on occasion, also probed the subject of Catholicism in relation to communism.[57]

Midgley developed his theme on other occasions. In his speech to an Apprentice Boys meeting in Londonderry in 1953 he argued that there was a 'fundamental resemblance between the two great systems of authoritarian control engaged in a mighty struggle for supremacy – the Vatican and the Kremlin'. Both, he said, had 'similar structures of power, devices of deification, thought control, education control, discipline and devotion, management of truth, the strategy of penetration, and both meant the negation of democracy'.[58]

This theory had the benefit of tying up neatly what Midgley saw as the twin enemies of the Ulster-British, Protestant way of life. The message was simple: be vigilant and active in defence of your liberty lest it be subverted by authoritarian forces both spiritual and material. If the theoretical attack on Ulster's would-be assailants was new, the practical measures prescribed to counter them were very old, tried and trusted. It all came down again to 'No Surrender'.

III

The teething troubles involved in putting the 1947 Education Act into practice had largely evaporated by 1953–4. By this time an expansionist programme was well under way and a climate of relative optimism had been ushered in. Speaking at Stormont in May 1954, Midgley declared that they had passed away from 'the era of paper planning to one of visible progress'.[59] A capital investment target of £3,000,000 had been fully achieved in 1953, a year Midgley regarded as a significant turning point:

We have passed away from the period of confusion when too much was being attempted and too little done, and we are now engaged upon an ordered programme the success of which is daily becoming more and more established.[60]

Indeed it was. Thirty-three new schools, of all types, were opened in 1953/4; this figure exceeded the total for the previous years since 1948.[61] Among these new schools were the first secondary intermediate schools opened in new buildings as opposed to having been converted from old ones. In addition, more capital investment was diverted to the task of erecting the much-needed intermediate schools. By 31 July 1954, nineteen out of forty-eight new schools in the process of construction were secondary intermediate.[62] Further progress was made regarding the training of teachers, and a new teacher training college, the Ulster College of Physical Education, was opened in 1953.[63]

When the time came to present his estimates before the House the following year, 1955, Midgley was not quite so buoyant. He had to admit first of all that not enough progress had been made in the realm of technical education.[64] He then went on to say that the department had not quite reached its investment target for new building. The reasons, he said, were not far to seek: 'first, the switch-over from pre-fabricated to traditional building, and second, the gradual change from a predominantly primary to a predominantly secondary school programme'.[65]

He had no reason to be too downcast, however. Progress over the year 1954/5 had been steady and four more secondary intermediate schools had been opened.[66] His estimated expenditure for the following year –

£8,797,000[67] – was proof that the government regarded education as a
top priority. In general Midgley's estimates and his report were well
received by the House. From one unexpected quarter – the Nationalist
MP Joseph Connellan – came praise for the work done by the Ministry
for the education of the handicapped and the subnormal.[68] From Harry
Holmes, the Unionist member for Shankill, there came the following
personal tribute:

The successful working out of the Act [the 1947 Act] imposed a three-fold yoke
of partnership – on the Ministry, on the local education authorities, and on the
teachers. That so much harmony exists is a tribute to the Minister's diplo-
macy.[69]

Having weathered the earlier storm of criticism and pessimism, this
must have been sweet music to Midgley's ears.

By the end of the academic year 1955/6 Midgley had more achievements to boast of. Another eight intermediate schools had been opened
during that year, bringing the total number of pupils attending intermediate schools to 13,700.[70] Over 20,000 pupils were now attending
grammar schools on state scholarships.[71] The number engaged in
teacher training courses again rose,[72] and considerable progress was
made in the promotion of further (adult) education.[73]

In May 1956, on presentation of his estimates, Midgley claimed that
the Northern Ireland educational system was 'comparable with that in
Great Britain and, indeed, if it were claimed that in some respects we are
superior, who am I that I should deny it?'[74] Once again he was rewarded
with praise from his colleagues. The Unionist member, J. W. Morgan,
said: 'I think he [Midgley] has done remarkably well since 1947. He has
really done monumental work and deserves the credit not alone of this
committee but of the people of Northern Ireland.'[75] Midgley had
steered a path of progress and reform through an intricate maze of
difficulties. It was only fitting that his achievement in this respect should
be crowned by the raising, after such a long delay, of the school leaving
age to 15 on 1 April 1957.

Midgley presided over a period of critical educational reconstruction
in Northern Ireland. In his term of office a new system of secondary
education involving three distinct types of school – grammar, technical
and intermediate – was established. Not only were the innovations of the
1947 Act put into practice, but great improvements were also made to
the facilities which existed before the act. The extension of state control
in education met with strong resistence in some quarters. This was to be
expected given the tradition of independence enjoyed by many schools.

There were inevitable fears that government interference would result in falling standards and would destroy the tradition of excellence these schools felt they possessed. Some simply feared that too hasty a change-over from the old system to the new would cause irreparable harm to the education of many children. There was also, of course, the controversial question of denominational education and the implacable opposition of the Roman Catholic church to any form of government control over their schools. This attitude was to some extent mirrored in the outlook of those Protestants who petitioned the government loudly to make bible teaching compulsory. Quite apart from the conflict of views concerning the nature of the schools and the schools systems, there were fundamental problems of how educational development was to be financed and how far it would be practical to set about implementing the changes envisaged by the 1947 Act. Revenue had to be found; capital had to be invested; materials had to be available; and the co-operation of school managers, parents' associations, teachers, local authorities, builders, planners, and landowners, had to be secured.

Midgley picked his way through this political and administrative minefield sufficiently well to give life to the ideals of the 1947 Act. That he did so was testimony to his skill in government administration. He realised that he had to be pragmatic and that compromises had to be worked out. He was the first to compromise when he took the office in 1950. From that day he knew that his own educational ideals would not constitute the policy he would be attempting to put into practice. He was aware of the problems he faced but at no time did he lose the determination to come up with a solution. His persistence in this regard, combined with a willingness to be flexible and to preside over steady, if unspectacular, progress, issued tangible achievements and warm praise at the end of the day. Through the years of slow progress he had to bear the brunt of many people's disgruntlement. It was thus only fair that when seemingly intractable difficulties had been overcome, he should take most of the credit. It was also appropriate that the raising of the school leaving age should be his monument: few had fought harder or longer to secure a more thorough education for schoolchildren.

IV

The problems Midgley faced as Minister of Education were not all outside his department. Indeed one problem he never solved was how to work harmoniously with his civil servants, particularly his Permanent

Secretary, Reginald Brownell. Midgley may have exhibited administrative skills as a government minister, but his style of working could
hardly be labelled 'ministerial'. Few, if any, cabinet ministers in the
history of the Northern Ireland state can have been so unorthodox in
their approach to matters of government. Patrick Shea, an official in the
Education Department in the 1950s, recently published his memoirs in
which he wrote: 'The essence of Harry Midgeley's [sic] personality was
informality: ebullient, back-slapping informality.'[76] This was not the
style to which Brownell and his staff were accustomed. From the
beginning the two men were at loggerheads. Brownell's formal,
bureaucratic approach was totally at odds with Midgley's impetuosity
and impulsiveness. Midgley became distrustful, suspecting that
Brownell was running his own show behind his back.

The friction between Midgley and Brownell reached its apogee in
1956 over the issue of scholarship awards to a number of student
teachers. Midgley overruled objections by Brownell that seven scholarships had been awarded without the statutory requirements being
fulfilled. The requirements in these cases concerned medical fitness.
For Midgley, it seemed preposterous that doctors could have the last
word over the ministry. He thus insisted that the scholarships be
awarded. Brownell just as stubbornly insisted that the rules be obeyed.
After what Shea has called a 'tempestuous brawl',[77] Midgley overruled
Brownell. The latter then felt obliged to report the whole matter to the
Public Accounts Committee, a committee of the Northern Ireland
House of Commons.

This committee sat for four sessions – on 12, 19, 26 and 28 March
1957 – before coming the conclusion that in five of the cases the
scholarship payments were unlawful.[78] This ensured that the matter
would come up for discussion in the House of Commons with Midgley
obliged to explain his actions. As events transpired, the House was
never to hear his explanation.[79]

On Saturday 27 April 1957 Midgley attended the closing session of
the Ulster Teachers' Union conference in Newcastle, County Down.
Early on the Sunday morning after returning home he had a heart
attack. He was rushed to the Musgrave and Clark Clinic in Belfast
where he died on the morning of Monday 29 April. He was 64.

The funeral took place on 1 May. A service was held in Carlisle
Memorial Methodist Church and the body was laid to rest in
Carnmoney Cemetery. Crowds lined the route of the cortège along the
Antrim Road. There was a large attendance at the funeral with

representatives from all walks of life in Ulster. The many organisations with which Midgley had been connected were represented, among them the Co-operative Society, the trade union movement, ex-service organisations, the Belfast Corporation, Linfield FC, and the Orange Order. The minister who took the service said that he had lived 'with a zest and an exuberant vitality'.[80] Harry Midgley left with many people a memory just as vital.

Notes

1. *Northern Whig* 21 January 1950.
2. *Belfast Telegraph* 3 March 1950.
3. Akenson op. cit. p. 184.
4. N.I. House of Commons Debates XXXIV, 569.
5. *Report of the Ministry of Education* 1950/51, HMSO, p. 8.
6. CAB 4/818/5 PRONI.
7. CAB 4/818/12 PRONI.
8. Ibid.
9. N.I. House of Commons Debates XXXIV, 574.
10. CAB 4/813/9 PRONI.
11. CAB 4/825/11 PRONI.
12. CAB 4/837/3 PRONI.
13. CAB 4/837/4 PRONI.
14. *Belfast News-Letter* 7 February 1951.
15. N.I. House of Commons Debates XXXV, 163–4.
16. Ibid., 345.
17. Ibid., 350.
18. Ibid., 363.
19. Ibid., 398.
20. Ibid., 404.
21. Ibid., 400.
22. In March 1953 Midgley made clear his opposition to proposals put forward by the Director of the Belfast Education Authority, Dr J. Stuart Hawnt. Hawnt wanted to introduce a comprehensive experiment by integrating grammar and intermediate types of education in a limited number of schools. Midgley defended the tripartite secondary school system by asking what would become of all the material plans which had already been laid to develop this system. *Belfast Telegraph* 26 March 1953.
23. N.I. House of Commons Debates XXXV, 2286.
24. By February 1952 unemployment was 11 per cent in contrast to the rest of the UK where it averaged 2 per cent.
25. N.I. House of Commons Debates XXXVII, 147.
26. Ibid., 155.
27. Ibid., 164.
28. Akenson op. cit. pp. 184–185.
29. See, for example, *Northern Whig* 24 September 1953 and *Belfast Telegraph* 27 October 1952.

30. *Report of Ministry of Education 1952–53* pp. 12–19.
31. *Northern Whig* 17 April 1952. The project never got off the ground due to lack of finance.
32. *Belfast Telegraph* 30 September 1953.
33. This and all other statistics regarding the election are taken from S. Elliott, *Northern Ireland Election Results 1921–1972*.
34. The result was Porter 4,747; Hall-Thompson 4,402.
35. Speech in support of Sir David Campbell 30 October 1952. *Midgley Papers*.
36. *Ulster Protestant* June 1952.
37. Ibid., March 1951.
38. For a full account of this episode see J. H. Whyte, *Church and State in Modern Ireland 1923–1970*, Dublin, 1971, chapters 7 and 8.
39. Speech at Willowfield Hall 12 April 1951. *Midgley Papers*.
40. Maginness was at the centre of a storm of controversy in June 1952 when he initially banned, then permitted, an Orange march.
41. See *Ulster Protestant* August 1954. The 'Orange and Protestant Committee' had also held a meeting in January 1954 at which a vote of no confidence in the government had been passed. See Farrell op. cit. p. 208.
42. N.I. House of Commons Debates XXXIX, 2626.
43. *Irish Press* 5 February 1955.
44. It is possible, though doubtful, that the cabinet minutes of the years 1953–7 (at the time of writing, closed) will throw some light on the matter.
45. N.I. House of Commons Debates XXXX, 564.
46. *Ulster Protestant* May 1956.
47. N.I. House of Commons Debates XXXX, 544.
48. Ibid., 545.
49. Ibid. XXXXI, 489–91. It should be kept in mind that the speech was delivered at a time when a concerted IRA campaign against the Northern Ireland security forces was being waged.
50. Personal Diary 10 January 1953, *Midgley Papers*.
51. See J. H. Whyte op. cit. pp. 369–74.
52. See *Northern Whig* 4 April 1955. The British edition of the book published in 1954 carried a foreward written by the Westminster Unionist MP Col. H. Montgomery-Hyde.
53. P. Blanshard, *The Irish and Catholic Power*, London, 1953 pp. 233–4.
54. Press release of speech to Cromac Unionists 15 March 1950. *Midgley Papers*.
55. Press release of speech delivered in Newry Town Hall 17 February 1950. *Midgley Papers*.
56. Press release of speech to Summerisland Royal Black District Chapter No. 6, 30 August 1952. *Midgley Papers*.
57. See, for example, *Ulster Protestant* June 1954.
58. *Belfast News-Letter* 20 February 1953.
59. N.I. House of Commons Debates XXXVIII, 2052.
60. Ibid., 2056.
61. *Report of Ministry of Education 1953–54*, p. 8.
62. Ibid.
63. Ibid., p. 11.

64. N.I. House of Commons Debates XXXIX, 1174.
65. Ibid., 1175–6.
66. *Report of Ministry of Education 1954–55* p. 7.
67. N.I. House of Commons Debates XXXIX, 1176.
68. Ibid., 1195.
69. Ibid., 1205.
70. *Report of Ministry of Education 1955–56* pp. 9–10.
71. N.I. House of Commons Debates XXXX, 1093.
72. *Report of Ministry of Education 1955–56* p. 21.
73. Ibid. pp. 11–12.
74. N.I. House of Commons Debates XXXX, 1094.
75. Ibid., 1127.
76. Shea op. cit. p. 165. See also pp. 165–8.
77. Ibid., p. 176.
78. Special Report from the Select Committee on Public Accounts for the financial year 1955–56. H. C. 1247, HMSO, 1957, pp. 285–7.
79. When the case came up for debate in the Commons in June 1957, it was decided to permit the student teachers to continue their courses. See *Northern Whig* 21 June 1957.
Shea op. cit. p. 176 has no doubts that Midgley would have talked his way out of the whole affair: 'No-one who had seen him in action would have wagered a penny that the House would have endorsed the Committee's reprimand; Harry Midgeley [sic] in the full flight of his oratorical gifts was the most persuasive speaker I have ever heard.'
80. *Northern Whig* 2 May 1957.

Chapter Eleven
Conclusion: Success or failure?

The significance of Midgley's career in Northern Ireland politics lies mainly in his role, for so many years, as the leading figure in the Province's Labour movement. Midgley, more than anyone else in the history of the Northern Ireland state, epitomises the failure of those who have tried to break the sectarian cast of the state's politics.

Following him there have been other notable attempts, albeit from a different perspective, which have met with the same fate: the case of Gerry Fitt, a Belfast Catholic who represented the Dock constituency at Stormont and West Belfast at Westminster, and who now sits in the House of Lords; Paddy Devlin, a leading Catholic member of the NILP in the 1960s and until recently an Independent Socialist councillor in Belfast; and even Glen Barr, a prominent Loyalist figure in the present troubles who has sought alliances across the sectarian divide on the basis of class interest. Each has paid the price of trying to break tribal politics: each has suffered at the hands of his own 'tribe', and each has been reduced to a position of marginal influence.

Strictly in terms of his objectives as leader of the NILP, Midgley failed. He attempted to turn the party into a formidable political machine, backed strongly by the local trade unions and closely linked to the British Labour Party. He was forced to pursue this strategy in a guarded way in order that anti-partitionist and Catholic support would not defect *en masse*. By 1942 Midgley had come to the conclusion that only a firm declaration in favour of Northern Ireland remaining part of the UK would give the NILP a realistic prospect of political progress. He could not get the party's endorsement and was thus confronted with little choice but to leave. Midgley thus failed on two counts: first, to build the NILP into more than a weak third political force while remaining effectively neutral on the national question; and, secondly, to persuade the party to abandon that neutrality and to challenge the Unionist Party on the basis of a unionist Labour position.

In his autobiography, Patrick Shea makes the following observation about Midgley: 'When he died one thought sadly of the young, fighting iconoclast and wondered what mountains he might have climbed had his character been shaped in a more mature environment and the circumstances which influenced his political life been less parochial.'[1] Shea seems to be implying that a political environment characterised – as in Britain – by class rather than ethnic divisions might have proved more congenial to Midgley's undoubted talents.

Certainly it might be argued that the only realistic way of minimising the importance of the national question in the minds of the Northern Ireland people would have been to integrate the Province politically with the rest of the UK. Just as sectarian tensions did not, in the main, find political expression in Glasgow and Liverpool, the wider political context of UK politics might similarly have diminished the force of sectarian appeals in Northern Ireland. This is not to suggest that the task would not have been much harder, or to gloss over the fact that sectarian tensions in Northern Ireland, unlike Glasgow and Liverpool, existed in the context of a conflict over national identity. It is simply to stress that provincial politics in Northern Ireland proved to be demonstrably unamenable to anything but sectarian considerations. Devolved government meant that most issues with a bearing on class interest were settled at Westminster; at Stormont there was no escaping the overriding importance of the national question. Had Northern Ireland been integrated with the rest of the UK this issue would probably not have been surrounded with such uncertainty, and, consequently, the respective fears and mutually exclusive aspirations of both communities would not have assumed such potent political force.

The British Labour Party might have had the most to gain from such an arrangement. The strong trade union organisation in Northern Ireland would have provided a good basis from which to build its strength in the Province; many individual trade unionists in Northern Ireland actually 'contracted in' to pay a levy to the party, which, of course, they had no chance of joining or voting for. A Labour party which stood a good chance of forming a government at Westminster to legislate in the interests of working class people might have been successful in overcoming sectarianism as it has done in both Glasgow and Liverpool. At the very least it can be argued that the British Labour Party would have had more success in such circumstances than the NILP enjoyed, locked as the latter was in provincial politics which had decidedly limited relevance to social and economic issues. In addition, it might be said that people like Midgley, Fitt and Devlin would have exerted a real influence through the medium of the British Labour Party instead of being faced, in effect, with the impotent isolation which seemed inevitably to befall frustrated Ulster socialists.

Midgley of course eventually escaped that fate. He moved from being a frustrated socialist to an ardent, if unorthodox, Ulster Unionist. As such his career following his departure from the NILP must be judged by different criteria. The verdict of failure is this time far more disputable.

Midgley's critics viewed the Commonwealth Labour Party simply as a bridge constructed to take him into the Unionist Party.[2] Certainly the CLP was a Protestant Labour Party in practice and Midgley's career began, at this juncture, to slide almost inexorably into the politics of Protestant exclusivism. In a sense this had been predictable – though certainly not inevitable – since the controversy surrounding the Spanish civil war and the consequent mutual antagonism between Midgley and the Catholic community.

However, if the CLP was a bridge to the Unionist Party, it has to be said that Midgley was very slow in crossing it. Far from using the party to pave his way towards the Unionists, Midgley made strenuous attempts, especially during the 1945 election, to distinguish the CLP ideologically from the Unionist Party and to discredit the latter as a reactionary political force out of step with a changing world. In resigning his government office in 1945 Midgley once again prepared to inherit political powerlessness. He knew that the power he desired lay in the Unionist Party and nowhere else. However, he did not take the crucial step into Unionist ranks until late in 1947 when he was convinced that the differences he had with the party over social and economic policies were not significant enough to justify splitting the vote of the Protestant community and thereby giving the possible appearance of ambivalence with regard to the constitution. He also took the decision knowing that he had antagonised many Unionists who would not be quick to forgive him his past. As it was, he had to wait two years before he once again enjoyed government office.

Midgley's political outlook genuinely changed during these years, but in such a way that, had he been involved in British politics, he would probably have moved only to the right of the Labour Party.[3] The peculiarities of Northern Ireland politics dictated that Midgley's shifts on the political spectrum should take him into the Unionist Party. Midgley was prepared to take the kind of political risk which, in Ulster, was commonly considered to be an act of political suicide: he changed his political allegiance. Moreover, Midgley changed it twice and survived to wield the power he wanted so much. That in itself was a signal success.

Midgley's performance in government in the 1950s says much about Northern Ireland politics and the Unionist Party. It was a period in which the minority could at least feel that it had made, and was making, some real material gains. Besides the British social welfare benefits, there was a marked expansion in the field of Catholic education borne out by the increase in the number of Catholic schools and Catholic student teachers. This development resulted in increased opportunities for young educated Catholics to enter the universities and the professions in the late 1950s and 1960s. For this expansion, of course, Midgley and his ministry were largely responsible, and Catholic prelates were not unwilling to recognise the fact.[4] Moreover, Midgley attempted personally to help individual Catholics with educational problems, despite his public anti-Catholic rhetoric. At least one of the five scholarship cases deemed unlawful by the Public Accounts Committee in 1957 concerned a Catholic student.[5]

The changing social conditions presented the Unionist Party with the best chance it had ever had of rendering militant republicanism or nationalism a marginal force on the fringe of the state's politics. By being seen to govern fairly at both local and parliamentary levels, the Unionists might have been able to stabilise properly the Northern Ireland state and to make their 'compare and contrast' exercises with the South seem more convincing to the minority. If they had so acted, the Unionists might have largely pre-empted much of the anger and frustration which the educated Catholics of the 1960s felt obliged to express on behalf of their community and, of course, themselves who, despite their education, were still looked upon by many Unionists as second-class citizens. What was needed in the 1950s in the Unionist Party were men far-seeing and shrewd enough to take advantage of an improved social and economic climate to the end of making the state more secure.

Midgley was one of the politicians of the time of whom more vision and more courage might have been expected. They were not forthcoming. Instead Midgley attempted to accommodate the opposing body of opinion: that of the extremist Protestant lobby. It is an open question whether he did so more out of personal sympathy with their position or of political expediency. It should be remembered that the chances of Brooke being ousted and Midgley becoming leader lay only in a lurch towards extremism. In the 1950s the liberal strand of opinion within the party firmly backed Brooke as Premier. If Midgley had hopes of extremist pressure leading to upheaval inside the party, then it has to be said, with the benefit of hindsight, that he misread the situation. Events of the late 1950s (the increased NILP vote in the 1958 election), and the early 1960s (the succession of the liberal O'Neill to Brooke), tend to suggest that the voice of extreme Protestantism was of less significance in this period than before or afterwards.

There was also something of a contradiction in Midgley's espousal of libertarian principles from a political home which was characterised by its defensiveness and intransigence towards the Catholic community, and its enduring appeal to crude Protestant tribalism. Midgley's public utterances, if not his actions in practice, reflected these features of Unionism. He was all too prone to the reflex actions of the 'Not an Inch' mentality when his concern for the rights and freedoms of the individual should have led him to criticise some of the more repressive and sterile aspects of Northern Ireland life.

In this last phase of his career – his years as Minister of Education – Midgley on the whole coped well with the demands of a particularly difficult office. He displayed a political maturity which saw him stick to his task in the face of considerable pressures and obstacles. This contrasted quite starkly with the Midgley of earlier years who was prone to temperamental impetuosity and outbursts of frustration. Such tendencies, in his time as Labour's leader, made him a difficult man to work with, his undoubted energy and ability notwithstanding. In government he learnt quickly that he had to develop a capacity to suffer setbacks and to learn from them.

While the Northern Ireland political world had a somewhat stifling effect on Midgley for a long time, it also suited his populist style. It was a world at once deadly serious and roguishly colourful. Political personalities mattered almost as much as parties in such a small society where so much was done on an informal basis. Ironically, Midgley embodied many of the features of a political environment which prevented him from making the most of his talents. The same might be said of Gerry Fitt.

The links between Midgley and Fitt do not, moreover, end there. Fitt grew up in the Dock Ward when Midgley was its MP at Stormont. He remembers, as a small boy, seeing Midgley address a street-corner meeting to an audience of people who, in their poverty, looked to him as their champion: 'I got the feeling', said Fitt, 'that there was someone the people loved.'[6] It was this experience of hearing Midgley's stirring oratory and sensing the crowd's adulation which inspired Fitt to set out on a political career of his own in which he too adopted the populist style of the 'old school' of political agitator.

Midgley was also very much of his own Protestant community. This community was – and is – much more pluralist in character than some commentators have suggested.[7] Within the framework of Protestant politics in Midgley's time there occurred several moments of class friction and ideological conflict; different traditions and tendencies jostled one another in a bid to dominate the overall blend. At various points in his political career Midgley can be seen as reflecting different aspects of his community's make-up: from a crusading radicalism through what might be termed a social democratic pragmatism to an intransigent Protestant exclusivism. Midgley personified some of his community's characteristics: he could be stubborn and self-righteous as well as magnanimous and resourceful. Perhaps in contrast to the received view of the Ulster Protestant community, he was also garrulous, expansive, volatile, and usually receptive to change and new ideas.

In terms of Labour politics in Northern Ireland, Midgley was perhaps the most interesting failure in an area where no-one has yet succeeded. In relation to Northern Ireland politics generally, and the business of government in particular, he was on balance a success. Over the span of his long and chequered career his overall influence was arguably for relative good. His name is still widely known and still provokes controversy. His imprint on Ulster's political history is both indelible and inimitable.

Notes

1. Shea op. cit. p. 177.
2. Letter to the writer from Jack MacGougan 12 July 1982.
3. Consider those former ILP firebrands Lord Shinwell and Baron Kirkwood.
4. See the comments of Eugene O'Doherty, Roman Catholic Bishop of Dromore, after Midgley's death. *Belfast Telegraph* 2 May 1957.
5. Special Report from the Select Committee on Public Accounts for the financial year 1955–56, H. C. 1247, HMSO 1957, p. 286.
6. *Observer Magazine* 20 December 1981.
7. See, for example, G. Bell, *The Protestants of Ulster*, London, 1976.

Appendix

'Declaration of Policy' outlined by Harry Midgley on 20 November 1942. Subsequently reproduced in *Ulster for the Commonwealth* (1943).

We accept the present political position in Northern Ireland and are prepared to work for a government in this area which will co-operate with Great Britain and the British Commonwealth of Nations

This means that we reject the claims of those who stand for separation from Great Britain and the Commonwealth.

This does not mean that we accept the doctrines or policy of the Conservative party; but it does mean that the Commonwealth Labour Party[1] will work for the establishment of a government which will seek to establish social justice and social security for all in Northern Ireland.

Those who believe that the mere removal of partition would solve any social or economic issue are living in a fool's paradise. Those, also, who profess to believe that it is wise, expedient or possible to build up a Northern Ireland divorced from political and economic association with the people of England, Scotland and Wales are living in the ideological realms of the past. The lesson to be learned from the new trend in world events and affairs is that no nation can live unto itself, and if there is to be any form of survival for the rule of law and the observance of justice amongst the nations, it must be on the basis of international co-operation, rather than on the basis of political or economic isolation. Those who claim that Ireland has nothing in common with the other democracies of the world and who refuse to take their place in the fight against Nazi-Fascist Totalitarianism, can have no claim to support in the Commonwealth Labour party.[1]

The real politics of our people are their economics, and our economic life and future salvation are bound up with the welfare and salvation of the people in the British Isles, the British Commonwealth and the Federation of the world.

Despite the wildly exaggerated assertions of abstentionists and isolationists there is much worth fighting for and retaining in our social life. Those who concentrate only on the iniquities of such Acts as the Special Powers Act (glossing over the fact that all countries have Special Powers Acts) conveniently ignore the rights and liberties we enjoy. All citizens enjoy the right to vote and to select candidates, on equal terms. We enjoy the right of a free press, subject only to the limitations imposed by considerations of national security. We enjoy (all of us in Northern Ireland) equality of social services with the people of England,

Scotland and Wales. These are, in the main, much superior to the social services prevailing in Eire, and they are destined to improve still more if the recommendations of the 'Beveridge Report' are accepted.

Our duty, therefore, is clear. We must use and improve our Northern Ireland Constitution so that within our area we can build up a fine free social order in which social security and equality of opportunity shall prevail.

Note

1. When he delivered this statement on 20 November 1942 Midgley was still in the Northern Ireland Labour Party. The Commonwealth Labour Party was not formed until 19 December. The above version of the statement is taken from the pamphlet, *Ulster for the Commonwealth.*

Primary sources

Manuscript and printed materials

Personal Papers of H. C. Midgley, privately held
Personal Papers of Mr Samuel Napier, privately held
Patrick Agnew Papers, Public Record Office of Northern Ireland PRONI D1676
Joseph Cunningham Papers, PRONI D1288
Diaries of Sir Wilfrid Spender, PRONI D715
William Walker Documents, PRONI T1241
Desmond Ryan Papers, University College Dublin (UCD) Archives LA10
John de Courcy Ireland Papers, UCD Archives P/29
Alexander Riddell Collection, Belfast Central Library
Correspondence between H. C. Midgley and the British Labour Party, British Labour Party Archives, London WG/SPA
NILP Documents, British Labour Party Archives 329.14 (416)
NILP Documents, PRONI D2474
Belfast Trades Council Minutes, PRONI MIC. 193
Belfast City Council Minutes, Belfast Central Library
Ulster Unionist Council Material, PRONI D3441 and D1736
Unionist Parliamentary Party Minute Book 1921–43, PRONI D1327
USDAW Records, USDAW Archives, Manchester
Northern Ireland Government Cabinet Minutes 1943–45; 1949–51, PRONI CAB 4
Ministry of Public Security Files, PRONI HA 18/3
Northern Ireland House of Commons Debates (HMSO)
Westminster House of Commons Debates (HMSO)
Northern Ireland Ministry of Education Reports 1949/1957 (HMSO)
Ulster Year Books (HMSO)
Special Report from the Select Committee on Public Accounts for the Financial Year 1955–56, H. C. 1247, HMSO 1957
Independent Labour Party, Annual Conference Report 1920
British Labour Party, Annual Conference Report 1937
Labour Party (Scottish Council), Annual Conference Report 1941
Business Directory of Belfast and the Principal Towns of the Province of Ulster 1865–66, Belfast, 1865

Henderson's Belfast Directory 1846–47, Belfast, 1846
Soldiers Died in the Great War Part 4 HMSO, 1981.

Newspapers and periodicals

Belfast:

Belfast Gazette
Belfast Labour Chronicle
Belfast News-Letter
Belfast Telegraph
Commonwealth
Irish Democrat
Irish News
Justice
Labour Advocate
Labour Opposition in
    Northern Ireland
Labour Progress
Northern Ireland
    Labour Bulletin
Northern Star
Northern Whig
Sunday News
The Ulster Protestant
The Unionist

Dublin:

Ireland and the War
Irish Freedom
The Irish People
Irish Press
Irish Times
Irish Workers' Voice
Irish Workers' Weekly

The Irishman
The Torch
The Voice of Labour
The Watchword and the
    Voice of Labour
The Worker
The Workers' Republic

London:

Daily Herald
Evening News
Evening Standard
New Statesman and
    Nation
Observer
Reynolds News
Sunday Empire News
The Times

Manchester:

Manchester Guardian
New Dawn
New Leader

Glasgow:

Forward

Others:

Bangor Spectator
Carrickfergus Advertiser
Coleraine Chronicle
Derry Journal
Londonderry Sentinel
Newtownards Chronicle
Portadown Times

Secondary sources

Contemporary books and pamphlets

Blanshard, P., *Communism, Democracy and Catholic Power*, Boston, 1950.
　The Irish and Catholic Power, London, 1954.
Clarkson, J. D., *Labour and Nationalism in Ireland*, New York, 1925.
Commonwealth Labour Party, *Ulster For The Commonwealth*, Belfast, 1944.
　Ulster Education and Democracy, Belfast, 1946.
Corkey, Rev. W., *Episode in the History of Protestant Ulster*, Belfast, n.d.
Gemmell, H., *Socialism for Ulster*, n.d.
Hinden, R., (ed.), *Fabian Colonial Essays*, London, 1945.
Labour Party, *The Book of the Labour Party* Vol. 3, London, n.d.
Midgley, H. C., *Thoughts from Flanders*, Belfast, 1924.
　Food for Thought, Belfast, 1933.
　The Labour Movement and Ulster, Belfast, 1933
　Important Facts for Old and Young, Belfast, 1934.
　A Bombshell of Facts on Home and Foreign Affairs, Belfast, 1936.
　Spain: The Press, the Pulpit and the Truth, Belfast, 1936.
　Give Labour a Chance, Belfast, 1937.
　The Great Betrayal, Belfast, 1938.
　Labour in Northern Ireland, Belfast, 1941.
　The Pilgrimage of Hope, Belfast, 1942.
O'Donnell, P., *Salud! An Irishman in Spain*, London, 1937.
Ulster Unionist Council, *Twenty Questions for Mr. de Valera*, 1948.
　Ulster Unionists Are Telling the World, 1948.
Wilkie, W., *One World*, Edinburgh, 1943.

Later works

Addison, P., *The Road to 1945*, London, 1977.
Akenson, D. H., *Education and Enmity: The Control of Schooling in Northern Ireland*, Newton Abbot, Devon, 1973.
Aunger, E., 'Religion and occupational class in Northern Ireland', *Economic and Social Review*, 7, I (1975) 1–18.
Baker, S., 'Orange and green', in H. J. Dyos and M. Wolfe (ed), *The Victorian City*, vol. 2, London, 1973.

Bell, G., *The Protestants of Ulster*, London, 1976.

Bell, J. Bowyer, 'Ireland and the Spanish civil war 1936–1939', *Studia Hibernica* 9 (1969) 137–163.

The Secret Army: A History of the IRA 1916–1970, London, 1972.

Bell, T., *The Struggle of the Unemployed in Belfast, October 1932*, Cork, n.d.

Bew, P., Gibbon, P., and Patterson, H., *The State in Northern Ireland*, Manchester, 1979.

Bew, P., and Norton, C., 'The Unionist state and the outdoor relief riots of 1932', *Economic and Social Review*, 10, 3 (1979) 255–65.

Birrell, D., and Murie, A., *Policy and Government in Northern Ireland*, Dublin, 1980.

Blake, J. W., *Northern Ireland in the Second World War*, Belfast, 1956.

Bleakley, D., 'The Northern Ireland trade union movement', *Journal of the Social and Statistical Inquiry Society of Ireland*, 19 (1953–4) 159–69.

Boyd, A., *Holy War in Ulster*, Tralee, 1969.

Boyle, J. W., 'The Belfast Protestant Association and the Independent Orange Order 1901–1910', *Irish Historical Studies*, 13 (1962–3) 117–52.

'William Walker', in J. W. Boyle (ed.), *Leaders and Workers*, Cork, 1967.

British and Irish Communist Organisation, *Irish Action*, Belfast, 1979.

Brown, T., *Ireland: A Social and Cultural History, 1922–79*, London, 1981.

Buckland, P., *The Factory of Grievances*, Dublin, 1979.

A History of Northern Ireland, Dublin, 1981.

Irish Unionism 1, Dublin, 1972.

Irish Unionism 2: Ulster, Dublin, 1973.

James Craig, Dublin, 1980.

'The unity of Ulster unionism', *History* 60 (1975) 211–23.

Budge, I., and O'Leary, C., *Belfast: Approach to Crisis*, London, 1973.

Calder, A., *The People's War*, London, 1971.

Carr, R., *The Spanish Tragedy*, London, 1977.

Clifford, A., 'Labour politics in Northern Ireland', parts 3, 5, 8 and 9, in *The Irish Communist*, nos. 162, 165, 173 and 176 (1979–80).

The Poor Law in Ireland, Belfast, 1983.

Connolly, J., *Ireland on the Dissecting Table*, Cork, 1975.

The Connolly–De Leon Controversy, Cork, n.d.

The Connolly–Walker Controversy, Cork, n.d.

Cook, C., and Stevenson, J., *The Slump*, London, 1977.

Cronin, S., *Frank Ryan*, Dublin, 1980.

Cullen, L. M., *An Economic History of Ireland Since 1660*, London, 1972.

Devlin, P., *Yes, We Have No Bananas*, Belfast, 1981.

Dewar, M. W., Brown, J., and Long, S. E., *Orangeism: A New Historical Appreciation*, Belfast, 1967.

Donoughue, B., and Jones, G. W., *Herbert Morrison: Portrait of a Politician*, London, 1973.

Dowse, R. E., *Left in the Centre*, London, 1966.

Edwards, O. Dudley, *The Sins of Our Fathers*, Dublin, 1970.

Edwards, O. Dudley, and Ransom, B., (eds), *James Connolly: Selected Political Writings*, New York, 1974.

Elliott, S., *Northern Ireland Parliamentary Election Results, 1921–1972*, Chichester, 1973.

Farrell, M., *Northern Ireland: The Orange State*, London, 1976.

Gibbon, P., *The Origins of Ulster Unionism*, Manchester, 1975.

Goldstrom, J. M., 'The industrialization of the north east', in L. M. Cullen, *The Formation of the Irish Economy*, Cork, 1968.

Gray, T., *The Orange Order*, London, 1972.

Green, E. R. R., *The Lagan Valley*, London, 1949.

'Industrial decline in the nineteenth century', in L. M. Cullen, *The Formation of the Irish Economy*, Cork, 1968.

Harbinson, J. F., *The Ulster Unionist Party 1882–1973*, Belfast, 1973.

Harkness, D. W., 'Difficulties of devolution: the post-war debate at Stormont', *Irish Jurist* xii part 1 (summer 1977) 176–86.

Johnson, D. S., 'The Belfast boycott 1920–1922', in J. M. Goldstrom and L. A. Clarkson (eds.), *Irish Population, Economy and Society*, Oxford, 1982.

'The economic history of Ireland between the wars', *Economic and Social History*, i (1974) 49–61.

Jones, A. Creech (ed), *New Fabian Colonial Essays*, London, 1959.

Jones, E., *A Social Geography of Belfast*, Oxford, 1960.

'Late Victorian Belfast', in J. Beckett and R. E. Glasscock (eds), *Belfast: The Growth of a City*, Belfast, 1967.

Knight, J., and Baxter-Moore, N., *Northern Ireland: The Elections of the Twenties*, London, 1972.

Lawrence, R. J., *The Government of Northern Ireland: Public Finance and Public Services 1921–64*, Oxford, 1965.

Lyons, F. S. L., *Ireland Since the Famine*, London, 1973.

Malby, A., *The Government of Northern Ireland 1922–72: A Catalogue and Breviate of Parliamentary Papers*, Dublin, 1974.

Midgley, J. F., *Midgleyana*, Cape Town, n.d.

Miliband, R., *Parliamentary Socialism*, London, 1961.

Mitchell, A., *Labour in Irish Politics 1890–1930*, Dublin, 1974.

O'Riordan, M., *Connolly Column*, Dublin, 1980.

Patterson, H., *Class Conflict and Sectarianism*, Belfast, 1981.

Probert, B., *Beyond Orange and Green*, London, 1978.

Ranson, B., *Connolly's Marxism*, London, 1980.

Rumpf, E., and Hepburn, A. C., *Nationalism and Socialism in Twentieth Century Ireland*, Liverpool, 1977.

Schneider, F., 'British Labour and Ireland 1918–21: the retreat to houndsditch', *Review of Politics* 40 (1978) 368–91.

Shea, P., *Voices and the Sound of Drums*, Belfast, 1981.

Skidelsky, R., *Politicians and the Slump*, London, 1967.

Stewart, A. T. Q., *Edward Carson*, Dublin, 1981.
The Ulster Crisis, London, 1967.
Thomas, H., *The Spanish Civil War*, London, 1961.
Walker, G. S., 'The Commonwealth Labour Party in Northern Ireland, 1942–47', *Irish Historical Studies* 24 (May 1984) 69–90.
Whyte, J. H., *Church and State in Modern Ireland 1923–1970*, Dublin, 1971.
Wilson, A., *P. R. Urban Elections in Ulster 1920*, London, 1972.
Wright, F., 'Protestant ideology and politics in Ulster', *European Journal of Sociology* 12 (1973) 213–80.

Theses

Bleakley, D. W., 'Trade union beginnings in Belfast and district', MA, Queen's University of Belfast, 1955.
Donaghy, T., 'A study of the secondary school system of Northern Ireland 1947–69', MA, Queen's University of Belfast, 1970.
Elliott, S., 'The electoral system in Northern Ireland since 1920', Ph.D., Queen's University of Belfast, 1971.
Harbinson, J. F., 'A history of the Northern Ireland Labour party 1891–1949', M.Sc., Queen's University of Belfast, 1966.
Holmes, E., 'Public opinion and educational reform in the north of Ireland 1900–1954', MA, Queen's University of Belfast, 1968.
Milotte, M., 'Communist politics in Ireland 1916–1945', Ph.D., Queen's University of Belfast, 1977.
Morgan, A., 'Politics, the labour movement and the working class in Belfast 1905–1923', Ph.D., Queen's University of Belfast, 1978.
Whitford, F. J., 'Joseph Devlin: Ulsterman and Irishman', MA, London University, 1959.

Interviews

Mr S. H. Bell, Dr J. M. Benn, Lord Blease of Cromac, Mr A. Boyd, Mr T. Boyd, Mr J. Boyd, Dr J. Boyle, Mr M. Gray, Mr F. Hanna, Mr J. Hewitt, Dr J. de Courcy Ireland, Mr & Mrs S. B. Ireland, Mr J. J. Kelly, Mr & Mrs W. Kennedy, Mr J. P. Kyle, Mr W. W. Logan, Mr S. McAughtry, Mr G. McBride, Mr W. McMullen, Mr & Mrs W. J. Midgley, Mr S. Napier, Rev. Dr I Paisley, Miss S. Patterson, Mr P. Scott, Mr P. Shea, Mr R. Thompson, Mr T. Watters, and Mr D. Wylie.

I benefited through information and opinions offered to me by many people in passing conversation or in correspondence. I am grateful in particular to: Miss M. Grant Cormack, Paddy Devlin, Mr H. Montomery Hyde, Jack MacGougan, Mr J. McWade, Murtagh Morgan, Paedar O'Donnell, Mrs O. Patten, and the late Betty Sinclair.

Index

Abyssinia, 81, 116
Acland, Sir Richard, 158
Adams, Alex., 22, 51, 156
Agnew, Rev. A. L., 36, 40n
Agnew, Patrick, 105, 115, 130, 132, 134, 135, 151
America, 4, 6, 8–9, 160–1, 182–3
  Labour movement in, 8, 45
Ancient Order of Hibernians, 53
Anderson, Edward, 101–2
Andrews, J. M., 65, 70, 72, 123, 128, 130, 131, 143, 147–8, 149, 163, 177, 177n, 207
Anglo-Irish Treaty (1921), 23
Anti-Partition League (A.P.L.), 172, 174, 182, 189
Antrim, County of, 16, 51
  North Antrim Constituency, 104, 118
Apprentice Boys, 208
Armagh, County, 1, 16, 201
  Cental Constituency, 167–8
  Labour Party Branch, 68, 99, 100, 115, 116, 122
  South Armagh Constituency, 105, 112n
Armstrong, Robert, 105
Australia, 183
Austria, 75, 116

Baird, James, 19–22
Baldwin, Stanley, 88, 89
Ballymena, 172
Ballynafeigh ward, 167
  Unionist Association, 181
Bangor, 156, 172
Barr, Glen, 216

Bates, Sir Richard Dawson, 62, 65, 76, 77, 80, 107, 147
Beattie, Jack, 55n
  elections, (1925), 46–7; (1929), 51; (1933), 68, 70; (1938), 105, 107; (1943), 147; (1945), 168; (1949), 189, 196n
  expulsion from N.I.L.P., 74, 168
  Midgley's election agent, 35
  position in the N.I.L.P., 33, 67–8, 74
  and possible 'coalition' government, 130, 151
  readmission to N.I.L.P., 132–3
  relations with Nationalists, 72–4
  rivalry with Midgley, 22, 26n, 83n, 150, 169–70
  role in split between Midgley and N.I.L.P., 134–8, 145n, 146n
  and Spanish civil war, 101
Belfast
  City Hall, 21
  and German air-raids, 123, 128, 154, 171
  growth as a city, 1
  housing conditions in, 2, 154–5
  Labour movement in, 3–5, 6–8, 12n, 14–16, 20–1, 23–5, 48–50
    (see also I.L.P. (Belfast); N.I.L.P., Trade Union Movement (Ulster))
  May Day rallies in, 17, 18
  Midgley's funeral in, 212
  and the nature of the N.I.L.P., 51, 119
  and Outdoor Relief riots, 61–7
  public speaking in, 3

Queen's University of, 163, 200
residential segregation in, 16
sectarian conflict in, 2, 19, 75–81
and William Walker, 48–9, *see also*
    entries for East, West, North and
    South Belfast, individual wards,
    streets, areas)
'Belfast Boycott', 19–20
Belfast Celtic F.C., 113n
Belfast Central (electoral ward), 72,
Belfast Co-operative Society, 15,
    22–3, 41, 54, 171, 213
Belfast Corporation, 17, 18, 38–9,
    41–2, 52–3, 57n, 68, 71, 82n,
    109, 131, 134, 154–5, 172, 178n,
    180n, 191, 196n, 213
Belfast Labour Party, 15, 17–18,
Belfast News-Letter, 20, 126, 127,
    149, 175
Belfast Telegraph, 108, 127, 149, 175
Belfast Trades Council, 3, 15, 57n,
    59, 63, 77, 118
Belgium, 119
    Kemmel Hill, 10
Belton, Patrick, 89
Beveridge Report, 139, 149, 157–8,
    159, 168, 223
Bevin, Ernest, 121, 130
Bing, Geoffrey, 172
Black, Sir Arthur, 125
Black, Norman, 167–8
Blakiston-Houston, Major C., 68–9
Blanshard, Paul, 207–8
Blueshirts, 89, 102
Bolshevism, 30, 35, 52
Boundary Commission, 23, 34, 35,
    37, 47
Boyd, Tom, 105, 107
Boyle, John, 132
Bradford, 60, 61
Bradley, Cathal, 105, 107
Brisbane, William, 176
British Commonwealth, 100, 102,
    112n, 120, 124, 133, 134, 135,
    142, 157, 160, 161, 174, 183,
    202, 222–3
British Empire Union, 19
British Imperialism, 101–2

Brooke, Sir Basil (Lord
    Brookeborough)
    becomes Prime Minister and
    forms government, 147–8, 177n,
    178n
and 'devolutionist' debate, 171–2
and education controversy, 192–5,
    199, 200
elections (Willowfield), 126;
    (1945), 167–8; (1949), 187–8
head of wartime 'coalition',
    148–56, 162–7
Midgley's admiration for, 159,
    179n
Midgley's letter of application to,
    181
Midgley's letter of resignation to,
    166–7, 179n
Minister of Commerce, 123
and propaganda campaign, 183
and Protestant extremists, 205
sectarian speeches of, 73, 76, 149
Browne, Noel, 204
Brownell, Reginald, 212
Butler, R. A.,
    Education Act, 165
Byrne, John, 105, 107
Byrne, Richard, 51, 74, 107

Callaghan, Frank, 105
Campbell, David, 7
Campbell, John, 51, 59, 67, 83n
Campbell, T. J., 73–4, 106
Canada, 187
Capitalism, 58–9, 67, 203
Carson, Sir Edward, 7, 9, 19, 24, 25n,
    35
Chamberlain, Neville, 120, 143n
China, 52, 81
Civil Service (N.I.), 55n, 80
Churchill, Winston
    and wartime coalition
    government, 120, 121
Clann na Poblachta, 182–3, 188
Clark, G. A., 105–8
Clifton ward
    election (1953), 202
    Labour party branch, 51

Coates, Sir William, 53
Coleraine, 104, 153, 156
    Labour Party, 145n
Collins, James, 74, 105–8, 113n, 132, 168
Commonwealth Labour Party (C.L.P.), 136, 142, 148, 149, 156–61, 162, 163, 166, 167–70, 172–7, 190, 206, 218
    Justice, 156, 158, 159, 172
    Ulster for the Commonwealth, 157, 222–3
Commonwealth Party, 159–61, 176
Communism, 88–9, 91–3, 167, 187, 203, 207–9
Communist Party of Ireland, 26n, 76, 84n, 99, 104, 111n, 115, 117, 123, 150, 168
    Irish Workers' Weekly, 120, 122
Connellan, Joseph, 210
Connolly, James, 4–5, 6–9, 13n, 18, 24, 47–50, 55n, 56n, 101–2, 106
    Connolly Hall, 88
    James Connolly Battalion, 89
    Labour in Irish History, 68
Conscription (W.W.II), 117, 128, 133, 143n
Conservative Party (U.K.), 58, 120, 127
Cook, A. J., 43–4
Cook-Maxton Manifesto (1928), 43–4, 46
Corrigan, Joseph, 104, 131, 132, 133, 136, 189
Court ward
    Labour Party branch, 51, 56n
Craig, Sir James (Lord Craigavon), 7, 21, 24, 31, 36, 51, 62, 80, 82n, 104, 120, 123, 127, 128
Czechoslovakia, 116

Dail Eireann, 18
Daily Herald, 90
Dallas, George, 103, 115
Derry, County of, 16
    Derry Journal, 94–5, 149–50
de Valera, Eamon, 16, 30, 67, 88, 102, 104, 117, 120, 183, 187, 188

Devine, P., 115
Devlin, Joseph, 16, 21, 25n, 29, 30, 36, 37, 49, 53, 72–4
Devlin, Paddy, 77, 78, 80, 216, 218
Diamond, Harry, 73, 169, 170, 201, 207
    Socialist Republican Party, 168
Diaz, Captain Luis, 98
Dixon, Herbert, 30
    Lord Glentoran, 127, 147, 163
Dock ward
    Catholic community in, 2, 190
    conditions in, 2, 41
    council seat, 38–9, 41, 52–3
    elections (1929), 51; (1933), 68–9; (1934), 74; (1938), 105–8, 125, 132, 141, 186; (1945), 168; (1949), 189
    and Gerry Fitt, 216, 220–1
    Labour Party branch, 44, 51, 56n, 100
    Midgley's 'Open Letter', 80
    Northern Ireland Parliamentary seat, 60–1
Donaghy, J., 118–9
Donald, Thompson, 30–1
Donaldson, W. J., 67, 68, 70
Donnelly, James, 189
Dornan, Robert, 34, 59
Dorricott, Jack, 132
Douglas, William, 52
Down, County of, 16, 22, 56n
    East Down Constituency, 188
    North Down Constituency, 123
    South Down Constituency, 106
Downey, Hugh, 131, 145n, 168
Dublin, 9, 18, 26n, 55n, 73, 88, 106, 188
Duncairn ward, 80
    Duncairn Gardens, 54, 171, (National School) 2
    Unionist Association, 204
Dundalk, 26n, 49
Dungannon, 206

East Belfast, 20, 21, 51
    East Belfast Labour Party, 105
    Westminster Constituency, 143n

Education
  in Belfast corporation, 41–2
  Commonwealth Labour Policy on,
    158–9, 167
  in Council Elections, 53
  Education Act (1947), 191–5,
    199–200, 202–3, 205
  Education (Amendment) Act
    (1951), 198–9, 200
  Education (Amendment) Act
    (1953), 201
  expansion in Catholic community,
    219
  issue in by-election, 73
  Midgley's opposition to Hall
    Thompson on, 165–6, 172–4,
    175
  Midgley as Minister of, 198–202,
    209–12, 220
Eire
  immigrants from, 121, 164–5
  neutrality during the war, 132–3,
    139, 154, 172, 177, 183
  social welfare benefits, 158
  the Treaty Ports agreement, 120
Engineering, 1, 9, 58
  Amalgamated Engineering Union,
    59
  Engineering Strike (1919), 17, 24
English, Thomas, 38
Expelled Workers Relief Committee,
  19–20, 26n, 107
ex-servicemen, 15, 17, 18, 21, 22

Fabian Society, 3, 13n
Falls Road (Falls ward), 16, 29, 31–2,
  34–6, 38, 51, 52, 105, 107, 168
Family Allowances Bill (N.I.), 175
Fascism, 75, 81, 88, 90–3, 95, 102,
  108, 110, 117, 124
Faulkner, Brian, 188
Fermanagh, County of, 16, 74, 201
Fianna Fail, 88, 183, 188
Fine Gael, 183, 188
Finley, G. I., 167–8
First World War, 8, 9–11, 30–1, 78,
  126, 152
Fitt, Gerry, 216, 218, 220–21

Floud, Sir Francis, 155
Flynn, Charlie, 69
Forward (Glasgow), 6, 33, 44, 49, 53,
  60, 63, 77, 154
France, 9–10, 52, 88, 119, 124
France, Anatole, 45
Franco, General, 88, 89, 90, 94, 106,
  112n, 208
'Friends of Ireland', 172, 174
Fripp, Rev. Edgar J., 36

Gage, Connolly H., 169
Geddes, Sam, 103–4
Geehan, Tommy, 49, 56n, 59, 63, 65
Gemmell, Hugh, 47–9, 54, 56n, 59,
  156
General Strike (1926), 43, 44, 46
George, Henry, 3
Germany, 9, 18, 67, 75, 88, 90, 102,
  116, 123, 153
  and Nazism, 117, 118, 120, 121,
    139, 142
Getgood, Bob, 54, 104, 116, 137, 151,
  168, 189
Glasgow, 6, 15, 33, 61, 217
Glass, John, 83n, 105, 107, 119
Gordon, Dawson, 51, 56n
Gordon, Milton, 131, 137, 156
Government of Ireland Act (1920),
  18, 157
Graham, A., 106, 107
Grant, William, 17, 72, 126, 149, 153,
  170, 171, 191
Gray, Samuel, 52
Greenisland Unionist Hall, 183–5
Grimley, James, 49

Hall-Thompson, S. B., 148, 165–6,
  181–2, 191–5, 197n, 202–3
Hanna, Frank, 132
Hanna, John, 19–22
Hardie, Keir, 3
Harkin, Brendan, 186
Harland and Wolff, 1, 11, 55n
Hawnt, J. Stuart, 213n
Hazlett, Sam, 56n, 93, 101
Healy, Cahir, 195, 201
Henderson, Tommy, 70, 177n

Hirst, Stanley, 115
Hitler, Adolf, 67, 88, 100, 116, 119, 120
Hogan, Luke, 69
Holland, 119
Holmes, Harry, 210
Housing, 153, 154–5, 158, 167, 172, 190
  Housing Bill, 163, 175
  Housing Trust, 154, 163
Hunter, Alexander, 199

Independent Labour Party (I.L.P.), 15, 43–4, 48, 60
Independent Labour Party (Belfast), 3, 7–8, 13n, 15, 19, 28, 44, 47, 48, 55n, 56n, 60, 93, 156
  The Labour Opposition in Northern Ireland, 47, 48, 54
Independent Labour Party of Ireland (I.L.P.(1)), 7–8
Independent Unionists, 51, 52, 56n, 70, 107, 123, 129, 151, 168, 170, 189
Ireland Bill (1949), 190
Irish Christian Front, 89
Irish Civil War, 23
Irish Democrat, 99, 101–2
Irish Free State
  and Boundary Commission, 23
  conditions of social welfare in, 47
  Constitution of (1937), 104
  election in (1927), 49
  Midgley's view of, 102
  National Anthem of, 106
  and Spanish Civil War, 88, 111n, (*see also* Eire; Irish Republic)
Irish Home Rule, 4–5, 6–7, 15, 18, 47–8, 49
Irish Labour Party, 7, 34, 39n, 49, 106, 115, 188, 189, 202
Irish Linenlappers and Warehouse Workers Union, 11, 56n
Irish National Teachers Organisation (I.N.T.O.), 55n, 75, 83n
Irish Nationalism, 4–5, 15, 33, 50, 85, 100, 102, 106, 124, 133, 134, 136, 177, 183, 185, 187, 219

Irish Nationalists, 9, 16, 21, 85–7, 99, 115, 117, 132, 142, 189, 202 (*see also* Nationalist Party)
Irish News, 20, 32, 35, 36, 38, 52, 106, 149
  Spanish Civil War controversy, 88–99
Irish People, 85
Irish Press, 205–6
Irish Republic (from 1948), 188, 204, 207–8
Irish Republican Army (I.R.A.), 18, 76, 121, 133, 151, 191, 214n
Irish Republicanism, 22, 31, 134, 136, 219
  Republican Congress, 76
  Republican Socialism, 22, 49–50, 112n, 114
Irish Republicans, 22, 23, 70, 73, 85–7, 105, 202
Irish Socialist Republican Party, 4
Irish Trades Union Congress (I.T.U.C.), 7, 34
Irish Transport and General Workers Union (I.T.G.W.U.), 4, 55n
Irwin, George, 8
Italy, 75, 88, 90, 102, 116

Jagger, John, 69
Japan, 116
Johnson, Thomas, 7
Johnston, Loftus, 59
Johnston, Tom, 154

Kater, Jimmy, 59
Kennedy, James, 167–8
Kennedy, William, 136, 156, 167–8
King George V Silver Jubilee celebrations, 76, 79
Kipling, Rudyard, 10
Koestler, Arthur, 207
Kyle, Sam, 15, 20, 33, 34, 51, 54, 55n, 56n
  as leader of N.I.L.P., 42–4, 46–8
  takes up residence in Dublin, 59
  views on partition, 18
  views on pogroms (1920–2), 24
  and Unionist propaganda, 38

Labour Advocate, 84n, 86
Labour movement (British), 4, 6, 13n,
    23–4, 28, 48, 50 (*see also* Labour
    Party (British))
Labour movement (Irish), 4, 18, 23–4
    (*see also* Irish Labour Party; Irish
    Trades Union Congress)
Labour movement (Ulster), 3–5, 6–8,
    11, 12n, 15–16, 23–5, 216–18 (*see
    also* Northern Ireland Labour
    Party; Trade Union movement
    (Ulster); Belfast Trades Council)
Labour Party (British), 28, 30, 34,
    37–8, 46, 50, 82n
  and British Commonwealth, 112n,
    161
  Conference (1948), 186–7
  and Cook-Maxton manifesto, 43–4
  disaffiliation of I.L.P., 60
  and Expelled Workers Committee,
    19, 22
  in government, (1924), 36;
    (1929–31), 58, 116–17; (wartime
    coalition), 120, 126; (1945–51),
    165, 169, 171–2, 190
  and Irish Home Rule, 18
  and League of Nations, 116
  and prolongation of N.I.
    parliament, 131
  prospects in Northern Ireland,
    217–18
  relations with N.I.L.P., 34, 75,
    86–7, 99–101, 102–4, 106, 112n,
    115–16, 118, 138, 140, 188–9,
    196n, 216
Larne, 32, 34, 35
Lavery, F. J., 126–8
League of Nations, 116
Leeburn, William, 117, 118, 131,
    134–5, 137, 138, 141, 151, 188–9
Left Book Club (Belfast), 114
Liberal Party (British), 58
Linen Industry, 1, 19, 42, 58
Linfield F.C., 54, 109, 113n, 171
Lisburn, 156, 185
Liverpool, 61, 160, 217
Lloyd-Dodd, F. T., 200
Lloyd George, David, 18

Loftus, Annie, 51
Logan, William, 13n
London, 16, 98, 131, 149
    Evening News, 170
Londonderry, 51, 74, 104, 208
    Labour Party, 137, 156
Lowry, William, 151, 154, 164
Lurgan, 1, 156
Lyle, William, 163
Lynn, Sir Robert, 29–32, 34–6, 39n,
    70
Lyttle, Billy, 160

MacBride, Sean, 183, 188
McBrinn, Bob, 167–8
McCann, P. J., 105, 112n
McCarroll, J. J., 72, 74, 94–5, 98
McCormick, Major Henry, 83n
McCoubrey, Margaret, 56n
McCoubrie, T. J., 61, 67, 76, 110
McCullough, William, 92
MacDonald, Ramsay, 35, 43, 58
McElroy, A. H., 101, 167–8, 176
MacGougan, Jack, 101, 105, 107, 132
McLean, Davie, 114
McLung, Bob, 12n, 156
McMullen, William, 7, 9, 33, 46,
    49–50, 51, 55n, 59, 73
MacRory, Cardinal J., 89, 121, 151
McSparran, James, 174
McSparran, Father J., 98–9
MacSwiney, Mary, 35, 40n
MacSwiney, Terence, 40n
Madrid, 88, 15
Maginness, Brian, 163–4, 171, 203,
    214n
Manchester, 61
Manchuria, 116
Martin, Thomas, 167–8
Maxton, James, 43–4
May, Morris, 203
Messines, Battle of, 10
Mexico, 52
Midgley, Alexander Snr, 1, 2
Midgley, Alexander Jnr, 2, 9, 10
Midgley, Eddie, 2, 9
Midgley (*née* Adgey), Eleanor, 11, 156
Midgley, (*née* Cassidy), Elizabeth, 1, 2

Midgley, Elizabeth, 1
Midgley, Harry Junior, 156–7, 159
Midgley, John, 1
Midgley, Marie, 156
Midgley, Minnie, 1
Millar, J., 119
Milne-Barbour, J., 147, 163
Mola, General, 88, 90
Mond-Turner discussions (1928),
    43–4
Montgomery-Hyde, H., 214n
Moore, Robert, 171
Morgan, J. W., 210
Morgan, Murtagh, 13n, 49, 53
Morrison, Herbert, 144n, 153–4,
    162–3
Morrow, James, 169
Mosley, Oswald, 75
Mulcahy, Richard, 188
Music, Midgley's love of, 54, 202
Mussolini, Benito, 88
Mylchreest, Alex, 160

Nash, Patrick, 34–6
National Government (U.K.), 58, 61,
    116
National Insurance, 7
National Insurance Bill (N.I.), 175
National Unemployed Workers'
    Movement (N.U.W.M.), 63, 82n
National Union of Distributive and
    Allied Workers (N.U.D.A.W.),
    52, 56n, 60, 69, 76, 110, 125, 133,
    136, 203
National Union Protestants (N.U.P.),
    202–3
Nationalist Party
    and the Anti-Partition League, 172
    attendance at Stormont, 87, 129
    elections (1921), 21–2; (1929),
        51–2; (1933), 70; (Belfast Central
        1934), 72–4; (Dock, 1938),
        105–7; (1938), 107; (1945), 168;
        (1953), 202
    elections boycott (1923), 29;
        (1924), 34
    Midgley's relations with, 53, 72–4,
        80, 174, 187, 198, 203

and the N.I.L.P., 49, 51, 115, 132
policy of abstention, 24, 47, 140
position in Belfast Catholic
    community, 16
and sectarianism, 38, 78, 85
and wartime 'coalition'
    government, 151 (*see also* Irish
    Nationalists)
New Statesman and Nation, 79
Newry, 51
Newtownards, 51, 156, 167–8, 172
New York, 8
New Zealand, 117, 124–5, 183
Nixon, J. W., 70, 177n
Nolan, Sean, 101
North Belfast, 1, 123
    I.L.P. branch in, 3, 19
    parliamentary constituency, 4,
        20–1, 34
Northern Ireland Government
    'abuse of power' allegation, 84n
    and conscription, 117
    and internees, 22
    and the minority, 207
    and Outdoor Relief crisis, 62–7
    and Protestant extremists, 80–1
    and Second World War, 120, 121,
        123–4, 129–30
    and Spanish Civil War, 89
    'step by step' policy on social
        legislation, 38, 171–2
    wartime 'coalition', 148–56, 161–7
    and Willowfield by-election, 125–9
    (*see also* Ulster Unionist Party)
Northern Ireland Labour Party
    (N.I.L.P.)
    character of in the 1920s, 46–51
    Commonwealth Labour view of,
        157, 174
    condition at the outset of 1930s,
        53–4
    and the depression, 59–61
    elections (1924), 34–8; (1929),
        51–2; (1933), 67–70; (1934),
        72–4; (1938), 104–8;
        (Willowfield), 125–9; (1943),
        147; (1945), 167–9; (1949),
        188–90; (1953), 202; (1958), 220

expulsion of Beattie, 74
failure of, 216–18
image in parliament, 71
inception of, 34
internal friction, 99–101, 108–10,
    114–15, 118–20, 122, 132–7
limitations of provincial status, 38
Midgley's position in the 1920s,
    42–6
Midgley's style of leadership, 74–5
and Outdoor Relief crisis, 63–7
outlook after Willowfield, 130–2
relations with British Labour,
    86–7, 99–101, 102–4, 106, 112n,
    115–16, 196n, 216
relations with Midgley after 1945,
    170
and Second World War, 117–18,
    119–22, 123–4
and sectarian riots in Belfast, 76–81
and Spanish Civil War, 93–4,
    109–10
split with Midgley, 22, 135–43
and wartime 'coalition'
    government, 150–1 (*see also* ward
    branches)
Northern Ireland Parliament, 18, 20,
    24, 46–7, 49, 70–2, 85, 164, 190
at Stormont (from 1932), 14, 72,
    74, 87, 95, 101, 108, 109, 127–34
    passim, 138, 148–50, 155, 158,
    163–75 *passim*, 187, 193, 194–5,
    198–201, 203–9 *passim*, 212,
    216–17, 220
Northern Ireland State, 24, 48, 216
and the Boundary Commission, 23
government committees of, 46
sectarian political mould of, 23
Northern Whig, 20, 30, 31, 32, 35, 38,
    126, 127, 149
Norton, William, 188
Nugent, Sir Roland, 171

O'Donnell, Paedar, 111n
O'Duffy, Eoin, 89
O'Neill, Terence, 220
Oldpark ward, 47, 51, 70, 105, 107,
    168
Orange Order, 5–6, 36, 53, 62, 174,
    192, 195n, 197n, 213
    Orangeism, 5–6, 25, 102, 109,
        181–2, 185
    Orange Parade (1935), 76–7, 79,
        181–2
    'Orange and Protestant
        Committee', 205, 214a
Ormeau ward
    Council seat, 172
    Unionist Association, 181, 196n
Orwell, George, 207
O'Shannon, Cathal, 24, 26n

Paisley, Rev. Ian, 177n, 178n
Pearse, Patrick, 185
Pollock, Hugh, 62
Poor Law relief, 40n, 53, 59
    Means Test, 59, 63
    Outdoor Relief Crisis and riots,
        61–7, 75
    Outdoor Relief and Poor Law
        Guardians, 41–2, 61–7
    Outdoor Relief rates in Belfast and
        other U.K. cities, 61
Portadown, 172, 207
    Portadown Times, 207
Porter, Norman, 202–3, 205, 206
Porter, S. C., 18
Pottinger ward
    elections (1929), 51; (1933), 70;
        (1938), 105, 107; (1945), 168
    Labour Party branch, 51
Proportional Representation
    in local government elections, 18
    N.I.L.P. support for, 99
Protestantism
    and communism, 208–9
    and education, 191–5, 200
    extremism, *see* National Union of
        Protestants; *Ulster Protestant;* Ulster
        Protestant League and the
        Orange Order, 181–2, 203–4,
        219–20 and socialism, 52
Public Accounts Committee, 212,
    215n, 219

Queen Elizabeth II, 202

Redmond, John, 9
Reformation 5, 182, 185
Revolutionary Workers' Groups
  (R.W.G.s), 59, 82n
  role in Outdoor Relief struggle,
  62–7
Richhill, 172
Robinson, William, 69
Roman Catholic Church
  Catholicism, 5–6, 185–6
  and communism, 207–9
  in Constitution of Irish Free State,
  102
  and education, 165–6, 172–4,
  191–5, 200, 211
  elections (1933), 69; (1949),
  188–90
  Eucharistic Congress, 78
  and Irish Home Rule, 4
  Midgley's opposition to, 102,
  108–10, 204–9
  and Spanish Civil War, 88–99
  and socialism, 52
  Truth Society Festival in Belfast,
  73, 78
  and Unionist propaganda, 37
Royal Black Preceptory, 181
Royal Engineers, 10
Royal Inniskilling Fusiliers, 9, 10
Royal Ulster Constabulary (R.U.C.),
  62–3, 80, 121
Russia, 17, 18, 20, 52, 123, 124
Ryan, Msgr Arthur, 96–8, 106
Ryan, Desmond, 101

Safeguarding of Employment Act
  (N.I.), 165
St. Anne's ward, 68, 70, 83n
Sandy Row (Belfast), 2, 29, 31, 32, 34,
  36
Searight, Norman, 202
Seaview Street (Belfast), 1, 2
Second World War, 116–167 *passim*,
  177
Shankill Road (ward), 29, 31, 34–6,
  70, 210

Labour Party branch, 51
Shaw, George Bernard, 175
Shea, Patrick, 46, 49, 98, 212, 217
Shepherd, G. R., 60, 75, 115, 136
Shinwell, Manny, 186, 221n
Shipbuilding Industry, 1, 19, 42, 58
  Shipbuilding and Engineering
  Federation, 34
Short Stand (Belfast), 47, 101, 189
Sinclair, J. Maynard, 153, 206
Sinclair, Upton, 45, 54
Sinn Fein, 16, 18, 19, 21, 22, 25n, 30,
  31, 34–6
Smithfield ward, 38, 52–3
  Labour Party branch, 51
Socialism, 3–10 *passim*, 35, 38–9,
  45–6, 52, 58, 93, 100, 120, 122,
  132, 136, 158, 159, 164–5, 171–6
  passim, 183, 218
Socialist Party (Northern Ireland)
  (S.P.(N.I.)), 60, 94, 99–101,
  114–5
Socialist Sunday School, 13n
Somme, battle of, 10
South Belfast, 20, 21
  1945 British election, 169
*Spain: The Press, The Pulpit and the
  Truth*, 95–6, 111n
Spanish Civil War, 13n, 87–99, 101,
  102, 105–10, 116, 135, 143, 173,
  186, 218
Special Powers Act (N.I.), 121, 122,
  124, 144n, 222
Spender, Sir Wilfrid, 62, 128, 147,
  154, 155
Stewart, Joe, 205, 206

Textile Trades Federation, 17
Thornbray, Frank, 26n
Thompson, Bob, 126, 134–5, 137,
  138, 141, 146n
Thoughts from Flanders, 10–11
Tiger's Bay (Belfast), 2
Todd, H., 118
Trades Union Congress (British), 3,
  19, 44
Trade Union Movement (Ulster), 3,
  15–16, 213

allegations against Unionist
   government, 186–7
and the British Labour Party, 217
Midgley's base of support in, 54,
   67, 114, 122
relationship with the N.I.L.P.,
   86–7, 103–4
and skilled Protestant workers, 125
and Willowfield by-election, 126–7
Tregenna, R., 21
Tyrone, County of, 16, 74, 201
South Tyrone constituency, 106

Ulster College of Physical Education,
   209
Ulster Division (British Army), 9, 10
Ulster Hall, 21, 28
Ulster Medical Aid for Spain
   Committee, 93
Ulster Protestant, 203–6, 208
Ulster Protestant League (U.P.L.),
   75–81, 83n, 84n, 108
Ulster Savings Committee, 117
Ulster Teachers' Union, 171, 212
Ulster Unionist Council, 146, 183
Ulster Unionist Labour Association
   (U.U.L.A.), 15, 16, 25n, 181, 187
Ulster Unionist Party (Ulster
   Unionism)
and Commonwealth Labour Party,
   157–60, 166
and communism, 76
death of Craig and succession of
   Andrews, 123
'devolutionist' debate in, 163–4,
   171–2
and education controversy, 191–5,
   198–202
and Eire immigrants, 121
elections (1906), 4; (1918), 16;
   (1921), 21–2; (1923), 11, 29–32;
   (1924), 34–8; (1925), 47; (1929),
   51–2; (1933), 68–70; (1938),
   107–8, 113n; (1941), 125–9;
   (1945), 167–9; (1949), 188–90;
   (1953), 202
and Engineering strike, 17, 24
fall of Andrews, succession of

Brooke, 147–8
and gerrymandering, 172
and Government of Ireland Act, 18
and Irish Home Rule, 5–7
members hostile to Midgley, 148,
   161–4, 170
Midgley moves towards, 174–7
Midgley joins, 181
Midgley's impact on in the 1950s,
   203–9, 218–20
and Midgley's split with N.I.L.P.,
   136–8, 140, 216
and the N.I.L.P., 50–1, 87
opposition to Andrews, 143
propaganda campaign, 183–7
and Protestant working class, 25,
   32–3, 70
question of Midgley joining, 148–9
relationship with Orange Order,
   181–2
and sectarianism, 15, 78–81, 85
and style of government, 71–2 (*see
   also* Northern Ireland
   Government)
Ulster Volunteer Force (U.V.F.), 9
Unbought Tenants' Association, 56n
Unemployment, 17, 30, 42, 53, 58,
   63, 76, 84n, 120, 144n, 152, 213n
Unemployment benefit cuts, 61
United Irishmen, 5

Victoria ward, 105, 107, 167–8

Walker, William, 3–5, 6–7, 8, 12n,
   47–50, 56n, 101
Wallace, Henry, 160–1
Wallace, Rev. J. Bruce, 20–2, 36
Walsh, H. R., 172
Warnock, Edmond, 120, 127,
   129–30, 149, 166
Watters, Tommy, 26n, 59
Weate, Harold, 69
Wedgewood, Col J. C., 28
Weir, Robert, 17
West Belfast
   Catholic community in, 16
   Labour Party branch, 119, 145n
   parliamentary constituency, 11, 20,

21, 26n, 29–37, 49, 147, 216
Westminster Parliament, 29, 30, 38,
  87, 103–4, 115, 131, 132, 163,
  169, 171, 172, 216, 217
Wexford, 32
Whitehouse, 156
Wilkie, Wendell, 160–1
Wilkinson, Ellen, 60, 69
Williams, Tom, 121
Willowfield ward
  elections (1941), 125–9, 132, 136,
    137, 138, 140, 160; (1945),
    167–8, 169; (1949), 188–90;
    (1953), 202

Labour group, 134, 136
Unionist Association, 181, 204
Unionist Hall, 167
Wilton, William, 70
Windsor ward, 167–8
Woodvale ward, 70
Workers' Party of Ireland (W.P.I.),
  56n
Workman and Clark, 1, 3, 84n

Yorkshire, 1, 12n
York Street (Belfast), 40n, 77, 81 (*see
  also* Dock ward)
Ypres, 10